FREEDMEN, THE FOURTEENTH AMENDMENT, AND THE RIGHT TO BEAR ARMS, 1866–1876

FREEDMEN, THE FOURTEENTH AMENDMENT, AND THE RIGHT TO BEAR ARMS, 1866–1876

Stephen P. Halbrook

Westport, Connecticut
London

Library of Congress Cataloging-in-Publication Data

Halbrook, Stephen P.
    Freedmen, the Fourteenth Amendment, and the right to bear arms,
    1866–1876 / Stephen P. Halbrook.
        p.   cm.
    Includes bibliographical references and index.
    ISBN 0–275–96331–4 (alk. paper)
    1. United States. Constitution. 14th Amendment—History.
    2. Civil rights—United States—History. 3. State rights—History.
    4. Firearms—Law and legislation—United States—History.
    I. Title.
    KF4749.H34   1998
    344.73'0533—DC21   98–15622

British Library Cataloguing in Publication Data is available.

Library of Congress Catalog Card Number: 98–15622
ISBN: 0–275–96331–4

First published in 1998

Praeger Publishers, 88 Post Road West, Westport, CT 06881
An imprint of Greenwood Publishing Group, Inc.

Printed in the United States of America

The paper used in this book complies with the
Permanent Paper Standard issued by the National
Information Standards Organization (Z39.48–1984).

10 9 8 7 6 5 4 3 2 1

Copyright Acknowledgment

The author and publisher gratefully acknowledge permission to publish a
revised version of Stephen P. Halbrook, "Personal Security, Personal Liberty,
and 'The Constitutional Right to Bear Arms': Visions of the Framers of the Fourteenth Amendment," 5 SETON HALL LAW SCHOOL CONSTITUTIONAL LAW JOURNAL,
No. 2, 341–434 (Spring 1995). Reprinted with permission of Seton Hall Law
School.

Contents

Preface

The same two-thirds of Congress that passed the Fourteenth Amendment to the United States Constitution also adopted the Freedmen's Bureau Act, which protected the "full and equal benefit of all laws and proceedings concerning personal liberty, personal security, and . . . estate . . . , including the constitutional right to bear arms."[1] Does the Fourteenth Amendment, which protects the individual rights to personal security and personal liberty from state violation,[2] incorporate the Second Amendment, which declares that "the right of the people to keep and bear arms, shall not be infringed," against the states?[3]

In three cases decided in the last quarter of the nineteenth century, the United States Supreme Court stated in dicta that the First, Second, and Fourth Amendments do not directly limit state action,[4] but did not rule on whether the Fourteenth Amendment prohibited state violation of the rights declared therein.[5] Since then, the Supreme Court has held that most Bill of Rights freedoms are incorporated into the Fourteenth Amendment, but has done so with little historical analysis and no discussion of the intent of the framers of that amendment.[6] Yet despite the specific declaration of two-thirds of Congress in the Freedmen's Bureau Act, the Court has failed to address whether the Second Amendment was likewise incorporated.

The first local and state prohibitions in U.S. history on firearms possession by the citizenry at large — the Morton Grove, Illinois handgun ban and California's prohibition on "assault weapons" (primarily repeating rifles) — were upheld by the United States Courts of Appeals for the Seventh and Ninth Circuits in 1982 and 1992, respectively. Both opinions refused to consider the intent of the Fourteenth Amendment's framers, relying instead upon century-old Supreme Court precedent to reject incorporation of the right to keep and bear arms into that amendment.[7]

Judicial reluctance to consider seriously whether the Fourteenth Amendment protects the right to keep and bear arms from state infringement perhaps reflects a tendency to view the Second Amendment, with its apparent guarantee of gun ownership, as embarrassing and politically incorrect.[8] Under the twentieth-century "State's rights" view, "the people" have no right to keep or bear arms, but the states have a collective right to have the National Guard.[9] However, the weight of serious scholarship supports the historical intent of the Second Amendment to protect individual rights and to deter governmental tyranny.[10] From the *Federalist Papers*[11] to explanations when the Bill of Rights was introduced,[12] it is clear that the purpose of the Second Amendment was to protect individual rights.

Historically, the right to keep and bear arms has been a key Bill of Rights guarantee related to the defense of African Americans from racist violence.[13] The Southern slave codes were the only significant prohibitions on firearm ownership in the antebellum United States.[14] Any historical analysis of the Fourteenth Amendment must take account of its origins in abolitionist thought, a fundamental tenet of which was that "the people" in the Second Amendment included individuals of all races, and that freedom for the slaves meant protection in their personal right to keep and bear arms.[15]

Previous studies document, primarily through floor speeches, that the framers of the Fourteenth Amendment did intend to protect Bill of Rights guarantees in general,[16] and the right to keep and bear arms in particular, against state action.[17] Critics have argued for the past 50 years over whether speeches by individual framers of the Fourteenth Amendment and other evidence is sufficient to demonstrate a consensus to incorporate the Bill of Rights.[18]

No comprehensive study exists, however, concerning the significance, for purposes of whether the Fourteenth Amendment prohibits state infringement of the right to keep and bear arms, of the declaration of the Freedmen's Bureau Act that the rights to personal security and personal liberty include the "constitutional right to bear arms."[19] Nor does any study trace the constitutional, statutory, and judicial developments of the rest of the Reconstruction period that pertain to whether the Fourteenth Amendment protects the right to keep and bear arms.

This study traces the adoption of, and investigates the interrelationship between, the Fourteenth Amendment and the civil rights legislation passed during Reconstruction, particularly focusing on the right to keep and bear arms. It begins with a day-by-day account of congressional proceedings in the Thirty-Ninth Congress leading to the passage of the Civil Rights and Freedmen's Bureau Acts of 1866 and the proposal of the Fourteenth Amendment.

The sources for this study include the texts of, and debates on, the Fourteenth Amendment and statutory enactments as they proceeded through Congress. The secret journal of the Joint Committee of Fifteen on Reconstruction, which drafted the Fourteenth Amendment, is also examined. Occasional references to press reports are made. Executive communications concerning conditions in the South and the role of the Freedmen's Bureau are also scrutinized.

This study interweaves the public proceedings before the Joint Committee of Fifteen with the contemporary congressional debates pertaining to the Fourteenth Amendment's adoption. This unique methodology, which, until now, had been missing from Fourteenth Amendment historiography, is crucial to the incorporation debate. As Benjamin B. Kendrick aptly surmised:

The testimony taken by the joint committee on reconstruction served as the *raison d'être* of the fourteenth amendment and as a campaign document for the memorable election of 1866. 150,000 copies were printed in order that senators and representatives might distribute them among their constituents

That this testimony was read by the people generally in the North, is proved by the fact that the newspapers of the time published copious extracts from it, as it was made public, together with editorial comments upon it.[20]

As Kendrick further remarked: "The testimony in regard to the treatment of the freedmen will tend to show why Congress was determined to pass such measures as the Freedmen's Bureau bill, the Civil Rights bill, and the civil rights resolution for amending the Constitution."[21] Besides exhibiting what thoughts were on the minds of members of Congress who asked many searching questions at the hearings, the testimony reveals which materials were considered relevant by the congressmen who voted for the Fourteenth Amendment and demonstrates the perceived evils that the public wanted remedied.

Lamentably, Reconstruction and constitutional law scholars have too often considered the Fourteenth Amendment and corresponding legislative enactments in isolation. This study takes a different tack. By chronologically examining committee hearings and records, floor debates on civil rights legislation and the Fourteenth Amendment, and contemporary public opinion, this study accurately reflects as a continuous process the adoption of the Freedmen's Bureau Act, the Civil Rights Act, and the Fourteenth Amendment.

Although these events were perhaps the most critical of the entire Reconstruction period, the constitutional, legislative, and judicial developments that followed were also of great significance. As this study demonstrates, the understanding of the Fourteenth Amendment's intent was expounded and clarified in reaction to the resistance in the states to the recognition of freedmen's rights and to the constitutional amendment. This work includes a state-by-state account of the conventions in the Southern States that were required to draft constitutions consistent with the Fourteenth Amendment.

Ratification of the Fourteenth Amendment gave rise to enactment of the Enforcement Act of 1870 and the Civil Rights Act of 1871, the legislative histories of which are saturated with expressions of the intent to protect the rights of freedmen to keep and bear arms. The rest of Reconstruction was, as far as this topic is concerned, consumed with the outer limits of the state action requirement of the Fourteenth Amendment, and in particular whether it could be made a federal crime to conspire to deprive freedmen of the rights to assemble and to bear arms. This drama was played out in the Ku Klux Klan trials in South Carolina and the trials stemming from the Grant Parish massacre in Louisiana. The Supreme Court's 1876 decision in the *Cruikshank* case was the climax of the debate and heralded the end of Reconstruction.

This book concludes with an analysis of the unfinished jurisprudence of the Supreme Court concerning the Second and Fourteenth Amendments. After dissecting post-*Cruikshank* cases, the study outlines twentieth-century developments by tracing the incorporation of substantive Bill of Rights guarantees into the Fourteenth Amendment, the court's pronouncements on the Second Amendment, and the role of the Freedmen's Bureau Act as an interpretative source of the Civil Rights Act of 1866 and the Fourteenth Amendment.

Although this study concentrates on the right to keep and bear arms, it also includes a comprehensive analysis pertinent to the general topic of incorporation of the Bill of Rights into the Fourteenth Amendment. Because it entailed trusting former slaves with firearms, application of the arms guarantee was the cutting edge of what it meant to take civil rights seriously. The history of the recognition of the right of freedmen to keep and bear arms in the period 1866–76 provides unique insights into the intent of the framers of the Fourteenth Amendment to protect Bill of Rights guarantees from state infringement generally and supplies a broader context to the question of the extent to which U.S. political society was willing to ensure the same liberties to all without regard to race or previous condition of slavery.

NOTES

The author thanks the following persons for their inspiration, suggestions for the direction of this study, or helpful comments on parts of the manuscript: Akhil Reed Amar, David I. Caplan, Robert J. Cottrol, Michael Kent Curtis, Robert Dowlut, Richard E. Gardiner, and George S. Knight. In addition, the following research assistants provided invaluable help: David W. Fischer, Lisa Halbrook-Stevenson, Noreen A. Cary, and Peter Robbins.

   1.   Act of July 16, 1866, 14 STATUTES AT LARGE 173, 176.
   2.   Griswold v. Connecticut, 381 U.S. 479, 485 n. (1965).
   3.   The Second Amendment provides: "A well regulated Militia, being necessary to the security of a free State, the right of the people to keep and bear Arms, shall not be infringed."
      The Fourteenth Amendment provides in pertinent part:

   §1. All persons born or naturalized in the United States, and subject to the jurisdiction thereof, are citizens of the United States and of the state wherein they reside. No state shall make or enforce any law which shall abridge the privileges or immunities of citizens of the United States; nor shall any state deprive any person of life, liberty or property without due process of law, nor deny to any person within its jurisdiction the equal protection of the laws.
   §5. The congress shall have power to enforce, by appropriate legislation, the provisions of this article.

   4.   United States v. Cruikshank, 92 U.S. 542, 551, 553 (1876) (private harm to rights to assemble and bear arms held not to be a federal offense); Presser v. Illinois, 116 U.S. 252, 265, 267 (1886) (requirement of license for armed march on public streets in city held not to violate right to assemble or bear arms); Miller v. Texas, 153 U.S. 535, 538 (1894) (refusal to consider whether Fourteenth Amendment protects Second and Fourth Amendment rights because claim not made in trial court).
   5.   Miller v. Texas, 153 U.S. 535, 538 (1894).
   6.   For example, Chicago, B.&Q.R.Co. v. Chicago, 166 U.S. 226, 238–39 (1897) (just compensation); Gitlow v. New York, 268 U.S. 652, 666 (1925)

(speech and press); DeJonge v. Oregon, 299 U.S. 353, 364 (1937) (assembly); Wolf v. Colorado, 338 U.S. 25, 27–28 (1949) (search and seizure); Robinson v. California, 370 U.S. 660, 666 (1962) (cruel and unusual punishment); Gideon v. Wainwright, 372 U.S. 335, 341 (1963) (counsel).

7.   Quilici v. Village of Morton Grove, 695 F.2d 261, 270 n.8 (7th Cir. 1982), *cert. denied* 464 U.S. 863 (1983) ("the debate surrounding the adoption of the second and fourteenth amendments . . . has no relevance on the resolution of the controversy before us."); Fresno Rifle & Pistol Club v. Van de Kamp, 965 F.2d 723, 730 (9th Cir. 1992) (refusing to consider "remarks by various legislators during passage of the Freedmen's Bureau Act of 1866, the Civil Rights Act of 1866, and the Civil Rights Act of 1871").

8.   S. Levinson, *The Embarrassing Second Amendment*, 99 YALE L. J. 637 (1989).

9.   See, for example, United States v. Warin, 530 F.2d 103 (6th Cir.), *cert. denied*, 426 U.S. 948 (1976); Burton v. Sills, 53 N.J. 86, 248 A.2d 521 (1967), *appeal dismissed*, 394 U.S. 812 (1969). However, no court has cited historical authority that actually supports this theory. See S. Halbrook, THAT EVERY MAN BE ARMED: THE EVOLUTION OF A CONSTITUTIONAL RIGHT 187–92 (1994); N. Lund, *The Second Amendment, Political Liberty, and the Right to Self-Preservation*, 39 ALABAMA LAW REVIEW 103 (1987) (concluding that "states' rights" theory of Second Amendment is "essentially baseless").

10.   For example, William van Alstyne, *The Second Amendment and the Personal Right to Arms*, 43 DUKE LAW JOURNAL 1236 (1994); S. Levinson, *The Embarrassing Second Amendment*, 99 YALE L. REV. 637 (1989); A. Amar, *The Bill of Rights as a Constitution*, 100 YALE L. REV. 1131, 1162–73 (1991); E. Scarry, *War and the Social Contract: Nuclear Policy, Distribution, and the Right to Bear Arms*, 139 U. OF PA. L. REV. 1257 (1991). The individual rights interpretation of the Second Amendment has been characterized as the "standard model." G. H. Reynolds, *A Critical Guide to the Second Amendment*, 62 TENN. L. REV. 461 (1995). For the most detailed accounts of the intent of the framers of the Second Amendment, see S. Halbrook, *Encroachments of the Crown on the Liberty of the Subject: Pre-Revolutionary Origins of the Second Amendment*, 15 UNIV. OF DAYTON L. REV. 91 (Fall 1989) and S. Halbrook, *The Right of the People or the Power of the State: Bearing Arms, Arming Militias, and The Second Amendment*, 26 VALPARAISO UNIV. L. REV. 131 (Fall 1991). On the English common-law background, see J. Malcolm, TO KEEP AND BEAR ARMS (Harvard Univ. Press 1994).

11.   For example, *The Federalist* No. 46 (James Madison) (contrasting the American people, who retained "the advantage of being armed," which they "possess over the people of almost every other nation," with European governments, which were "afraid to trust the people with arms") in THE FEDERALIST PAPERS (Arlington House ed. n.d.).

12.   Ten days after the Bill of Rights was proposed in the House of Representatives, Tench Coxe, a prominent Federalist and colleague of James Madison,

published his "Remarks on the First Part of the Amendments to the Federal Constitution," *Federal Gazette*, June 18, 1792, at 2, col. 1, which explained what became the Second Amendment as follows, "As civil rulers, not having their duty to the people duly before them, may attempt to tyrannize, and as the military forces which must be occasionally raised to defend our country, might pervert their power to the injury of their fellow citizens, the people are confirmed by the next article in their right to keep and bear their private arms."

13. R. Cottrol and R. Diamond, *The Second Amendment: Toward an Afro-Americanist Reconsideration*, 80 GEORGETOWN L. J. 309 (Dec. 1991).

14. For a state-by-state analysis of the antebellum slave codes, see S. Halbrook, A RIGHT TO BEAR ARMS: STATE AND FEDERAL BILLS OF RIGHTS AND CONSTITUTIONAL GUARANTEES (Greenwood Press 1989).

15. See S. Halbrook, THAT EVERY MAN BE ARMED 99–106 (1994).

16. A. Amar, *The Bill of Rights and the Fourteenth Amendment*, 101 YALE L. J. 1193 (Apr. 1992); M. Curtis, NO STATE SHALL ABRIDGE: THE FOURTEENTH AMENDMENT AND THE BILL OF RIGHTS (1986); H. Flack, THE ADOPTION OF THE FOURTEENTH AMENDMENT (1908).

17. S. Halbrook, "Freedom, Firearms, and the Fourteenth Amendment," in THAT EVERY MAN BE ARMED: THE EVOLUTION OF A CONSTITUTIONAL RIGHT 107–53 (1984); S. Halbrook, "The Fourteenth Amendment and The Right To Keep and Bear Arms: The Intent of The Framers," in THE RIGHT TO KEEP AND BEAR ARMS: REPORT OF THE SUBCOMMITTEE ON THE CONSTITUTION, Senate Judiciary Committee, 97th Cong., 2d Sess., at 68–82 (1982).

18. The first great clash in this debate pitted Charles Fairman, *Does the Fourteenth Amendment Incorporate the Bill of Rights?* 2 STANFORD L. REV. 5 (Dec. 1949) (arguing against incorporation) against W. Crosskey, *Charles Fairman, "Legislative History," and the Constitutional Limitations on State Authority*, 22 UNIV. OF CHICAGO L. REV. 1 (Autumn 1954) (arguing for incorporation). Most recently the key gladiators have been M. Curtis, NO STATE SHALL ABRIDGE: THE FOURTEENTH AMENDMENT AND THE BILL OF RIGHTS (1986) (advocating incorporation) and R. Berger, THE FOURTEENTH AMENDMENT AND THE BILL OF RIGHTS (1989) (denying incorporation).

19. Supra note 1 and accompanying text. The significance of this declaration to support incorporation of the Second Amendment as well as other parts of the Bill of Rights into the Fourteenth Amendment is recognized in three of the best studies on the Fourteenth Amendment. See A. Amar, supra note 8, at 1245 n. 228; M. Curtis, supra note 8, at 72; H. Flack, supra note 8, at 17.

20. B. Kendrick, JOURNAL OF THE JOINT COMMITTEE OF FIFTEEN ON RECONSTRUCTION 264–65 (1914).

21. Id. at 269.

1

The Civil Rights and Freedmen's Bureau Acts and the Proposal of the Fourteenth Amendment

THAT NO FREEDMAN SHALL KEEP OR CARRY FIREARMS: THE BLACK CODES AS BADGES OF SLAVERY

Numerous antebellum commentators interpreted the Second Amendment as guaranteeing an individual right to keep and bear arms free from both state and federal infringement.[1] In his famous criminal law commentaries, Joel P. Bishop wrote in 1865: "The constitution of the United States provides, that, 'a well-regulated militia being necessary to the security of a free State, the right of the people to keep and bear arms shall not be infringed.' This provision is found among the amendments; and, though most of the amendments are restrictions on the General Government alone, not on the States, this one seems to be of a nature to bind both the State and National legislatures."[2]

Bishop's references to state "statutes relating to the carrying of arms by negroes and slaves"[3] and an "act to prevent free people of color from carrying firearms"[4] exemplified the need for a constitutional guarantee to protect the rights of all persons, regardless of race, to keep and carry firearms. After the Civil War these slave codes, which limited the access of blacks to land, firearms, and the courts, began to reappear as "black codes."[5] Congress quickly turned its attention to these efforts to reenslave the freedmen.

E. G. Baker, a white Mississippi planter, wrote a letter to members of the state legislature on October 22, 1865, warning of a possible negro insurrection. He added: "It is well known here that our negroes through the country are well equipped with fire arms, muskets, double barrel shot guns & pistols, — & furthermore, it would be well if they are free to prohibit the use of fire arms until they had proved themselves to be good citizens in their altered state."[6] Forwarding a copy of the letter to the Union commander in Northern Mississippi, Governor Benjamin G. Humphreys warned that "unless some measures are taken to disarm [the freedmen] a collision between the races may be speedily looked for."[7]

White fears of armed ex-slaves led to the quick enactment of the 1865 Mississippi "Act to Regulate the Relation of Master and Apprentice Relative to Freedmen, Free Negroes, and Mulattoes." In addition to prohibiting seditious speeches and unlicensed preaching by freedmen, the statute contained a firearms prohibition that would serve as a model for the black codes of other Southern States:

Section 1. Be it enacted, . . . That no freedman, free negro or mulatto, not in the military service of the United States government, and not licensed so to do by the board of police of his or her county, shall keep or carry fire-arms of any kind, or any ammunition, dirk or bowie-knife, and on conviction thereof in the county court shall be punished by fine, not exceeding ten dollars, and pay the costs of such proceedings, and all such arms or ammunition shall be forfeited to the informer; and it shall be the duty of every civil and military officer to arrest any freedman, free negro, or mulatto found with any such arms or ammunition, and cause him or her to be committed to trial in default of bail.

Section 3. . . . If any white person shall sell, lend, or give to any freedman, free negro, or mulatto any fire-arms, dirk or bowie-knife, or ammunition, or any spirituous or intoxicating liquors, such person or persons . . . shall be fined not exceeding fifty dollars, and may be imprisoned, at the discretion of the court, not exceeding thirty days.

Section 5. . . . If any freedman, free negro, or mulatto, convicted of any of the misdemeanors provided against in this act, shall fail or refuse for the space of five days, after conviction, to pay the fine and costs imposed, such person shall be hired out by the sheriff or other officer, at public outcry, to any white person who will pay said fine and all costs, and take said convict for the shortest time.[8]

Two weeks after the Mississippi prohibition passed, Calvin Holly, a black private assigned to the Freedmen's Bureau in Mississippi, wrote to Bureau Commissioner O. O. Howard, relating in his letter an article in the *Vicksburg Journal* about an incident involving blacks with a gun, and noting that "they was forbidden not to have any more but did not heed."[9]

"The Rebbles," Holly warned, "are going about in many places through the State and robbing the colored people of arms[,] money and all they have and in many places killing."[10] Holly continued: "They talk of taking the arms away from (col[ored]) people and arresting them and put them on farms next month and if they go at that I think there will be trouble and in all probability a great many lives lost."[11]

When the Thirty-Ninth Congress convened in December 1865, Republican leaders quickly sought to establish committees charged with the task of drafting protections for the freedmen. On December 6, the House resolved that the Speaker appoint a Select Committee on Freedmen.[12] A few minutes later, Representative John A. Bingham (R-Ohio) introduced a joint resolution to amend the Constitution "to empower Congress to pass all necessary and proper laws to secure to all persons in their rights, life, liberty, and property."[13] Bingham's bill would become, of course, the Fourteenth Amendment.

The House Select Committee on Freedmen consisted of Thomas D. Eliot of Massachusetts, William D. Kelley of Pennsylvania, Godlove S. Orth of Indiana, Bingham of Ohio, Nelson Taylor of New York, Benjamin F. Loan of Missouri, Josiah B. Grinnell of Iowa, Halbert E. Paine of Wisconsin, and Samuel S. Marshall of Illinois.[14] Other significant committees were the Senate Judiciary Committee, chaired by Lyman Trumbull of Illinois,[15] and the House Judiciary Committee, chaired by James F. Wilson of Iowa.[16]

On December 12, the Senate concurred with a House resolution to appoint a Joint Committee of Fifteen to investigate the condition of the Southern States.[17] This committee would later hear extensive testimony on the violations of freedmen's rights and eventually drafted the Fourteenth Amendment.

The enactment of the black code provisions prompted initiation of civil rights legislation that culminated in the proposal of the Fourteenth Amendment. Among the first proposals was S. 9, which declared as void all laws or other actions by the rebel states "whereby or wherein any inequality of civil rights and immunities among the inhabitants of said states is recognized, authorized, established, or maintained, by reason or in consequence of any distinctions or differences of color, race or descent, or by reason or in consequence of a previous condition or status of slavery or involuntary servitude of such inhabitants."[18]

Senator Henry Wilson, the bill's sponsor, led the debate, which was the first substantive discussion of civil and constitutional rights in the Thirty-Ninth Congress. Wilson deplored enforcement of the black codes:

In Mississippi rebel State forces, men who were in the rebel armies, are traversing the State, visiting the freedmen, disarming them, perpetrating murders and outrages on them; and the same things are done in other sections of the country. . . . I am told by eminent gentlemen connected with the Freedmen's Bureau that where they have the power they arrest the execution of these laws, but as the laws exist they are enforced in the greater portions of those States. If we now declare those laws to be null and void, I have no idea that any attempt whatever will be made to enforce them, and the freedmen will be relieved from this intolerable oppression.[19]

Wilson grounded his bill in the federal military power rather than the Thirteenth Amendment, which abolished slavery.[20] Senator Edgar Cowan of Pennsylvania wanted to secure "the natural rights of all people," but maintained that a constitutional amendment was necessary to provide Congress the power to enforce these rights.[21] Senator John Sherman argued that legislation "should be in clear and precise language, naming and detailing precisely the rights that these men shall be secured in, so that in the southern States there shall be hereafter no dispute or controversy."[22]

On December 13, the House took its first action on a civil rights issue. Representative John Farnsworth moved to refer to the Joint Committee of Fifteen a resolution to protect freedmen in "their inalienable rights" and to "secure to the colored soldiers of the Union their equal rights and privileges as citizens of the United States."[23] John W. Chandler (D-N.Y.) opposed the motion because "the people of the United States" as used in the Constitution referred to whites only.[24] The resolution was referred to the committee.[25]

The House members appointed to serve on the Joint Committee included John Bingham, Thaddeus Stevens of Pennsylvania, Elihu B. Washburne of Illinois, Justin S. Morrill of Vermont, Henry Grider of Kentucky, Roscoe Conkling of New York, George S. Boutwell of Massachusetts, Henry T. Blow of Missouri, and Andrew J. Rogers of New Jersey.[26] Grider and Rogers were the only Democrat members. On December 18, the House resolved that the committee consider legislation securing to freedmen in the Southern States "the political and civil rights of other citizens of the United States."[27]

The next day, Senator Trumbull announced that he would introduce a bill that would enable the Freedmen's Bureau "to secure freedom to all persons in the United States, and protect every individual in the full enjoyment of the rights of persons and property and furnish him with the means for their vindication."[28] Trumbull justified his bill under the pending

Thirteenth Amendment,[29] which prohibited slavery and empowered Congress to enforce the prohibition.

Minutes later, President Andrew Johnson transmitted to the Senate the report of Major General Carl Schurz, whom the president had sent to tour the South.[30] A heated debate ensued on the importance of that report.[31] Schurz's widely publicized report, upon which Congress placed great credence,[32] reviewed in detail abuses committed against freedmen, including deprivations of the right to keep and bear arms.[33] To restore slavery in fact, planters advocated that "the possession of arms or other dangerous weapons [by the freedmen] without authority should be punished by fine or imprisonment and the arms forfeited."[34] The report brought to Congress' attention an ordinance enacted in Opelousas and other Louisiana towns, which provided: "No freedman who is not in the military service shall be allowed to carry firearms, or any kind of weapon, without the special permission of his employer, in writing, and approved by the mayor or president of the board of police." Punishment was forfeiture of the weapon and either five days imprisonment or a fine of $5.[35] A Freedmen's Bureau report denounced the ordinance as a violation of the Emancipation Proclamation and as "slavery in substance."[36]

With the holiday adjournment nearing, the Senate appointments to the Joint Committee were finally made and included William P. Fessenden of Maine, J. W. Grimes of Iowa, Ira Harris of New York, Jacob M. Howard of Michigan, Reverdy Johnson of Maryland, and George H. Williams of Oregon.[37] Johnson was the sole Democrat. Meanwhile, S. 9, Senator Wilson's civil rights bill, continued to be debated with great animosity.[38]

INTRODUCTION OF THE FREEDMEN'S BUREAU AND CIVIL RIGHTS BILLS

On January 5, 1866, Trumbull introduced S. 60, a bill to enlarge the powers of the Freedmen's Bureau, and S. 61, the Civil Rights Bill, both of which were referred to the Judiciary Committee.[39] These bills would become of unprecedented importance in regard to both the passage of the Fourteenth Amendment and to recognition of the right to keep and bear arms. In the House, Eliot introduced a bill to amend the existing law that established the Freedmen's Bureau, and it was referred to the Select Committee on Freedmen.[40]

On January 11, Trumbull, chairman of the Committee on the Judiciary, reported S. 60 and S. 61.[41] The following day, at Trumbull's request, the Senate considered S. 60, the Freedmen's Bureau Bill. S. 60 provided the

Bureau with jurisdiction in areas where the war had interrupted the ordinary course of judicial proceedings and,

Wherein, in consequence of any State or local law, ordinance, police, or other regulation, custom, or prejudice, any of the civil rights or immunities belonging to white persons (including the right to make and enforce contracts, to sue, be parties, and give evidence, to inherit, purchase, lease, sell, hold, and convey real and personal property, and *to have full and equal benefit of all laws and proceedings for the security of person and estate*) are refused or denied to negroes, mulattoes, freedmen, refugees, or any other persons, on account of race, color, or any previous condition of slavery or involuntary servitude.[42] (emphasis added)

Trumbull then opened consideration of S. 61, the Civil Rights Bill. It contained virtually identical language as S. 60, likewise protecting the right "to full and equal benefit of all laws and proceedings for the security of person and property."[43]

While the Senate was considering statutory protections, the Joint Committee behind closed doors began to examine constitutional amendments to protect the same rights. It is instructive to compare the Freedmen's Bureau Bill with the draft of a constitutional amendment proposed by Bingham to the Joint Committee that same day: "The Congress shall have power to make all laws necessary and proper to secure to all persons in every state within this Union equal protection in their rights of life, liberty and property."[44] Stevens proposed a similar guarantee: "All laws, state or national, shall operate impartially and equally on all persons without regard to race or color."[45] These proposals resemble what became the due process and equal protection clauses of the Fourteenth Amendment. A subcommittee consisting of Bingham, Stevens, Fessenden, Howard, and Conkling was appointed to consider proposed constitutional amendments.[46]

That same day (January 12), the House continued consideration of H.R. 1, a bill to allow black suffrage in the District of Columbia. Chandler quoted from a speech by Michael Hahn of Louisiana to the National Equal Suffrage Association, in which Hahn stated:

It is necessary . . . to see that slavery throughout the land is effectually abolished, and that the freedmen are protected in their freedom.
    "The right of the people to keep and bear arms" must be so understood as not to exclude the colored man from the term "people."[47]

Proponents thus saw both suffrage and the right to keep and bear arms as related rights of citizenship.

On January 13 *Harper's Weekly* informed its readers of Mississippi's prohibition on firearms possession by freedmen: "The militia of this country have seized every gun and pistol found in the hands of the (so called) freedmen of this section of the country. They claim that the statute laws of Mississippi do not recognize the negro as having any right to carry arms. They commenced seizing arms in town, and now the plantations are ransacked in the dead hours of night. . . . The civil laws of this State do not, and will not protect, but *insist* upon infringing on their [the freedmen's] liberties."[48] Such reports generated demands that Congress take action to prevent the states from infringing on the freedmen's right to bear arms.

On January 18, Senator William M. Stewart of Nevada called S. 60 "a practical measure . . . for the benefit of the freedmen, carrying out the constitutional provision to protect him in his civil rights."[49] That bill and S. 61, Stewart averred, "will give full and ample protection under the constitutional amendment to the negro in his civil liberty, and guaranty to him civil rights."[50] The same day in the House, Chairman Eliot of the Select Committee on Freedmen reported H.R. 87,[51] the House version of S. 60.

The following day (January 19) in the Senate, Thomas A. Hendricks (D-Ind.) attacked S. 60. Hendricks feared that § 7 of the bill, which guaranteed civil rights to all, including "the full and equal benefit of all laws and proceedings for the security of person and estate,"[52] might apply in Indiana: "We do not allow to colored people there many civil rights and immunities which are enjoyed by the white people."[53] Hendricks was aware that the Indiana Constitution provided that "the people have a right to bear arms for the defence of themselves and the State,"[54] which protected the open carrying of firearms.[55] Hendricks may have feared that, should S. 60 pass, blacks would have this right.

Trumbull denied that the Freedmen's Bureau jurisdiction would extend to Indiana because it had not been in rebellion and its courts were open.[56] Willard Saulsbury (D-Del.) noted that his state was the last slaveholding state in the United States, and "I am one of the last slaveholders in America."[57] Trumbull responded that although Delaware was not in rebellion, the bureau would protect freedmen in any state where they congregated in large numbers.[58] Bureau judicial authority under § 7 of the bill, by contrast, would exist only in ex-Confederate states where the civil tribunals had been overthrown.[59]

Trumbull argued that the Thirteenth Amendment, because it abolished slavery, would justify congressional legislation to eradicate the slave codes and other incidents of slavery anywhere.[60] The slave codes prohibited, of course, the keeping and carrying of firearms by slaves. Noting that some free states had laws abridging the rights of blacks, Trumbull declared that these discriminatory laws could also be eradicated by Congress pursuant to the Thirteenth Amendment.[61] Referring respectively to the Freedmen's Bureau and Civil Rights Bills, Trumbull continued: "Its provisions are temporary; but here is another bill on your table, and somewhat akin to this, which is intended to be permanent, to extend to all parts of the country, and to protect persons of all races in equal civil rights."[62]

In the House, Connecticut Representative Henry Deming introduced a constitutional amendment similar to Bingham's that declared: "That Congress shall have power to make all laws necessary and proper to secure to all persons in every State equal protection in their rights of life, liberty, and property."[63] This would guarantee, according to Deming, "that the freedman shall be secured an absolute equality with the white man before the civil and criminal law, and shall be endowed with every political right necessary to maintain that equality."[64]

On January 20 the Joint Committee's subcommittee considering drafts of constitutional amendments reported to the full Joint Committee an expanded form of the Bingham proposal that read as follows: "Congress shall have power to make all laws necessary and proper to secure to all citizens of the United States, in every State, the same political rights and privileges; and to all persons in every State equal protection in the enjoyment of life, liberty and property."[65] A wholly separate proposed amendment would have stated, in addition to the above: "All provisions in the Constitution or laws of any State, whereby any distinction is made in political or civil rights or privileges, on account of race, creed or color, shall be inoperative and void."[66] The word "creed" was deleted by the full committee, perhaps to exclude atheists or Confederate sympathizers.[67] Stevens proposed and subsequently withdrew a constitutional amendment that defined United States citizens as "all persons born in the United States, or naturalized, excepting Indians."[68]

CONSTITUTIONAL PROTECTION IN KEEPING ARMS, IN HOLDING PUBLIC ASSEMBLIES

On January 22 Charles Sumner of Massachusetts presented on the Senate floor a Memorial from the Colored Citizens of the State of South Carolina, assembled in convention, that urged Congress to take action to protect the lives, liberty, and personal rights of South Carolina freedmen. Paraphrasing the memorial, Sumner noted: "They also ask that government in that State shall be founded on the consent of the governed, and insist that can be done only where equal suffrage is allowed. . . . *They ask also that they should have the constitutional protection in keeping arms*, in holding public assemblies, and in complete liberty of speech and of the press"[69] (emphasis added).

The convention, held at Charleston in November 1865, included prominent South Carolina blacks, several of whom would later be among America's first black congressmen.[70] Agents of the Freedmen's Bureau and pro-Republican newspaper publishers were among the delegates.[71] Although Sumner's above account embellished the memorial to include the First Amendment, the memorial actually mentioned only the Second: "We ask that, inasmuch as the Constitution of the United States explicitly declares that the right to keep and bear arms shall not be infringed — and the Constitution is the Supreme law of the land — that the late efforts of the Legislature of this State to pass an act to deprive us or [*sic*] arms be forbidden, as a plain violation of the Constitution."[72] The memorial was referred to the Joint Committee on Reconstruction.[73]

Subcommittees of the Joint Committee began to hold hearings later that morning. These hearings documented countless violations of the freedmen's rights, including the right to keep and bear arms. Analysis of these hearings as they occurred contributes to an understanding of the legislative process as it unfolded on the floor of Congress. In a preview of the testimony to come, the first witness testified about murders and acts of violence against freedmen in the Southern States.[74]

When the Senate debated S. 60 (the Freedmen's Bureau Bill) that day, Senator Wilson referred to the laws of South Carolina, Mississippi, Louisiana, and other states as "codes of laws that practically make the freedman a peon or a serf."[75] The next day, January 23, Saulsbury attacked § 7 of S. 60, which included protection for the right "to full and equal benefit of all laws and proceedings for the security of person and property," as Congressional usurpation of state functions.[76]

Even the Freedmen's Bureau Bill's opponents recognized many of the same fundamental rights as its proponents, differing only as to whether freedmen were entitled to all the rights of citizenship and whether the federal government should enforce these rights. Senator Garrett Davis, for example, a self-described Kentucky "old-line Whig," declared the following as the principles of the Founding Fathers: "They were for the subordination of the military to the civil power in peace, in a war, and always. They were for the writ of *habeas corpus*. They were for the trial by jury according to the forms of the common law. *They were for every man bearing his arms about him and keeping them in his house, his castle, for his own defense.* They were for every right and liberty secured to the citizens by the Constitution"[77] (emphasis added).

Davis did not object to any of the bill's statements of rights, offering only unrelated amendments.[78] Trumbull rejoined that such rights are meaningless in places where the civil power is overthrown and the courts are not in operation.[79] A vote was then taken, and the Freedmen's Bureau Bill passed 37 to 10.[80]

On January 24, while the debate over S. 60 was taking place, the Joint Committee considered Bingham's proposed constitutional amendment. Motions by Howard and Boutwell to guarantee suffrage were defeated.[81] A subcommittee composed of Bingham, Boutwell, and Rogers (D-N.J.) — who had led the opposition in the House — was appointed to review the proposal further.[82]

Meanwhile, members of the Joint Committee heard testimony concerning the repression of freedmen by state militias. On January 26 an army general noted that in Alabama, "the roads and public highways are patrolled by the State militia, and no colored man is allowed to travel without a pass from his employer."[83] "The arming of the militia," the general testified, "is only for the purpose of intimidating the Union men, and enforcing upon the negroes a species of slavery."[84] Members of the Joint Committee, particularly Howard, who would introduce the proposed Fourteenth Amendment in the Senate, asked questions concerning the intimidation of unarmed people.[85]

On January 27 the Joint Committee considered a draft of the constitutional amendment reported by the subcommittee of Bingham, Boutwell, and Rogers. It now read: "Congress shall have power to make laws which shall be necessary and proper to secure all persons in every state full protection in the enjoyment of life, liberty and property; and to all citizens of the United States in every State the same immunities and also equal political rights and privileges."[86] Johnson lost his motion to strike the privileges and immunities clause.[87] Further consideration was postponed until the next meeting.[88]

On January 29 the Senate began consideration of S. 61, the Civil Rights Bill. Trumbull opened debate by arguing that it enforced the Thirteenth Amendment, which would be a dead letter if the Southern States could retain "badges of slavery" in their legal codes. Trumbull cited the Mississippi and other black codes that "prohibit[ed] any negro or mulatto from having fire-arms," emphasizing that it was "the intention of this bill to secure those rights" and other "privileges which are essential to freemen" from state deprivation.[89] Trumbull quoted § 7 of the bill, which referred to "full and equal benefit of all laws and proceedings for the security of person and property."[90] He referred to "the great fundamental rights set forth in this bill . . . as appertaining to every freeman."[91] Trumbull clearly assumed that both positive rights and equal protection were to be guaranteed and that a prohibition on firearms possession was a badge of slavery.

Saulsbury led the attack on the Civil Rights Bill.[92] Raising the specter of black suffrage, he complained that the bill would provide blacks "every security for the protection of person and property which a white man has," including the ballot.[93] Saulsbury also complained that the bill would prevent the states from disarming blacks:

This bill positively deprives the State of its police power of government. In my State for many years, and I presume there are similar laws in most of the southern States, *there has existed a law of the State based upon and founded in its police power, which declares that free negroes shall not have the possession of firearms or ammunition. This bill proposes to take away from the States this police power*, so that if in any State of this Union at anytime hereafter there shall be such a numerous body of dangerous persons belonging to any distinct race as to endanger the peace of the State, and to cause the lives of its citizens to be subject to their violence, the State shall not have the power to disarm them without disarming the whole population.[94] (emphasis added)

Actually, the bill was even more sweeping, because it guaranteed "*full and equal*" — not just equal — "benefit of all laws and proceedings for the security of person and property." The states could not, by the Civil Rights Bill's language and Trumbull's logic, equally infringe the right to bear arms of the whole population.

On January 30 the House took up consideration of the Freedmen's Bureau Bill. Chairman Eliot reported the committee substitute.[95] As an example of black codes the bill was designed to nullify, Eliot quoted the ordinance of Opelousas, Louisiana, that required freedmen to have a pass, prohibited their residence in the town, prohibited their religious and other meetings, and infringed their right to keep and bear arms: "No freedman who is not in the military service shall be allowed to carry fire-arms, or any kind of weapons, within the limits of the town of Opelousas without the special permission of his employer, in writing, and approved by the mayor or president of the board of police. Anyone thus offending shall forfeit his weapons, and shall be imprisoned and made to work five days on the public streets, or pay a fine of five dollars in lieu of said work."[96]

In the Joint Committee that day, in response to questions by Boutwell, Brevet Major General Clinton B. Fisk told of the paranoia in the South concerning blacks with firearms: "I went myself into northern Mississippi to look after a reported insurrection of negroes there, and found the whole thing had grown out of one negro marching through the woods with his fowling-piece [shotgun] to shoot squirrels to feed his family."[97] Fisk pointed out the need to protect the right of freedmen to keep and bear arms: "One of the causes for the late disturbances in northern Mississippi was the arming of their local militia. They were ordered by the adjutant general of the State to disarm the negroes and turn their arms into the arsenals. That caused great dissatisfaction and disturbance. We immediately issued orders prohibiting the disarming of the negroes, since which it has become more quiet."[98]

When the hearings continued the following day, the committee obtained the report of Brigadier General Charles H. Howard to his brother and head of the Freedmen's Bureau, Major General O. O. Howard.[99] Dated December 30, 1865, the report provided a detailed account of how state-armed and -organized militias were disarming the freedmen:

The militia organizations in the opposite county of South Carolina (Edgefield) were engaged in disarming the negroes. This created great discontent among the latter, and in some instances they had offered resistance.

In southwestern Georgia, I learned that the militia had done the same, sometimes pretending to act under orders from United States authorities.

General Howard recommended the abolition of these militias, which "give the color of law to their violent, unjust, and sometimes inhuman proceedings."[100]

Senator Howard examined perhaps most of the witnesses at the hearings. A federal tax commissioner from Fairfax County, Virginia, responded to a question by the Senator concerning the disposition of whites toward freedmen as follows: "The corporate authorities of Alexandria refused to grant them licenses to do business, the law of the State not allowing it; and attempts were made in that city to enforce the old law against them in respect to whipping and carrying fire-arms, nearly or quite up to the time of the establishment of the Freedmen's Bureau in that city."[101]

S. 60 AMENDED TO RECOGNIZE "THE CONSTITUTIONAL RIGHT OF BEARING ARMS"

On February 1, 1866, Senator Benjamin G. Brown of Missouri introduced, and the Senate adopted, a resolution that the Joint Committee consider an amendment to the Constitution "so as to declare with greater certainty the power of Congress to enforce and determine by appropriate legislation *all the guarantees contained in that instrument*"[102] (emphasis added). This resolution thus anticipated the intent of the Fourteenth Amendment to incorporate the Bill of Rights.

Debate on the Civil Rights Bill centered on whether citizenship would be race neutral, with some Western senators wishing to exclude Indians and Chinese from citizenship. Williams of Oregon argued that if Indians were citizens, then state laws that prohibited whites from selling arms and ammunition to Indians would be void.[103] At a time when the suppression of Indians and the seizure of their lands was proceeding in earnest, it was considered unacceptable to recognize a right of Indians to keep and bear arms. Thus, the Senate voted to define all persons born in the United States, without distinction of color, as citizens, "excluding Indians not taxed."[104]

In the House, debate on the Freedmen's Bureau Bill, S. 60, began with a procedural ruling that delayed the offering of amendments. Nathaniel P. Banks, a former governor of Massachusetts and Union general, stated: "I shall move, if I am permitted to do so, to amend the seventh section of this bill by inserting after the word 'including' the words 'the constitutional right to bear arms'; so that it will read, 'including the constitutional right to bear arms, the right to make and enforce contracts, to sue, &c.'"[105] The section would thus have recognized "the civil rights belonging to white persons, including the constitutional right to bear arms."

The House then returned to debate on the bill. Supporting its passage, Representative Ignatius Donnelly noted that "there is an amendment offered by the distinguished gentleman from Ohio [Mr. Bingham] which provides in effect that Congress shall have power to enforce by appropriate legislation *all the guarantees of the Constitution*."[106] Once again, Bingham's draft of the Fourteenth Amendment was seen as protecting Bill of Rights guarantees.

On February 2, Davis introduced a substitute for S. 61, the Civil Rights Bill. It declared that any person "who shall subject or cause to be subjected a citizen of the United States to the deprivation of *any privilege or immunity in any State to which such citizen is entitled under the Constitution* and laws of the United States" shall have an action for damages, and that such conduct would be a misdemeanor[107] (emphasis added). Davis' substitute suggests that even opponents of the Civil Rights Bill were willing to concede that the explicit guarantees of the Bill of Rights should be protected. Davis grounded his compromise bill in the privileges and immunities clause of article IV.[108]

Senator Wilson of Massachusetts argued the necessity of the Civil Rights Bill on the basis that military decrees were still necessary to overturn the black codes: "General Sickles has just issued an order in South Carolina of twenty-three sections, more full, perfect, and complete in their provisions than have ever been issued by an official in the country, for the security of the rights of the freedmen."[109] General D. E. Sickles' order, which was quoted in full in later floor debates, recognized "the constitutional rights of all loyal and well disposed inhabitants to bear arms," and the same right for ex-Confederates who had taken the amnesty oath.[110] After further debate, the Civil Rights Bill passed the Senate by a vote of 33 to 12.[111]

On February 3 Representative L. H. Rousseau of Kentucky quoted § 7 of S. 60, including the terms "all laws and proceedings for the security of person and estate," and then referred in part to "the security to person and property from unreasonable search."[112] This suggested that the Fourth Amendment and other Bill of Rights provisions were encompassed in the "laws and proceedings for the security of person and estate," and indeed the Freedmen's Bureau Bill would later pass stating that "the constitutional right to bear arms" was encompassed within this language.[113]

On the same day in the Joint Committee, Bureau official J. W. Alvord, who had visited most of the Southern States, told Senator Howard that some blacks had arms, and the following exchange ensued:

Question. Do they keep them publicly in their houses so that they can be seen, or are they concealed.

Answer. It may be that some of them are concealed, but generally they are proud of owning a musket or fowling-piece. They use them often for the destruction of vermin and game.[114]

The Joint Committee met in secret that day to consider the proposed constitutional amendment. Bingham offered the following substitute for the subcommittee draft: "The Congress shall have power to make all laws which shall be necessary and proper to secure to the citizens of each state all privileges and immunities of citizens in the several states (Art. 4, Sec. 2); and to all persons in the several States equal protection in the rights of life, liberty and property (5th Amendment)."[115] Bingham's substitute was agreed to on a nonpartisan vote of 7 to 6, with Democrat Rogers joining with Howard in voting in the affirmative.[116] Ironically, Rogers then cast the deciding vote against the amendment as such.[117]

In House debate on February 5, Representative Lawrence Trimble, a Democrat, argued that S. 60 (the Freedmen's Bureau Bill) was based on military rule and violated the Fourth, Fifth, and Sixth Amendments, which he called "inalienable rights of an American freeman."[118] In response, bill supporters pointed to the rights violated under current law in Trimble's own state. Representative Grinnell noted that "a white man in Kentucky may keep a gun; if a black man buys a gun he forfeits it and pays a fine of five dollars, if presuming to keep in his possession a musket which he has carried through the war."[119] In Kentucky, according to the Report of the Commissioner of the Freedmen's Bureau, "the civil law prohibits the colored man from bearing arms," and "their arms are taken from them by the civil authorities. . . . Thus, the right of the people to keep and bear arms as provided in the Constitution is *infringed*."[120] Representative Samuel McKee of Kentucky noted that 27,000 black soldiers from Kentucky "have been returned to their homes by the order of the Secretary of War, approved by the President, and they are allowed to retain their arms. I suppose those men, who are now freedmen, would like to have this law to protect them. . . . As freedmen they must have the civil rights of freemen."[121]

As instructed by the Select Committee on the Freedmen's Bureau, Chairman Eliot offered a substitute for S. 60.[122] Eliot proceeded "to explain the changes proposed by the select committee," including the following: "The next amendment is in the seventh section, in the eleventh line, after the word 'estate,' by inserting the words 'including the constitutional right to bear arms,' so that it will read, 'to have full and equal benefit of all laws and proceedings for the security of person and estate, including the constitutional right to bear arms.'"[123] Representative Banks had suggested identical language four days earlier, although he would then have placed the term "the constitutional right to bear arms" first in the list of civil rights.[124] The above language seems to have received unanimous Republican support in the House.

Bingham, whose proposed constitutional amendment was being debated, was also a member of the Select Committee on Freedmen, which had instructed Eliot to report the substitute for S. 60. Although the House debated other provisions, no one objected to the proposed amendment to S. 60 explicitly recognizing the right to bear arms.

Arguing for adoption of the Freedmen's Bureau Bill, Eliot quoted from a report by General Fisk to General Howard, commissioner of the Freedmen's Bureau, that outlined circumstances in Kentucky, stating in part: 'On the very day last week that [Senator] Garrett Davis [of Kentucky] was engaged in denouncing the Freedmen's Bureau in the United States

Senate, his own neighbors, who had fought gallantly in the Union Army, were pleading with myself for the protection which the civil authorities failed to afford. *The civil law prohibits the colored man from bearing arms; returned soldiers are, by the civil officers, dispossessed of their arms and fined for violation of the law"* [125] (emphasis added). Eliot also quoted from a letter received from a teacher at a freedmen's school in Maryland. Because of attacks on the school, the teacher wrote, "both the mayor and sheriff have warned the colored people to go armed to school, (which they do,). . . . The superintendent of schools came down and brought me a revolver."[126] The next day, February 6, a vote was taken in the House on final passage of S. 60. The Select Committee's substitute as reported by Eliot, which included "the constitutional right to bear arms" as a "civil right,"[127] passed by a resounding vote of 136 to 33.[128] In the Senate the following day, Trumbull moved that the House amendments to S. 60 be referred to the Committee on the Judiciary.[129]

In the Joint Committee on February 8, Senator Harris questioned a Mississippi judge about laws passed in his state concerning freedmen. The judge responded in part: "They also enacted they [the freedmen] should be disarmed, which grew out of an excitement in the country at the time there was likely to be an insurrection. . . . It was believed to exist by the officer of the Freedmen's Bureau for the State, but which I think was without foundation, and is now so understood."[130]

That same day, Trumbull informed the Senate that he was instructed by the Committee on the Judiciary to report back S. 60 and to recommend that the Senate concur in the House amendments.[131] Explaining the amendments, Trumbull noted: "There is also a slight amendment in the seventh section, thirteenth line. That is the section which declares that negroes and mulattoes shall have the same civil rights as white persons, and have the same security of person and estate. The House have inserted these words, 'including the constitutional right of bearing arms.' *I think that does not alter the meaning"*[132] (emphasis added). Thus, the author of the Freedmen's Bureau and Civil Rights Bills verified that the common language of both bills protected the constitutional right to bear arms.

Once again, opponents objected that S. 60 was based on military rule and denied jury trial.[133] No one objected to the acknowledgment of the right to keep and bear arms. The Senate then concurred in S. 60 as amended without a recorded vote.[134] Unrelated Senate amendments were approved by the House the next day.[135] Congress had at last passed the Freedmen's Bureau Bill.

FROM ENFORCEMENT OF THE SECOND
AMENDMENT TO THE VETO OF S. 60

As passed, the Freedmen's Bureau Bill provided in § 7 that, in areas where ordinary judicial proceedings were interrupted by the rebellion, the president shall extend military protection to persons whose rights are violated. The contours of rights violations were described by the bill in part as follows:

Wherein, in consequence of any State or local law, ordinance, police or other regulation, custom, or prejudice, any of the *civil rights or immunities* belonging to white persons, including the right to make and enforce contracts, to sue, be parties, and give evidence, to inherit, purchase, lease, sell, hold and convey real and personal property, and to have *full and equal benefit of all laws and proceedings for the security of person and estate, including the constitutional right of bearing arms*, are refused or denied to negroes, mulattoes, freedmen, refugees, or any other persons, on account of race, color, or any previous condition of slavery or involuntary servitude.[136] (emphasis added)

On February 13, 1866, it was reported in both houses of Congress that the Joint Committee had recommended adoption of a constitutional amendment to read as follows: "The Congress shall have power to make all laws which shall be necessary and proper to secure to the citizens of each State all privileges and immunities of citizens in the several States; and to all persons in the several States equal protection in the rights of life, liberty, and property."[137] This appears to be the first reported draft of what would become § 1 of the Fourteenth Amendment. Now that the Freedmen's Bureau Bill had been passed, Congress turned its attention to a constitutional provision generalizing the same rights.

The Memorial of Citizens of Tennessee, the unionists in control of the state seeking recognition, was that day referred to the Joint Committee.[138] It included acts passed by the Union legislature, including an apparent exemption in favor of all loyalists, perhaps including freedmen, from the state's prohibition on carrying concealed weapons: "That all discharged Union soldiers, who have served either as State or Federal soldiers, and have been honorably discharged [from] the service, and all citizens who have always been loyal, shall be permitted to carry any and all necessary side-arms, being their own private property, for their personal protection and common defence."[139] The Tennessee legislature also passed a resolution ratifying the Thirteenth Amendment.[140] The memorialists complained of acts of Tennessee's ex-Confederate government, such as "the disarming and conscripting of the people."[141] They pleaded to be represented again in Congress.[142]

Witnesses from other states paraded before the Joint Committee. A Virginia music professor related an incident where "two Union men were attacked. . . . But they drew their revolvers and held their assailants at bay."[143] The professor himself was armed for protection.[144] Senator Howard questioned an assistant commissioner in the Freedmen's Bureau from Richmond, Virginia. If the Bureau were to be removed, asked Howard, what would be the result of the increased violence toward blacks? The following exchange took place:

Answer: I think it would eventually result in an insurrection on the part of the blacks; black troops that are about being mustered out, and those that have been mustered out, will all provide themselves with arms; probably most of them will purchase their arms; and will not endure those outrages, without any protection except that which they obtain from Virginia.

Question: Are there many arms among the blacks?

Answer: Yes, sir; attempts have been made, in many instances, to disarm them.

Question: Who have made the attempts?

Answer: The citizens, by organizing what they call "patrols" — combinations of citizens.

Question: Has that arrangement pervaded the State generally?

Answer: No sir; it has not been allowed; they would disarm the negroes at once if they could.[145]

On February 17 Representative Burton C. Cook of Illinois, noting the importance of the Freedmen's Bureau and Civil Rights Bills, rhetorically asked about the Thirteenth Amendment: "Did this mean only that they [slaves] should no longer be bought and sold like beasts in shambles, or did not mean that they should have the civil rights of freedmen?"[146] Cook went on to advocate adoption of further constitutional amendments to secure these rights.[147]

Representative William Lawrence of Ohio discussed the need to protect freedmen, quoting General Sickles' General Order No. 1 (dated January 1, 1866) for the Department of South Carolina, which negated the state's prohibition on possession of firearms by blacks and, at the same time, recognized the right of the conquered to bear arms:

I. To the end that civil rights and immunities may be enjoyed, . . . the following regulations are established for the government of all concerned in this department.

XVI. The constitutional rights of all loyal and well disposed inhabitants to bear arms, will not be infringed; nevertheless this shall not be construed to sanction the unlawful practice of carrying concealed weapons; nor to authorize any person to enter with arms on the premises of another without his consent. No one shall bear arms who has borne arms against the United States, unless he shall have taken the Amnesty oath prescribed in the Proclamation of the President of the United States, dated May 19th, 1865 or the Oath of Allegiance, prescribed in the Proclamation of the President of the United States, dated December 8th, 1863, within the time prescribed therein. And no disorderly person, vagrant, or disturber of the peace shall be allowed to bear arms.[148]

This "most remarkable order," repeatedly printed in the headlines of the *Loyal Georgian*,[149] a prominent black newspaper, was thought to have been "issued with the knowledge and approbation of the President if not by his direction."[150] The first issue to print the order included the following editorial:

Editor Loyal Georgian:
    Have colored persons a right to own and carry fire arms?
    A Colored Citizen
Almost every day we are asked questions similar to the above. We answer *certainly* you have the *same* right to own and carry arms that other citizens have. You are not only free but citizens of the United States and as such entitled to the same privileges granted to other citizens by the Constitution.
    Article II, of the amendment to the Constitution of the United States, gives the people the right to bear arms, and states that this right shall not be infringed. Any person, white or black, may be disarmed if convicted of making an improper or dangerous use of weapons, but no military or civil officer has the right or authority to disarm any class of people, thereby placing them at the mercy of others. All men, without distinction of color, have the right to keep and bear arms to defend their homes, families or themselves.[151]

The last paragraph, taken from a Freedmen's Bureau circular, was printed numerous times in the *Loyal Georgian*.[152] Other black newspapers also defended the right to keep and bear arms.[153] The first draft of the Fourteenth Amendment was proposed about the same time as publication of the above issue of the *Loyal Georgian*, which followed the congressional debates carefully.[154] The freedmen readership of such newspapers could only have concluded that the new amendment would protect their right to keep and bear arms as well as other constitutional rights.

In the Joint Committee on February 17 Representative Boutwell asked an Arkansas state official whether any danger of negro insurrection existed if blacks were properly treated. The official replied: "No sir, but if they are told that they have no rights which white men are bound to respect, and if federal bayonets are turned against them, they will secrete arms for the purpose of defending themselves."[155] Boutwell then examined Arkansas Supreme Court Justice Charles A. Harper, who stated about blacks in Arkansas: "He has all the civil rights of the white man *with the exception of suffrage and bearing arms.* That was our purpose in the convention, and we think we have made sufficient change in our bill of rights to carry it out. We think the negro can hold real estate and that his testimony is admissible; but we did not grant him suffrage nor the privilege of bearing arms. . . . We certainly could not have carried our constitution if we had given the negro all the rights of the white man"[156] (emphasis added).

In the Senate on February 19, Wilson introduced S.R. 32, a joint resolution to disband the militia forces in most Southern states.[157] Wilson quoted detailed accounts of militia abuses, including the report of General Howard that had been submitted to the Joint Committee that Southern militias "were engaged in disarming the negroes. This created great discontent among the latter."[158]

In opposition to referring the joint resolution to committee, Senator Saulsbury argued that the power of Congress under Article I, § 8 to organize, arm, and discipline the militia

Does not give power to Congress to disarm the militia of a State, or to destroy the militia of a State, because in another provision of the Constitution, the second amendment, we have these words:

"A well-regulated militia being necessary to the security of a free State, the right of the people to keep and bear arms shall not be infringed."

The proposition here . . . is an application to Congress to do that which Congress has no right to do under the second amendment of the Constitution.

Saulsbury complained that the Freedmen's Bureau had ordered judges to return seized firearms to blacks convicted of carrying them concealed. Further, abuses by freedmen using firearms were ignored by radical Republicans, but "if a few letters are written to members here that oppression has been practiced against negroes, then the whole white population of a State are to be disarmed."[159]

Senator Wilson responded that ex-Confederates went "up and down the country searching houses, disarming people, committing outrages of every kind and description."[160] He concluded: "Congress has power to disarm ruffians or traitors, or men who are committing outrages against law or the rights of men on our common humanity."[161] The resolution was then referred to committee.[162]

Both senators upheld the peaceful citizen's right to keep and bear arms, but they disagreed over who in the South were aggressors and consequently had lost this and other rights. Wilson had complained two months earlier about the deprivations of arms of freedmen in Mississippi, pursuant to that state's firearms prohibition law that applied only to blacks.[163] Although just three weeks earlier Saulsbury had opposed the Civil Rights Bill because it would prohibit states from disarming free negroes,[164] he now invoked the Second Amendment to protect the right of "the whole white population" not only to be armed but also to organize and operate as militia.

A few days later, Wilson reported his bill to disband the Southern State militias,[165] but it was not taken up until the next session, where it passed in a form not creating any infringement of the individual right to keep and bear arms.[166] On both sides of the aisle, the personal right to have arms was more fundamental than the power of the state to maintain a militia.

By now members of Congress were startled to learn that President Johnson had just vetoed the Freedmen's Bureau Bill. Johnson objected that the Freedmen's Bureau Bill relied on military rule and violated the right to trial by jury.[167] The president complained that § 8 "subjects any white person who may be charged with depriving a freedman of 'any civil rights or immunities belonging to white persons' to imprisonment or fine, or both, without, however, defining the 'civil rights and immunities' which are thus to be secured to the freedmen by military law."[168] Johnson did not, however, object to the civil suit provision in § 7, or to its specific protection of "the constitutional right to bear arms." The reading of the veto message caused such an uproar that the Senate galleries had to be cleared.[169]

Meanwhile in the Joint Committee, Boutwell was eliciting further testimony concerning how the Union constitutional convention in Arkansas recognized the civil rights of freedmen, with the notable exceptions of bearing arms and suffrage. The witness, Senator William D. Snow of Arkansas, explained in part about "the civil and political rights of negroes":

The old constitution and the new constitution are identical in this: The old constitution declares, "that the free white men of the State shall have a right to keep and to bear arms for their common defence." The new constitution retains the words "free white" before the word "men." . . . At the time this new constitution was adopted we were yet in the midst of a war. . . . There was also some uncertainty in

the minds of timid men as to what the negro might do, if given arms, in a turbulent state of society, and in his then uneducated condition; and to allay what I was
confident was an unnecessary alarm, that clause was retained. . . . The idea
prevailed that that clause, being simply permissive, would not prevent the legislature, if at a future time it should be deemed advisable, from allowing the same
rights to the colored man.[170]

The old and new constitutions had been adopted in 1836 and 1864 respectively.[171] Ironically, the 1861 secessionist constitution had extended the
right to bear arms to Indians.[172]

On February 20, the Senate debated whether to override the veto of the
Freedmen's Bureau Bill. Davis made an impassioned speech on the bill's
unconstitutionality.[173] Trumbull expressed great surprise at the veto,
pointing out that the bill's purpose was to protect constitutional rights.[174]
Trumbull again detailed the oppression of the freedmen, quoting the letter
from Colonel Samuel Thomas in Vicksburg, Mississippi, that "nearly all
the dissatisfaction that now exists among the freedmen is caused by the
abusive conduct of this militia," which typically would "hang some freedman or search negro houses for arms."[175] Trumbull appealed to the Thirteenth Amendment, which empowered Congress to stamp out the badges
of slavery.[176]

The proponents of S. 60 sought to override the veto, but it failed by a
vote of 30 to 18, just 2 votes shy of the necessary two-thirds.[177] This
defeat mooted any need for a House override vote. The veto, the first
break between President Johnson and the Congress, began a saga that
would culminate in the unsuccessful impeachment of the president.[178]
Republican newspapers, both radical and conservative, denounced the
veto and supported the principles of the Freedmen's Bureau Bill.[179] At
least one state legislature, Wisconsin, praised Congress for passing the bill
and decried the veto.[180]

Meanwhile it was business as usual in the Joint Committee. Major
General Alfred Terry related that he refused the demands of members of
the Virginia legislature "to take the arms of the blacks away from
them."[181] Lieutenant Colonel H. S. Hall, an official with the Freedmen's
Bureau, told how Texas Governor Jack Hamilton authorized armed
patrols to suppress an alleged negro insurrection: "Under pretense of the
authority given them, they passed about through the settlements where
negroes were living, disarmed them — took everything in the shape of
arms from them — and frequently robbed them of money, household
furniture, and anything that they could make of any use to themselves.

Complaints of this kind were very often brought to my notice by the negroes from counties too far away for me to reach."[182]

The next day (February 21) Senator Howard examined General Rufus Saxton, former Assistant Commissioner of the Freedmen's Bureau in South Carolina. Saxton explained: "I have had men come to my office and complain that the negroes had arms, and I also heard that bands of men called Regulators, consisting of those who were lately in the rebel service, were going around the country disarming negroes. I can further state that they desired me to sanction a form of contract which would deprive the colored men of their arms, which I refused to do. The subject was so important, as I thought, to the welfare of the freedmen that I issued a circular on this subject."[183]

General Saxton then furnished the committee with a copy of his circular, which documented peonage contracts as well as the following:

It is reported that in some parts of this State, armed parties are, without proper authority, engaged in seizing all fire-arms found in the hands of the freedmen. Such conduct is in clear and direct violation of their personal rights as guaranteed by the Constitution of the United States, which declares that "the right of the people to keep and bear arms shall not be infringed." The freedmen of South Carolina have shown by their peaceful and orderly conduct that they can safely be trusted with fire-arms, and they need them to kill game for sustenance, and to protect their crops from destruction by birds and animals.[184]

After asserting that South Carolina whites sought a "disarmed and defenseless" black population, General Saxton testified that the probable effect of disarming the freedmen would be to "leave their condition no better than before they were emancipated."[185]

PERSONAL SECURITY, PERSONAL LIBERTY, AND THE CIVIL RIGHTS ACT

The first draft of the proposed Fourteenth Amendment was debated in the House for three days, beginning on February 27, 1866. Bingham, its author, argued on its behalf that previously "this immortal bill of rights embodied in the Constitution, rested for its execution and enforcement hitherto upon the fidelity of the States."[186]

Representative Robert Hale of New York saw no need for the amendment, because he interpreted the existing Bill of Rights to bind not just Congress but also the States: "Now, what are these amendments to the Constitution, numbered from one to ten, one of which is the fifth article in question? . . . They constitute the bill of rights, a bill of rights for the protection of the citizen, and defining and limiting the power of Federal and State legislation."[187]

Bingham responded that the proposed amendment would "arm the Congress . . . with the power to enforce this bill of rights as it stands in the Constitution today."[188] Representative Frederick E. Woodbridge of Vermont characterized the sweep of the proposed Fourteenth Amendment as empowering Congress to protect "the natural rights which necessarily pertain to citizenship."[189]

In debate on February 28 on the representation of the Southern States in Congress, Senator James Nye of Nevada opined that the Bill of Rights already applied to the States, and that Congress has power to enforce it against the States. He stated:

In the enumeration of natural and personal rights to be protected, the framers of the Constitution apparently specified everything they could think of — "life," "liberty," "property," "freedom of speech," "freedom of the press," "freedom in the exercise of religion," "security of person," &c.; and then, lest something essential in the specifications should have been overlooked, it was provided in the ninth amendment that "the enumeration in the Constitution of certain rights should not be construed to deny or disparage other rights not enumerated." . . . All these rights are established by the fundamental law.

Will it be contended, sir, at this day, that any State has the power to subvert or impair the natural and personal rights of the citizen?

Referring to blacks, Senator Nye continued: "As citizens of the United States they have equal right to protection, and to keep and bear arms for self-defense."[190]

Similarly, Senator Stewart repeated that the federal Constitution is "the vital, sovereign, and controlling part of the fundamental law of every State," and although the states may repeat parts of it in their own bills of rights, "no State can adopt anything in a State constitution in conflict."[191]

A significant debate in the House on S. 61, the civil rights bill, took place on March 1. Representative Wilson, chairman of the Judiciary Committee, explained the background to the bill's phraseology "civil rights and immunities" and "full and equal benefit of all laws and proceedings for the security of person and property."[192] Quoting Kent's *Commentaries*, Wilson explained: "I understand civil rights to be simply the absolute rights of individuals, such as — 'The right of personal security, the right of personal liberty, and the right to acquire and enjoy property.'"[193] Wilson added that "we are reducing to statute from the spirit of the Constitution,"[194] a clear reference to the Bill of Rights. Referring to "the great fundamental civil rights," Wilson pointed out:

[Sir William] Blackstone classifies them under three articles, as follows:

1. The right of personal security; which, he says, "Consists in a person's legal and uninterrupted enjoyment of his life, his limbs, his body, his health, and his reputation."

2. The right of personal liberty; and this, he says, "Consists in the power of locomotion, of changing situation, or moving one's person to whatever place one's own inclination may direct, without imprisonment or restraint, unless by due course of law."

3. The right of personal property; which he defines to be, "The free use, enjoyment, and disposal of all his acquisitions, without any control or diminution, save only by the law of the land."[195]

To protect "the principal absolute rights which appertain to every Englishman," Blackstone explained that there are "auxiliary" rights to "maintain inviolate the three great and primary rights, of personal security, personal liberty, and private property."[196] Blackstone included among these rights "that of having arms for their defence suitable to their condition and degree, and such as are allowed by law," that made possible "the natural right of resistance and self-preservation, when the sanctions of society and laws are found insufficient to restrain the violence of oppression."[197] Together with justice in the courts and the right of petition, "the right of having and using arms for self-preservation and defense" were available to preserve the rights to life, liberty, and property.[198]

The Freedmen's Bureau Bill likewise declared that the rights of personal security and personal liberty included what Blackstone referred to as "the right of having and using arms for self-preservation and defense."[199] Senator Wilson had the Second Amendment partly in mind when he stated that every right enumerated in the federal Constitution is "embodied in one of the rights I have mentioned, or results as an incident necessary to complete defense and enjoyment of the specific right."[200]

Opponents agreed. Representative Rogers declared that S. 61, the Civil Rights Bill, "is nothing but a relic of the Freedmen's Bureau bill,"[201] which declared explicitly that the rights of personal security and personal liberty included "the constitutional right of bearing arms." Even Rogers held that "the rights of nature" included "the right of self-defense, the right to protect our lives from invasion by others."[202]

Another Democrat, Representative Anthony Thornton of Illinois, argued in a speech on Reconstruction on March 3 that the South had no monopoly on violation of rights. In the North during the Civil War "freedom of speech was denied; the freedom of the press was abridged; the right to bear arms was infringed," yet these "inherent" rights were once again respected under the Constitution.[203]

On March 5 the Senate debated the basis of representation, which became § 2 of the Fourteenth Amendment. Senator Samuel Pomeroy of Kansas, a supporter of the proposed amendment, stated:

And what are the safeguards of liberty under our form of Government? There are at least, under our Constitution, three which are indispensable —

1. Every man should have a homestead, that is, the right to acquire and hold one, and the right to be safe and protected in that citadel of his love.

2. He should have the right to bear arms for the defense of himself and family and his homestead. And if the cabin door of the freedman is broken open and the intruder enters for purposes as vile as were known to slavery, then should a well-loaded musket be in the hand of the occupant to send the polluted wretch to another world, where his wretchedness will forever remain complete; and

3. He should have the ballot.[204]

Pomeroy was uncertain whether the proposed Fourteenth Amendment would pass, but argued that the right to bear arms could be secured through the Enforcement Clause of the Thirteenth Amendment: "Sir, what is 'appropriate legislation' on the subject, namely, securing the freedom of all men? It can be nothing less than throwing about all men the essential safeguards of the Constitution. The 'right to bear arms' is not plainer taught or more efficient than the right to carry ballots. And if appropriate legislation will secure the one so can it also the other. And if both are necessary, and provided for in the Constitution as now amended, why then let us close the question by congressional legislation."[205]

In the Joint Committee on March 5 Senator Howard questioned Captain Alexander Ketchum, assistant to General O. O. Howard, concerning South Carolina. The witness testified that the freedmen as a general rule did not have arms, but removal of the Freedmen's Bureau would subject them to oppressive state legislation and would result in armed conflict. The senator continued:

Question: Could they do otherwise than arm themselves to defend their rights?
Answer: No, sir; they would be bound to do it.

Question: Do not you think that in such an exigency it would be imperative upon these men to arm themselves to defend their rights, and that it would be cowardly in them not to do it?

Answer: Certainly I do. They could not do otherwise than organize to protect themselves.[206]

The subject then turned to contracts of peonage between the former masters and slaves. Ketchum noted: 'The planters are disposed, in many cases, to insert in their contracts tyrannical provisions, to prevent the negroes from leaving the plantation without a written pass from the proprietor; forbidding them to entertain strangers *or to have fire-arms in their possession, even for proper purposes*"[207] (emphasis added). Senator Howard then produced a model contract drafted by a committee of planters. Under its terms, freedmen agreed "to keep no poultry, dogs or stock of any kind, except as hereinafter specified; no firearms or deadly weapons."[208]

On March 6 President Johnson communicated to the Senate all reports made since December 1, 1865 by the assistant commissioners of the Freedmen's Bureau.[209] These reports were communicated to the House on March 20.[210] The reports included a circular promulgated by Assistant Commissioner for Georgia Davis Tillson on December 22, 1865, which stated: "Article 2 of the amendments to the Constitution of the United States gives the people the right to bear arms, and states that this right *'shall not be infringed.'* Any person, white or black, may be disarmed if convicted of making an improper and dangerous use of weapons; but no military or civil officer has the right or authority to disarm any *class* of people, thereby placing them at the mercy of others. All men, without distinction of color, have the right to keep arms to defend their homes, families, or themselves"[211] (emphasis added). The circular reported several "outrages committed upon colored persons in Kentucky,"[212] including arrests for possession of pistols.[213]

Assistant Commissioner Fisk wrote that in Kentucky "the civil law prohibits the colored man from bearing arms":[214] "Their arms are taken from them by the civil authorities, and confiscated for benefit of the Commonwealth. . . . Thus, the right of the people to keep and bear arms as provided in the Constitution is *infringed*."[215] Fisk's report noted further that "the town marshal takes all arms from returned colored soldiers, and is very prompt in shooting the blacks whenever an opportunity occurs."[216] As a result, outlaws throughout Kentucky "make brutal attacks and raids upon the freedmen, who are defenseless, for the civil law-officers disarm the colored man and hand him over to armed marauders."[217]

A report of Assistant Commissioner Wager Swayne from Alabama described the abuses committed by state militias and special constables, adding that "the weaker portion of the community should not be forbid[den] to carry arms, when the stronger do so as a rule of custom."[218] Swayne detailed instances where officials, ostensibly to prevent insurrection but really to compel blacks to enter into labor contracts, ordered militia units to break into the houses of blacks and seize firearms. These militias often took "not only fire-arms, but whatever their fancy or avarice desired."[219]

In another report, Swayne detailed the following incident: "Two men were arrested near here one day last week, who were robbing and disarming negroes upon the highway. The arrests were made by the provost marshal's forces. The men represented themselves as in the military service, and acting by my order. They afterwards stated, what was probable true, that they belonged to the Macon county militia."[220] Swayne expected to place the militiamen on trial for robbery, adding: "There must be 'no distinction of color' in the right to carry arms, any more than in any other right."[221]

On March 7 Eliot reintroduced the Freedmen's Bureau Bill, which was referred to the Select Committee on Freedmen.[222] This bill had a more refined formulation of the rights of personal security and personal liberty than the Civil Rights Bill as well as explicit recognition of "the constitutional right to bear arms."[223] The debates on the Civil Rights Bill, which quoted Blackstone in detail, apparently contributed to the more advanced draftsmanship in the Freedmen's Bureau Bill.

The Civil Rights Bill was debated on March 8 and 9. Representative John Broomall of Pennsylvania identified "the rights and immunities of citizens" as including the writ of habeas corpus and the right of petition.[224] Representative Henry Raymond of New York, the editor of the *New York Times* and a member of the Joint Committee, proposed an amendment to the bill declaring that all persons born in the United States are "citizens of the United States, and entitled to all rights and privileges as such."[225] This formulation is similar to what would become the Citizenship Clause of the Fourteenth Amendment. Raymond explained: "Make the colored man a citizen of the United States and he has every right which you or I have as citizens of the United States under the laws and constitution of the United States. . . . He has defined *status*; he has a country and a home; a right to defend himself and his wife and children; *a right to bear arms*"[226] (emphasis added).

Quoting *Barron* v. *Baltimore* (1833),[227] Representative Michael Kerr of Indiana argued that the Bill of Rights limited only Congress.[228] Martin

Thayer of Pennsylvania responded: "Of what value are those guarantees if you deny all power on the part of the Congress of the United States to execute and enforce them?"[229] Thayer's argument exhibited the intent of what would become the Fourteenth Amendment.

House members then discussed the meaning in the Civil Rights Bill of "all laws and proceedings for the security of person and property." Representative Wilson referred to "the fundamental rights of the citizen commonly called civil rights" and the rights, such as the right to testify in court, "necessary to protect his personal liberty, his personal security, his right to property."[230] As the language of the Freedmen's Bureau Bill attests, the right to keep and bear arms was also necessary to guarantee personal liberty and personal security.

The next day Bingham explained that the Civil Rights Bill would "enforce in its letter and its spirit the bill of rights as embodied in that Constitution."[231] Citing Aristotle, Bingham argued that, by virtue of being a citizen, one is guaranteed every right in the Constitution.[232] In *The Politics* and other writings familiar to nineteenth-century Americans, Aristotle postulated that true citizenship included the right to possess arms, and that those who are deprived of arms are oppressed by armed tyrants.[233]

Bingham quoted § 1 of the Civil Rights Bill, including the terms "full and equal benefit of all laws and proceedings for the security of person and property,"[234] and reiterated his support for "amending the Constitution of the United States, expressly prohibiting the States from any such abuse of power in the future."[235] He explained that "the seventh and eighth sections of the Freedmen's Bureau bill enumerate the same rights and all the rights and privileges that are enumerated in the first section of this [the Civil Rights] bill."[236] Bingham then quoted the seventh section of the Freedmen's Bureau Bill, which provided that all persons shall "have full and equal benefit of all laws and proceedings for the security of person and estate, including the constitutional right of bearing arms."[237]

Bingham wished to "arm Congress with the power to . . . punish all violations by State Officers of the bill of rights."[238] In drafting the first section of the Fourteenth Amendment, Bingham clearly sought to protect the same rights.

On March 9 in the Joint Committee, Representative Boutwell examined Brevet Major General Wager Swayne, assistant commissioner of the Freedmen's Bureau in Alabama. Swayne testified that the failure to redistribute land to freedmen as promised led to fear of insurrection, to prevent which militias were organized.[239] Militias "were ordered to disarm the freedmen, and undertook to search in their houses for this purpose."[240] Although "a bill for the disarming of freedmen was defeated in the legislature," the disarming and resultant outrages proceeded.[241] Swayne did not intervene initially. "But when, shortly after New Year, an order [to disarm the freedmen] came to my knowledge, I made public my determination to maintain the right of the negro to keep and to bear arms, and my disposition to send an armed force into any neighborhood in which that right should be systematically interfered with."[242] Swayne's threat effectively deterred further widespread disarmings.[243]

On March 10 Captain J. H. Matthews, a subcommissioner of the Freedmen's Bureau in Mississippi, described how militiamen, sometimes with their faces blackened, patrolled the country, flogging and mistreating freedmen and Union men. The following exchange took place between Matthews and Representative Boutwell:

Answer: About Christmas and New Year it was said there would be an insurrection, and orders were issued by the governor of the State to disarm the freedmen.

Question: Was that order executed?

Answer: Yes, sir; and mostly by the militia. And it was in the execution, or pretended execution, of that order, that the most of those outrages were committed.

Question: Have the United States authorities interfered in that district to prevent the disarming of the negroes, or was it completed so far as the militia chose to do it?

Answer: I think the United States authorities took no measures against it.[244]

In House debate on March 24, Representative Leonard Myers of Pennsylvania referred to Alabama, "whose aristocratic and anti-republican laws, almost reenacting slavery, . . . impose an imprisonment of three months and a fine of $100.00 upon any one owning fire-arms."[245] To nullify such laws, Myers recommended the following imperatives:

1.   That no law of any State lately in insurrection shall impose by indirection a servitude which the Constitution now forbids. . . .

2.   That each State shall provide for equality before the law, equal protection to life, liberty, and property, equal right to sue and be sued, to inherit, make contracts, and give testimony.[246]

Representative Roswell Hart of New York asserted that the United States had a duty to secure to the people of the Southern States a republican form of government, adding: "The Constitution clearly describes that to be a republican form of government for which it was expressly framed. A government . . . where 'the right of the people to keep and bear arms shall not be infringed.'"[247] Hart also mentioned rights under the First, Fourth, and Fifth Amendments.[248]

The Civil Rights Bill passed both houses,[249] but on March 27 President Johnson surprised everyone by vetoing it.[250] In the override debate in the Senate on April 4, Trumbull argued that every citizen has "inherent, fundamental rights which belong to free citizens or free men in all countries, such as the rights enumerated in this bill."[251] Trumbull quoted from Kent's *Commentaries* as follows: "The absolute rights of individuals may be resolved into the right of personal security, the right of personal liberty, and the right to acquire and enjoy property. These rights have been justly considered, and frequently declared, by the people of this country to be natural, inherent, and inalienable."[252]

These were the same rights generally recited in the Civil Rights Bill and explicitly expounded both by Blackstone and the Freedmen's Bureau Bill as including the right to bear arms. Trumbull's further quotation from Kent specifically states that the existence of these rights means that one may protect them: "The privileges and immunities conceded by the Constitution of the United States to citizens of the several States were to be confined to those which were, in their nature, fundamental, and belonged of right to the citizens of all free Governments. Such are the rights of protection of life and liberty, and to acquire and enjoy property."[253]

On April 6, 1866, the Senate voted to override Johnson's veto of the Civil Rights Bill.[254] An editorial in the *New York Evening Post* on the override vote referred to "the mischiefs for which the Civil Rights bill seeks to provide a remedy . . . that there will be no obstruction to the acquirement of real estate by colored men, no attempts to prevent their holding public assemblies, freely discussing the question of their own disabilities, keeping fire-arms."[255]

While the Senate was voting to override Johnson's veto, in the Joint Committee Senator Howard examined Brevet Lieutenant Colonel W.H.H. Beadle, superintendent of the Freedmen's Bureau in North Carolina. Beadle testified about police brutality in Wilmington. In one instance, two policemen repeatedly struck a petite black woman with baseball bats. The police claimed self-defense.[256] In another incident, a black man was beaten by police based on a bogus weapons charge, and the policeman's word was enough to exonerate him.[257] Beadle also testified: "Some of the local police have been guilty of great abuses by pretending to have authority to disarm the colored people. They go in squads and search houses and seize arms. . . . Houses of colored men have been broken open, beds torn apart and thrown about the floor, and even trunks opened and money taken. A great variety of such offenses have been committed by the local police."[258]

Representative Lawrence made the same arguments in the House override debate on April 7 as Trumbull had made in the Senate. Quoting the same passage from Kent on the rights of personal security and personal liberty, Lawrence explained:

It has never been deemed necessary to enact in any constitution or law that citizens should have the right to life or liberty or the right to acquire property. These rights are recognized by the Constitution as existing anterior to and independently of all laws and all constitutions.

Without further authority I may assume, then, that there are certain absolute rights which pertain to every citizen, which are inherent, and of which a State cannot constitutionally deprive him. But not only are these rights inherent and indestructible, but the means whereby they may be possessed and enjoyed are equally so.[259]

This expresses the postulate that the rights to life and liberty, and the right to have arms to protect these rights, are inherent and cannot be infringed by a state.[260] Lawrence recalled the testimony before the Joint Committee that General Terry had refused demands by Virginia state officials "to take the arms of the blacks away from them."[261]

Representative Sidney Clarke of Kansas denounced Alabama for prohibiting blacks from owning firearms, and Mississippi for seizing arms of blacks.[262] He continued: "Sir, I find in the Constitution of the United States an article which declares that 'the right of the people to keep and bear arms shall not be infringed.' For myself, I shall insist that the reconstructed rebels of Mississippi respect the Constitution in their local laws."[263]

On April 9, after both houses had mustered the requisite two-thirds vote to override Johnson's veto, the Civil Rights Act of 1866 became law.[264] As enacted, § 1 provided: "Citizens, of every race and color, without regard to any previous condition of slavery or involuntary servitude, . . . shall have the same right, in every State and Territory in the United States, to make and enforce contracts, to sue, be parties, and give evidence, to inherit, purchase, lease, sell, hold, and convey real and personal property, and to *full and equal benefit of all laws and proceedings for the security of person and property*, as is enjoyed by white citizens"[265] (emphasis added).

NO STATE SHALL ABRIDGE, DEPRIVE, OR DENY: THE PASSAGE OF THE FOURTEENTH AMENDMENT

In a secret meeting of the Joint Committee on April 21, 1866, Stevens proposed a plan of reconstruction.[266] Section one of the proposal stated: "No discrimination shall be made by any state, nor by the United States, as to the civil rights of persons because of race, color, or previous condition of servitude."[267] That language had been submitted to Stevens by Robert Dale Owen, an ex-Representative and civil rights reformer,[268] who was a leading advocate of the right to keep and bear arms.[269]

Equality was necessary but insufficient for Bingham, who moved to add the following language: "nor shall any state deny to any person within its jurisdiction the equal protection of the laws, nor take private property for public use without just compensation."[270] The first phrase would become the Equal Protection Clause of the Fourteenth Amendment. Because Stevens' proposal had already prohibited discrimination, Bingham's "equal protection" was more than mere equality — it was equal protection of rights, not equal deprivation of rights. Indeed, equal protection of "the laws" might well have included, in Bingham's mind, the Bill of Rights. The second phrase in Bingham's proposal, the "takings" clause of the Fifth Amendment, might have been intended to state explicitly only one of the Bill of Rights guarantees to be protected. This was similar to the recitation in the Freedmen's Bureau bill of the constitutional right to bear arms, mention of which was not intended to preclude protection of other guarantees.

Bingham's amendment failed, but the 5 to 7 vote was nonpartisan, with Democrats Johnson and Rogers voting with Bingham and Stevens in favor.[271] Stevens' original proposal was then adopted.[272] Bingham next introduced a proposal for a separate section, which ten members of the committee, including Johnson, approved: "No state shall make or enforce any law which shall abridge the privileges or immunities of citizens of the United States; nor shall any state deprive any person of life, liberty or property without due process of law, nor deny to any person within its jurisdiction the equal protection of the laws."[273] The committee also approved the Enforcement Clause.[274]

A week later on April 28 Bingham moved, and the Joint Committee voted, to delete Stevens' draft prohibiting race discrimination as to civil rights and to insert Bingham's draft guaranteeing privileges and immunities, due process, and equal protection. This language became § 1 of the proposed constitutional amendment.[275] Stevens himself voted affirmatively, but Howard wanted to keep both.[276] The committee voted to require the Southern States to ratify the amendment as a condition of read-mission into the Union.[277] Finally, the committee decided to report the proposal of the constitutional amendment to Congress and to lift the veil of secrecy by notifying the newspapers.[278] The work of the Joint Commit-tee was now over for all practical purposes.

Attention in Congress focused on the proposed Fourteenth Amendment and the second Freedmen's Bureau Bill. Three months had passed since the House considered a first draft of the constitutional amendment. On April 30 Stevens, the leader of the House delegation to the Joint Commit-tee, reported to the House a joint resolution proposing the constitutional amendment.[279] Stevens also introduced a bill from the Joint Committee that would require the Southern States to ratify the amendment and conform their constitutions and laws thereto as a condition of readmit-tance to the Union.[280]

On May 8 a report from the president written by Benjamin C. Truman on the condition of the Southern people was ordered to be printed by the Senate. Truman recalled the fear of a black insurrection in late 1865 and early 1866, commenting:

In consequence of this there were extensive seizures of arms and ammunition, which the negroes had foolishly collected, and strict precautions were taken to avoid any outbreak. Pistols, old muskets, and shotguns were taken away from them as such weapons would be wrested from the hands of lunatics. Since the holidays, however, there has been a great improvement in this matter; many of the whites appear to be ashamed of their former distrust, and the negroes are seldom molested now in carrying the fire-arms of which they make such a vain display. In one way or another they have procured great numbers of old army muskets and revolvers, particularly in Texas, and I have, in a few instances, been amused at the vigor and audacity with which they have employed them to protect themselves against the robbers and murderers that infest that State.[281]

This suggests that blacks exhibited their perceived entitlement to the right to keep and bear arms to the dismay of whites uncomfortable with allow-ing this liberty to ex-slaves.

What would become the Fourteenth Amendment was debated in the House on May 8 through 10. Stevens remarked that its provisions "are all asserted, in some form or another, in our DECLARATION or organic law. But the Constitution limits only the action of Congress, and is not a limitation on the States. This Amendment supplies that defect, and allows Congress to correct the unjust legislation of the States."[282] Representative Thayer stated that the proposed amendment "simply brings into the Constitution what is found in the bill of rights of every State," and that "it is but incorporating in the Constitution of the United States the principle of the civil rights bill which has lately become a law."[283]

Bingham averred that the amendment would protect "the privileges and immunities of all the citizens of the Republic and the inborn rights of every person within its jurisdiction."[284] He added that it would furnish a remedy against state injustices, such as infliction of cruel and unusual punishment.[285] By stating that Eighth Amendment violations would be prohibited, Bingham implied that the Fourteenth Amendment would prohibit deprivations of any rights recognized in the Bill of Rights.[286]

The proposed Fourteenth Amendment passed the House on May 10.[287] The *New York Evening Post* remarked: "The first section merely reasserts the Civil Rights Act."[288] That act had been perceived by the *Post* as protecting "public assemblies" and "keeping firearms,"[289] that is, First and Second Amendment rights.

On May 22, Representative Eliot, on behalf of the Select Committee on Freedmen's Affairs, reported the second Freedmen's Bureau Bill,[290] which would become H.R. 613. As before the new bill recognized "the constitutional right to bear arms."[291] Bingham, author of § 1 of the Fourteenth Amendment, was a member of the select committee that had drafted this bill.

The need to protect the right to bear arms persisted. That same day (May 22) the president transmitted a report on Southern state laws concerning freedmen to the House. The report included black code provisions that prohibited the possession of firearms by freedmen. South Carolina made it unlawful for "persons of color to keep a firearm, sword, or other military weapon," without a license, except a farm owner could keep a shotgun or rifle "ordinarily used in hunting."[292] Florida made it unlawful for a black to enter a white railroad car and to possess "any bowie-knife, dirk, sword, fire-arms, or ammunition of any kind" without a license.[293] Although these state laws were well known, it is significant that they were received again in Congress on May 23, the first day that the Senate considered H.R. 127, which would become the Fourteenth Amendment.

Howard introduced the proposed amendment in the Senate on behalf of the Joint Committee, explaining "the views and motives which influenced that Committee."[294] After acknowledging the important role of the testimony before the Joint Committee, Howard referred to "the personal rights guaranteed and secured by the first eight amendments of the Constitution; such as freedom of speech and of the press; . . . *the right to keep and bear arms*"[295] (emphasis added). Howard averred: "The great object of the first section of this amendment is, therefore, *to restrain the power of the States and compel them at all times to respect these great fundamental guarantees*"[296] (emphasis added).

In the ensuing debate, no one questioned Howard's premise that the Amendment made the first eight amendments applicable to the states.[297] Howard explained that Congress could enforce the Bill of Rights through the Enforcement Clause, "a direct affirmative delegation of power to Congress to carry out all the principles of all these guarantees."[298] Howard added: "It [the amendment] will, if adopted by the States, forever disable every one of them from passing laws trenching upon those fundamental rights and privileges which pertain to citizens of the United States, and to all persons who happen to be within their jurisdiction."[299]

Howard's explanation that the Fourteenth Amendment would protect "the personal rights guaranteed by the first eight amendments of the United States Constitution such as . . . the right to keep and bear arms" appeared on the front page of the *New York Times*[300] and *New York Herald*,[301] and were printed in the *National Intelligencer*[302] and *Philadelphia Inquirer*.[303] The *New York Times* found his speech "clear and cogent,"[304] while the *Chicago Tribune* found that it was "very forcible and well put, and commanded the close attention of the Senate."[305] "It will be observed," summarized the *Baltimore Gazette*, "that the first section is a general prohibition upon all of the States of abridging the privileges and immunities of the citizens of the United States, and secures for all the equal advantages and protection of the laws."[306] Other newspapers were impressed with the length or detail of Howard's explanation.[307]

While Howard was explaining in the Senate that the Fourteenth Amendment would protect the right to keep and bear arms from state infringement, the House was debating the second Freedmen's Bureau Bill,[308] § 8 of which protected "the constitutional right to bear arms."[309] Eliot observed that § 8 "simply embodies the provisions of the civil rights bill, and gives to the President authority, through the Secretary of War, to extend military protection to secure those rights until the civil courts are in operation."[310] The constitutional basis of the bill was the Thirteenth Amendment.[311]

Eliot cited Freedmen's Bureau reports, such as that of General Fisk, who wrote of 25,000 discharged Union soldiers who were freedmen returning to their homes: "Their arms are taken from them by the civil authorities and confiscated for the benefit of the Commonwealth. The Union soldier is fined for bearing arms. *Thus the right of the people to keep and bear arms as provided in the Constitution is infringed,* and the Government for whose protection and preservation these soldiers have fought is denounced as meddlesome and despotic when through its agents it undertakes to protect its citizens in a constitutional right"[312] (emphasis added). Fisk added that the freedmen "are defenseless, for the civil-law officers disarm the colored man and hand him over to armed marauders."[313]

The Fourteenth Amendment and the second Freedmen's Bureau Bill, H.R. 613, continued to be debated in the Senate and House respectively for several days. On May 29, the House passed H.R. 613 by a vote of 96 to 32, with 55 abstaining.[314] The House immediately proceeded to consideration of the proposed constitutional amendment.[315]

Noting the House's passage of the Freedmen's Bureau Bill, the *New York Evening Post* reprinted some of the black code provisions, which had been communicated to Congress by the president, including those punishing freedmen with flogging for keeping arms.[316] An editorial sarcastically stated:

In South Carolina and Florida the freedmen are forbidden to wear or keep arms.

We feel certain the President, who is, as he says, the peculiar friend and protector of the freedmen, was not aware of the code of South Carolina, or Florida, or Mississippi, when he vetoed that [Civil Rights] act. The necessity for such a measure, to secure impartial justice, will not be denied by any one who reads the extracts we have made.[317]

May 30 began with Senator Howard proposing to add the citizenship clause to § 1 of the Fourteenth Amendment as follows: "All persons born in the United States, and subject to the jurisdiction thereof, are citizens of the United States and of the States wherein they reside."[318] This language was designed to settle the issue raised in *Dred Scott* — that is, who are citizens and thus have the bundle of rights appertaining to citizenship. After a raucous debate over making Indians, coolies, and gypsies citizens, the Senate passed Howard's language.[319]

Supporters of what became known as the Howard Amendment repeatedly asserted the broad character of the rights it protected. Senator Luke Poland of Vermont analyzed § 1 on June 5 as follows:

It is essentially declared in the Declaration of Independence and in *all the provisions of the Constitution*. Notwithstanding this we know that State laws exist, and some of them of very recent enactment, in direct violation of these principles. Congress has already shown its desire and intention to uproot and destroy all such partial State legislation in the passage of what is called the civil rights bill. . . . It certainly seems desirable that no doubt should be left existing as to the power of Congress to enforce principles lying at the foundation of all republican government if they be denied or violated by the States.[320] (emphasis added)

The references to "all the provisions of the Constitution" and to recently enacted state laws again show the intent to protect Bill of Rights freedoms from state violation.

On June 8, Senator John B. Henderson of Missouri expounded the concept of citizenship by reference to *Dred Scott*.[321] In *Dred Scott*, according to Henderson, Chief Justice Roger Taney had conceded to members of the state communities "all the personal rights, privileges, and immunities guarantied to citizens of this 'new Government.' In fact, the opinion distinctly asserts that the words 'people of the United States' and 'citizens' are 'synonymous terms.'"[322] However, Taney had disregarded the plain meaning of the term "the people" by excluding blacks.[323]

Taney's opinion also explicitly declared that citizens are entitled to Bill of Rights guarantees, including those of the Second Amendment. The following passage from *Dred Scott* particularizes the rights discussed in the passages to which Henderson referred and illustrates the objectives sought by the Republicans in Congress: "For if they [blacks] were . . . entitled to the privileges and immunities of citizens, it would exempt them from the operation of the special laws and from the police regulations which they considered to be necessary for their own safety. It would give to persons of the negro race . . . the full liberty of speech in public and in private upon all subjects upon which its own citizens might speak; to hold public meetings upon political affairs, and *to keep and carry arms wherever they went*"[324] (emphasis added). Taney's logic was clear: if blacks were citizens, they would have a right to bear arms, and state laws prohibiting their possession of firearms would be void.

Senator Johnson favored the citizenship and due process clauses but opposed the privileges and immunities clause "because I do not understand what will be the effect of that."[325] However, as counsel for the slaveholder in *Dred Scott*, Johnson was fully aware of Taney's characterization of "the right to keep and carry arms" as a privilege and immunity of citizenship.[326] Johnson also conceded in Senate debate that reports of firearms seizures from blacks and other outrages were accurate.[327]

After further debate, the Fourteenth Amendment passed the Senate by a vote of 33 to 11,[328] or 75 percent of the votes, far more than the necessary two-thirds for a constitutional amendment. On June 13, the House passed the proposed Fourteenth Amendment as amended by the Senate by a vote of 120 to 32,[329] a margin of 79 percent, again far more than the necessary two-thirds.

CONGRESS OVERRIDES THE PRESIDENT'S VETO OF H.R. 613, THE SECOND FREEDMEN'S BUREAU BILL

On June 15, 1866, Senator Wilson urged quick action on H.R. 613, the second Freedmen's Bureau Bill, which had been reported out of committee.[330] Meanwhile, the House debated H.R. 543, which required the Southern States to ratify the Fourteenth Amendment. Indiana Representative George W. Julian argued the necessity of that bill to remedy the following: "Although the civil rights bill is now the law, . . . [it] is pronounced void by the jurists and courts of the South. Florida makes it a misdemeanor for colored men to carry weapons without a license to do so from a probate judge, and the punishment of the offense is whipping and the pillory. South Carolina has the same enactments; and a black man convicted of an offense who fails immediately to pay his fine is whipped. . . . Cunning legislative devices are being invented in most of the States to restore slavery in fact."[331] This again shows the common objective of the Civil Rights Act and the Freedmen's Bureau bill to protect the right to keep and bear arms and the need for the Fourteenth Amendment to provide a constitutional foundation.

On June 26 the Senate took up H.R. 613, the second Freedmen's Bureau Bill. Unrelated amendments resulted in § 8, which recited "the constitutional right to bear arms," being renumbered as § 14.[332] Senator Hendricks moved to strike the section because "the same matters are found in the civil rights bill substantially that are found in this section." Hendricks' proposal was rejected.[333]

Trumbull replied that, although the two bills protected the same rights, the Civil Rights Act would apply in regions where the civil tribunals were in operation, but the Freedmen's Bureau bill would apply in regions where the civil authority was not restored.[334] The bill then passed without a roll-call vote.[335]

Because the House did not concur in certain amendments made by the Senate to the second Freedmen's Bureau Bill,[336] a conference committee was necessary. Although the amendments were not germane to the topic here, the committee appointments again indicate the commonality of thought and intent of the prime movers of the second Freedmen's Bureau Bill and the Fourteenth Amendment. For the House, the speaker appointed Eliot, Bingham, and Hiram McCullough.[337] Eliot and Bingham were the respective authors of both Freedmen's Bureau Bills and the Fourteenth Amendment. The Senate chair appointed Wilson, Harris, and J. W. Nesmith.[338]

Senator Wilson, on behalf of the conference committee, reported on July 2 and the Senate concurred in the report.[339] Eliot raised the report in the House the next day, where William E. Finck (D-Ohio) made a last-minute attempt to kill the bill by moving to table the conference committee report. This motion was rejected by a vote of 25 to 102.[340] Because the report was then agreed to without another roll call vote, the recorded procedural vote represented yet another landslide vote (80 percent) in favor of passage of the bill.

As expected, Johnson vetoed the second Freedmen's Bureau Bill. The veto message was read to the House on July 16. The president conceded that previously, because the civil courts were closed in the South, the need existed for military tribunals to exercise "jurisdiction over all cases concerning the free enjoyment of the immunities and rights of citizenship, as well as the protection of person and property."[341] Now, Johnson claimed, Southern courts were again in operation and "the protection granted to the white citizen is already conferred by law upon the freedmen."[342] He trusted the protection of "the rights, privileges, and immunities of the citizens" to the civil tribunals, where one is entitled to trial by jury.[343] The president believed that the Civil Rights Act, which protected, *inter alia*, the "full and equal benefit of all laws and proceedings for the security of person and property," was sufficient.[344] Without further debate, the House overrode the president's veto by a vote of 104 to 33, or 76 percent.[345]

Word of the House's override quickly reached the Senate,[346] where Wilson urged immediate action. After momentary debate, the Senate easily overrode the veto by a vote of 33 to 12, or 73 percent.[347]

SUMMARY OF CONGRESSIONAL ACTION
ON THE FREEDMEN'S BUREAU ACT
AND THE FOURTEENTH AMENDMENT

As finally passed into law on July 16, 1866, the Freedmen's Bureau Act extended the Bureau's existence for two more years.[348] The full text of § 14 of the Act declared:

That in every State or district where the ordinary course of judicial proceedings has been interrupted by the rebellion, and until the same shall be fully restored, and in every State or district whose constitutional relations to the government have been practically discontinued by the rebellion, and until such State shall have been restored in such relations, and shall be duly represented in the Congress of the United States, the right to make and enforce contracts, to sue, be parties, and give evidence, to inherit, purchase, lease, sell, hold, and convey real and personal property, and to have *full and equal benefit of all laws and proceedings concerning personal liberty, personal security,* and the acquisition, enjoyment, and disposition of estate, real and personal, *including the constitutional right to bear arms, shall be secured to and enjoyed by all the citizens* of such State or district without respect to race or color or previous condition of slavery. And whenever in either of said States or districts the ordinary course of judicial proceedings has been interrupted by the rebellion, and until the same shall be fully restored, and until such State shall have been restored in its constitutional relations to the government, and shall be duly represented in the Congress of the United States, the President shall, through the commissioner and the officers of the bureau, and under such rules and regulations as the President, through the Secretary of War, shall prescribe, extend military protection and have military jurisdiction over all cases and questions concerning *the free enjoyment of such immunities and rights,* and no penalty or punishment for any violation of law shall be imposed or permitted because of race or color, or previous condition of slavery, other or greater than the penalty or punishment to which white persons may be liable by law for the like offense. But the jurisdiction conferred by this section upon the officers of the bureau shall not exist in any State where the ordinary course of judicial proceedings has not been interrupted by the rebellion, and shall cease in every State when the courts of the State and the United States are not disturbed in the peaceable course of justice, and after such State shall be fully restored in its constitutional relations to the government, and shall be duly represented in the Congress of the United States.[349] (emphasis added)

With the enactment of the Freedmen's Bureau Act, the civil rights revolution in the Thirty-Ninth Congress was won. The Fourteenth Amendment was passed by Congress, and the ratification process was the next step.

The following summarizes the roll-call voting behavior of Congressmen concerning the Freedmen's Bureau Act and the Fourteenth Amendment. Every Senator who voted for the Fourteenth Amendment also voted for the Freedmen's Bureau Bills, S. 60 and H.R. 613, and thus for recognition of the constitutional right to bear arms. The only recorded Senate vote on S. 60, the first Freedmen's Bureau Bill, as amended to include recognition of the right to bear arms, was the 30 to 18 veto override vote of February 20, just two votes shy of the necessary two-thirds.[350] On June 8 the Senate passed the proposed Fourteenth Amendment by a vote of 33–11.[351] H.R. 613, the second Freedmen's Bureau Bill, then passed the Senate by voice vote on June 26.[352] On July 16 the Senate overrode the President's veto of H.R. 613 by a vote of 33 to 12 (73 percent).[353]

An analysis of the roll call votes reveals that all 33 senators who voted for the Fourteenth Amendment also voted for either S. 60 or H.R. 613.[354]

Of the 33 senators who voted for the Fourteenth Amendment, 28 (85 percent) voted for both S. 60 and H.R. 613. The 11 senators who voted against the Fourteenth Amendment also voted against either S. 60 or H.R. 613, or both.[355]

Members of the House cast recorded votes overwhelmingly in favor of the Freedmen's Bureau Bills and in favor of the Fourteenth Amendment on two occasions. On February 6, a day after inserting the right to bear arms into the bill,[356] the House passed S. 60 by a vote of 136 to 33.[357] Because the Senate failed to muster the necessary two-thirds to override the president's veto, the House had no override vote. The proposed Fourteenth Amendment passed the House on May 10 by a vote of 128–37,[358] and again with the Senate amendments on June 13 by a vote of 120–32.[359] The House passed H.R. 613 on May 29 by a 96–33 margin,[360] and then on July 16 overrode the President's veto by a vote of 104–33, or 76 percent.[361]

The overwhelming majority of House members voted in the affirmative on all five recorded votes — once on S. 60, twice on the proposed Fourteenth Amendment, and twice on H.R. 613. Some voted only once on the proposed Fourteenth Amendment, or once or twice on the Freedmen's Bureau Bills. A total of 140 representatives voted at least once in favor of the proposed Fourteenth Amendment, and every one of the 140 voted at least once in favor of one of the Freedmen's Bureau Bills.[362] Of the 140 representatives who voted for the proposed Fourteenth Amendment, 120 (86 percent) voted for both S. 60 and H.R. 613.

Accordingly, to a man, the same two-thirds-plus members of Congress who voted for the proposed Fourteenth Amendment also voted for the proposition contained in both Freedmen's Bureau bills that the constitutional right to bear arms is included in the rights of personal liberty and personal security. No other guarantee in the Bill of Rights was the subject of this official approval by the same Congress that passed the Fourteenth Amendment.

The framers intended and opponents recognized the Fourteenth Amendment to guarantee the right to keep and bear arms as a right and attribute of citizenship that no state government could infringe. The passage of the Fourteenth Amendment accomplished the abolitionist goal that each state respect all the guarantees contained in the Bill of Rights.

Each clause of § 1 of the Fourteenth Amendment reflects the broad character of the rights for which protection was sought. That section provides: "All persons born or naturalized in the United States and subject to the jurisdiction thereof, are citizens of the United States and of the state wherein they reside. No State shall make or enforce any law which shall abridge the privileges or immunities of citizens of the United States; nor shall any State deprive any person of life, liberty, or property, without due process of law; nor deny to any person within its jurisdiction the equal protection of the laws."

Among other freedoms in the Bill of Rights, keeping and bearing arms was considered part of the definition of a citizen. Depicted as a civil right and a privilege and immunity in *Dred Scott*, the debates on the Fourteenth Amendment, and on related civil rights legislation, this liberty interest effectuated the defense and practical realization of the guarantees of "life, liberty, or property." This fundamental right under "the laws" (that is, the Bill of Rights) also qualified for "equal protection," but never for deprivation, whether equal or unequal. To the framers of the Fourteenth Amendment, these universally recognized rights, too numerous to list individually, were to be protected by the all-inclusive language that they proposed.

The Freedmen's Bureau Act declared that "the constitutional right to bear arms" is included among the "laws and proceedings concerning personal liberty, personal security," and property, and that "the free enjoyment of such immunities and rights" is to be protected.[363] This again suggests that the Fourteenth Amendment was intended to incorporate the Second Amendment, so as to invalidate state infringements of the right of the people to keep and bear arms. The Fourteenth Amendment protects the rights to personal security and personal liberty, which its authors declared in the Freedmen's Bureau Act to include "the constitutional right to bear arms." To the members of the Thirty-Ninth Congress, possession of arms was a fundamental, individual right worthy of protection from both federal and state violation.

The arms that the Fourteenth Amendment's framers believed to be constitutionally protected included the latest firearms of all kinds, from military muskets (which were fitted with bayonets) and repeating rifles to shotguns, pistols, and revolvers. The right of the people to keep arms meant the right of an individual to possess arms in the home and elsewhere; the right to bear arms meant to carry arms on one's person. The right to have arms implied the right to use them for protection of one's life, family, and home against criminals and terrorist groups of all kinds, whether attacking Klansmen or lawless law enforcement. Far from being restricted to official militia activity, the right to keep and bear arms could be exercised by persons against the state's official militia when it plundered and killed the innocent.

In the above sense, "the constitutional right to bear arms" was perhaps considered as the most fundamental protection for the rights of personal liberty and personal security, which may explain its unique mention in the Freedmen's Bureau Act. To the framers of the Fourteenth Amendment, human emancipation meant the protection of this great human right from all sources of infringement, whether federal or state.

NOTES

This chapter is an expanded version of the author's "Personal Security, Personal Liberty, and 'The Constitutional Right to Bear Arms': Visions of the Framers of the Fourteenth Amendment," 5 SETON HALL LAW SCHOOL CONSTITU-TIONAL LAW JOURNAL, No. 2, 341–434 (Spring 1995), and is reprinted with the kind permission of Seton Hall Law School.

　　1.　See S. Halbrook, THAT EVERY MAN BE ARMED, 89–106 (1994). In his widely read constitutional law treatise, U.S. Attorney William Rawle, who rejected President Washington's offer to become the first U.S. Attorney General, wrote:

In the second [amendment] it is *declared*, that a well regulated militia is necessary to the security of a free state. . . .

The corollary, from the first position, is that the right of the people to keep and bear arms shall not be infringed.

The prohibition is general. No clause in the Constitution could by any rule of construction be conceived to give to congress a power to disarm the people. Such a flagitious attempt could only be made under some general pretence by a state legislature. But if in any blind pursuit of inordinate power, either should attempt it, this amendment may be appealed to as a restraint on both.

W. Rawle, A VIEW OF THE CONSTITUTION 125–26 (2d ed. 1829).

　　2.　2 J. Bishop, COMMENTARIES ON THE CRIMINAL LAW § 124 (1865). The Texas Supreme Court cited Bishop's *Commentaries* in holding that the Second Amendment prohibits states from passing laws that ban the possession or carrying of militia-type firearms. See English v. State, 35 Tex. 473 (1872).

　　3.　Id. at 120 n. 6.

　　4.　Id. at 125 n. 2.

　　5.　W. Dubois, BLACK RECONSTRUCTION IN AMERICA 167, 172–73, 223 (1962); E. Coulter, THE SOUTH DURING RECONSTRUCTION 40, 49 (1947).

　　6.　FREE AT LAST: A DOCUMENTARY HISTORY OF SLAVERY, FREEDOM, AND THE CIVIL WAR 520–21 (I. Berlin et al. eds. 1992).

　　7.　Id. at 522.

　　8.　Laws of Miss., 1865, at 165 (Nov. 29, 1865); Ex.Doc. No. 6, 39th Cong., 1st Sess., at 195–96 (1867). J. Burgess, RECONSTRUCTION AND THE CONSTITUTION, 1866–1876, at 47, 51–52 (1902) states of the Mississippi Act: "This is a fair sample of the legislation subsequently passed by all the 'States' reconstructed under President Johnson's plan. . . . The Northern Republicans professed to see in this new legislation at the South the virtual re-enslavement of the negroes."

9.   FREE AT LAST: A DOCUMENTARY HISTORY OF SLAVERY, FREEDOM, AND THE CIVIL WAR 523 (I. Berlin et. al. eds. 1992).

10.   Id.

11.   Id. at 524.

12.   CONG. GLOBE, 39th Cong., 1st Sess. 14 (Dec. 6, 1865).

13.   Id.

14.   Id. at 22 (Dec. 11, 1865).

15.   Id. at 11 (Dec. 6, 1865).

16.   Id. at 21 (Dec. 11, 1865).

17.   Id. at 30 (Dec. 12, 1865).

18.   Id. at 39 (Dec. 13, 1865).

19.   Id. at 40.

20.   Id. at 39. The Thirteenth Amendment provides:

Section 1. Neither slavery nor involuntary servitude, except as a punishment for crime whereof the party shall have been duly convicted, shall exist within the United States, or any place subject to their jurisdiction.

        Section 2. Congress shall have power to enforce this article by appropriate legislation.

21.   CONG. GLOBE, 39th Cong., 1st Sess. 40–41 (Dec. 13, 1865).

22.   Id. at 42.

23.   Id. at 46.

24.   Id. at 47.

25.   Id. at 48.

26.   Id. at 57 (Dec. 14, 1865).

27.   Id. at 69 (Dec. 18, 1865).

28.   Id. at 77 (Dec. 19, 1865).

29.   Id.

30.   Id. at 78.

31.   Id. at 79.

32.   J. Burgess, RECONSTRUCTION AND THE CONSTITUTION, 1866–1876, 64 (1902).

33.   Sen. Exec. Doc. No. 2, 39th Cong., 1st Sess., pt. 1, at 40 (Dec. 13, 1865).

34.   Id. at 85.

35.   Id. at 93–95.

36.   Id. at 96.

37.   CONG. GLOBE, 39th Cong., 1st Sess., at 106 (Dec. 21, 1865).

38.   Id. at 109. See id. at 90–97.

39.   Id. at 129 (Jan. 5, 1866).

40. Id. at 135 (Jan. 8, 1866).

41. Id. at 184 (Jan. 11, 1866).

42. Id. at 209 (Jan. 12, 1866).

43. Id. at 211.

44. B. Kendrick, THE JOURNAL OF THE JOINT COMMITTEE OF FIFTEEN ON RECONSTRUCTION 46 (1914). Hereafter cited JOURNAL OF THE JOINT COMMITTEE.

45. Id.

46. Id. at 45–47.

47. CONG. GLOBE, 39th Cong., 1st Sess. 217 (Jan. 12, 1866).

48. *Harper's Weekly*, Jan. 13, 1866, at 3, col. 2.

49. CONG. GLOBE, 39th Cong., 1st Sess. 297 (Jan. 18, 1866).

50. Id. at 298.

51. Id. at 302.

52. Id. at 318 (Jan. 19, 1866).

53. Id. The Indiana Constitution provided: "No negro or mulatto shall come into, or settle in, the state after the adoption of this constitution." Ind. Const., Art. XIII, § 1 (1851).

54. Ind. Const., Art. I, § 32 (1851). A delegate at the constitutional convention that approved this provision, Hendricks had proposed that no law should "deprive" this right rather than "restrict" this right. JOURNAL OF THE CONVENTION OF THE STATE OF INDIANA TO AMEND THE CONSTITUTION 574 (1851).

55. State v. Mitchell, 3 Blackf. Ind. Rpts. 229 (1832).

56. CONG. GLOBE, 39th Cong., 1st Sess., 320 (Jan. 19, 1866).

57. Id. at 321.

58. Id.

59. Id. at 322.

60. Id.

61. Id.

62. Id.

63. Id. at 331.

64. Id.

65. JOURNAL OF THE JOINT COMMITTEE at 51.

66. Id. at 50.

67. Id. at 53.

68. Id. at 52–53.

69. CONG. GLOBE, 39th Cong., 1st Sess. 337 (Jan. 22, 1866).

70. 2 PROCEEDINGS OF THE BLACK STATE CONVENTIONS, 1840–1865, at 284 (P. Foner and G. Walker eds. 1980).

71. Id. at 303.

72. Id. at 302.

73. CONG. GLOBE, 39th Cong., 1st Sess. 337 (Jan. 22, 1866).

74. REPORT OF THE JOINT COMMITTEE ON RECONSTRUCTION, H.R. Rep. No. 30, 39th Cong., 1st Sess., pt. 3, at 3–4 (1866). Hereafter cited REPORT OF THE JOINT COMMITTEE.

75. CONG. GLOBE, 39th Cong., 1st Sess. 340 (Jan. 22, 1866).

76. Id. at 363 (Jan. 23, 1866).

77. Id. at 371.

78. Id. at 374–75. See also id. at 394–400 (Jan. 24, 1866).

79. Id. at 420.

80. Id. at 421.

81. JOURNAL OF THE JOINT COMMITTEE at 55.

82. Id. at 55–56.

83. REPORT OF THE JOINT COMMITTEE, pt. 3, at 8.

84. Id. at 10.

85. Id. at 20–22.

86. JOURNAL OF THE JOINT COMMITTEE at 56–57.

87. Id. at 57.

88. Id. at 58.

89. CONG. GLOBE, 39th Cong., 1st Sess. 474 (Jan. 29, 1866). Trumbull stated: "It is the intention of this bill to secure those rights. The laws in the slaveholding States have made a distinction against persons of African descent on account of their color, whether free or slave. I have before me the statutes of Mississippi. *[One] statute prohibit[s] any negro or mulatto from having firearms*; similar provisions are to be found running through all the statutes of the late slaveholding States. . . . The purpose of the bill under consideration is to destroy [this] discrimination" (Id., emphasis added).

90. Id.

91. Id. at 475.

92. Id.

93. Id. at 478.

94. Id.

95. Id. at 512.

96. Id. at 517.

97. REPORT OF THE JOINT COMMITTEE, pt. 3, at 30.

98. Id. at 32.

99. Id. at 39.

100. Id. at 46–47.

101. Id., pt. 2, at 21.

102. CONG. GLOBE, 39th Cong., 1st Sess. 566 (Feb. 1, 1866).

103. Id. at 573.

104. Id. at 574–75.

105. Id. at 585.

106. Id. at 586.

107. Id. at 595 (Feb. 2, 1866).

108. Id.

109. Id. at 603.

110. Id. at 908–9 (Feb. 17, 1866).

111. Id. at 606–7.

112. Id., App., at 69 (Feb. 3, 1866).
113. Act of July 16, 1866, 14 STATUTES AT LARGE 173, 176.
114. REPORT OF THE JOINT COMMITTEE, pt. 2, at 246.
115. JOURNAL OF THE JOINT COMMITTEE at 61.
116. Id.
117. Id.
118. CONG. GLOBE, 39th Cong., 1st Sess. 648 (Feb. 5, 1866).
119. Id. at 651.
120. Exec. Doc. No. 70, 39th Cong., 1st Sess., 233, 236 (1866).
121. CONG. GLOBE, 39th Cong., 1st Sess. 654 (Feb. 5, 1866).
122. Id.
123. Id.
124. Id. at 585 (Feb. 1, 1866).
125. Id. at 657 (Feb. 5, 1866).
126. Id. at 658.
127. Id. at 1292 (Mar. 9, 1866).
128. Id. at 688 (Feb. 6, 1866).
129. Id. at 702 (Feb. 7, 1866).
130. REPORT OF THE JOINT COMMITTEE, pt. 3, at 68.
131. CONG. GLOBE, 39th Cong., 1st Sess. 742 (Feb. 8, 1866).
132. Id at 743.
133. Id.
134. Id. at 748.
135. Id. at 775 (Feb. 9, 1866).
136. Id. at 1292.
137. Id. at 806, 813 (Feb. 13, 1866).
138. REPORT OF THE JOINT COMMITTEE, pt. 1, at 1.
139. Id. at 34.
140. Id. at 73.
141. Id. at 94. The Tennessee legislature had passed a war measure confiscating firearms. When the war ended, a person whose gun was seized successfully sued for its value. Smith v. Ishenhour, 43 Tenn. (3 Coldwell) 214, 217 (1866) held: "In the passage of this Act, the 26th section of the Bill of Rights, which provides, 'that the free white men of this State have a right to keep and bear arms for the common defense,' was utterly disregarded. This is the first attempt, in the history of the Anglo-Saxon race, of which we are apprised, to disarm the people by legislation."
142. REPORT OF THE JOINT COMMITTEE, pt. 1, at 94.
143. Id., pt. 2, at 110.
144. Id. at 112.
145. Id. at 127–28.
146. CONG. GLOBE, 39th Cong., 1st Sess. 903 (Feb. 17, 1866).
147. Id.

148.   Id. at 908–9. The proclamation's recognition of the same right of ex-Confederates as for freedmen not only stemmed from the constitutional guarantee but also was apparently in response to such situations as the following:

Mr. Ferebee [N.C.] . . . said that in his county the white citizens had been deprived of arms, while the negroes were almost all of them armed.
Gen. Dockery . . . stated that in his county the white residents had been disarmed, and were at present almost destitute of means to protect themselves against robbery and outrage.

1 DOCUMENTARY HISTORY OF RECONSTRUCTION 90 (Fleming ed. 1906), citing ANNUAL CYCLOPEDIA 627 (1865).
    149.   *The Loyal Georgian* (Augusta), Feb. 3, 1866, at 1, col 2.
    150.   Id. at 2, col. 2.
    151.   Id. at 3, col. 4.
    152.   Circular No. 5, Freedmen's Bureau, Dec. 22, 1865. See, for example, issues of *Loyal Georgian* for Jan. 20, 27, Feb. 3, 1866.
    153.   D. Sterling, THE TROUBLE THEY SEEN: BLACK PEOPLE TELL THE STORY OF RECONSTRUCTION 394 (1976). Sterling documents numerous instances of blacks using firearms for self-defense as well as instances of firearms seizures by whites from blacks.
    154.   For example, "The Constitutional Amendment in the Senate," *The Loyal Georgian*, Feb. 24, 1866, at 2, cols. 3–4.
    155.   REPORT OF THE JOINT COMMITTEE, pt. 3, at 72.
    156.   Id. at 73.
    157.   CONG. GLOBE, 39th Cong., 1st Sess. 914 (Feb. 19, 1866).
    158.   Id.
    159.   Id. at 914–15.
    160.   Id. at 915.
    161.   Id.
    162.   Id.
    163.   Id. at 40 (Dec. 13, 1865).
    164.   Id. at 478 (Jan. 29, 1866).
    165.   Id. at 1100 (Mar. 1, 1866).
    166.   See S. Halbrook, THAT EVERY MAN BE ARMED 136–42 (1984).
    167.   CONG. GLOBE, 39th Cong., 1st Sess. 916 (Feb. 19, 1866).
    168.   Id.
    169.   Id. at 917.
    170.   REPORT OF THE JOINT COMMITTEE, pt. 3, at 81.
    171.   Ark. Const., Art. I, § 21 (1836); Art. I, § 21 (1864).
    172.   Ark. Const., Art. I, § 21 (1861) ("That the free white men, and Indians, of this state shall have the right to keep and bear arms for their individual or common defence").
    173.   CONG. GLOBE, 39th Cong., 1st Sess. 934 (Feb. 20, 1866).
    174.   Id. at 936.

175. Id. at 941.

176. Id. at 941–42.

177. Id. at 943.

178. W. Rehnquist, GRAND INQUESTS 204 ff. (1992).

179. B. Kendrick, JOURNAL OF THE JOINT COMMITTEE 236 (1914). See "The Republican Press on the Veto Message," *New York Tribune*, Mar. 3, 1866, at 9, which reprinted 22 editorials from Republican newspapers.

180. House Misc. Docu. No. 64, 39th Cong., 1st Sess. (1866).

181. REPORT OF THE JOINT COMMITTEE, pt. 2, at 143.

182. Id., pt. 4, at 49–50.

183. Id., pt. 2, at 219.

184. Id. at 229.

185. Id. at 219.

186. CONG. GLOBE 1033–34 (Feb. 26, 1866).

187. Id. at 1064 (Feb. 27, 1866).

188. Id. at 1088 (Feb. 28, 1866). And see further comments of Bingham at 1089 ("the existing Amendments") and 1094 ("the law in its highest sense").

189. Id. at 1088.

190. Id. at 1072 (Feb. 28, 1866).

191. Id. at 1077.

192. Id. at 1117 (Mar. 1, 1866).

193. Id.

194. Id.

195. Id. at 1118.

196. 1 Blackstone, COMMENTARIES 140–41 (St. Geo. Tucker ed. 1803).

197. Id. at 143–44.

198. Id.

199. Id.

200. CONG. GLOBE, 39th Cong., 1st Sess. 1118–19 (Mar. 1, 1866).

201. Id. at 1121.

202. Id. at 1122.

203. Id. at 1168 (Mar. 3, 1866).

204. Id. at 1182 (Mar. 5, 1866). Pomeroy made several more interesting comments. For example, he referred to "the rights of an individual under the common law when his life is attacked. If I am assaulted by a highwayman, by a man armed and determined, my first duty is to resist him, and if necessary, use my arms also." Id. at 1183.

205. Id.

206. REPORT OF THE JOINT COMMITTEE, pt. 2, at 239.

207. Id. at 240.

208. Id. at 241.

209. Ex. Doc. No. 27, Senate, 39th Cong., 1st Sess., at 1 (1866).

210. Ex. Doc. No. 70, House of Representatives, 39th Cong., 1st Sess., at 1 (1866).

211.   Id. at 65.

212.   Id. at 203.

213.   Id. at 205–6. Another report noted in the circular was taken from a Lexington black man's deposition, wherein he testified that upon trying to sell his pistol to a white man, he was arrested, jailed, and subsequently ordered by a court to give his pistol to the white man at no cost. Id.

214.   Id. at 233.

215.   Id. at 236.

216.   Id. at 238.

217.   Id. at 239.

218.   Id. at 291.

219.   Id. at 292.

220.   Id. at 297.

221.   Id.

222.   CONG. GLOBE, 39th Cong., 1st Sess. 1238 (Mar. 7, 1866).

223.   Id. at 3412 (June 26, 1866).

224.   Id. at 1263 (Mar. 8, 1866).

225.   Id. at 1266 (Mar. 8, 1866).

226.   Id.

227.   32 U.S. (7 Pet.) 243, 250–51.

228.   CONG. GLOBE, 39th Cong., 1st Sess. 1270 (Mar. 8, 1866).

229.   Id.

230.   Id., App., at 157 (Mar. 8, 1866).

231.   Id. at 1291 (Mar. 9, 1866).

232.   Id.

233.   Aristotle, THE POLITICS 68, 71, 79, 136, 142, 218 (transl. T. A. Sinclair, 1962); Aristotle, ATHENIAN CONSTITUTION 43–47 (transl. H. Rackman, 1935).

234.   CONG. GLOBE, 39th Cong., 1st Sess. 1291 (Mar. 9, 1866).

235.   Id.

236.   Id. at 1292.

237.   Id.

238.   Id.

239.   JOURNAL OF THE JOINT COMMITTEE, pt. 3, at 140.

240.   Id.

241.   Id.

242.   Id.

243.   Id.

244.   Id. at 142.

245.   CONG. GLOBE, 39th Cong., 1st Sess., 1621 (Mar. 24, 1866).

246.   Id. at 1622.

247.   Id. at 1629.

248.   Id.

249.   Id. at 606 (Feb. 2, 1866) (Senate); 1367 (Mar. 13, 1866) (House).

250.   Id. at 1679 (Mar. 27, 1866).

251. Id. at 1757 (Apr. 4, 1866).

252. Id.

253. Id.

254. Id. at 1809 (Apr. 6, 1866).

255. "The Civil Rights Bill in the Senate," *New York Evening Post*, Apr. 7, 1866, at 2, col. 1. The page facing the editorial supporting enforcement of First and Second Amendment rights against the states included a prominent advertisement for Remington rifles, muskets, "pocket and belt revolvers," and other arms, with the admonition: "In these days of housebreaking and robbery every house, store, bank and office should have one of Remington's revolvers." Id. at 3, col. 10. The New York police were seen as being "employed in the service of the wealthy and prosperous corporations" while crime was rampant. Id., Apr. 16, 1866, at 2, col. 2, and May 10, 1866, at 2, col. 4.

256. REPORT OF THE JOINT COMMITTEE, pt. 2, at 271–72.

257. Id.

258. Id. at 272.

259. CONG. GLOBE, 39th Cong., 1st Sess. 1833 (Apr. 7, 1866).

260. See also id. (remarks of Representative Lawrence) (arguing that one cannot enjoy the rights to life, liberty, and property without "the benefit of laws for the security of person and property.")

261. Id. at 1834.

262. Id. at 1838.

263. Id.

264. Id. at 1861 (Apr. 9, 1866).

265. 14 Stat. 27.

266. JOURNAL OF THE JOINT COMMITTEE at 83. For a study of voting patterns in the committee, see E. Maltz, CIVIL RIGHTS, THE CONSTITUTION, AND CONGRESS, 1863–1869, at 82–92 (1990).

267. JOURNAL OF THE JOINT COMMITTEE at 83.

268. Id. at 295–303.

269. Owen was the most prominent advocate of civil rights for blacks and women at the Indiana constitutional convention of 1850. Supporting the right of "carrying of weapons," he added: "For if it were declared by Constitutional provision that the people should have the right to bear arms, no law of the Legislature could take away that right." REPORT OF THE DEBATES AND PROCEEDINGS OF THE CONVENTION OF THE REVISION OF THE CONSTITUTION OF THE STATE OF INDIANA 1385 (1850). In a U.S. Senate-commissioned report, Owen had written: "The most prized of personal rights is the right of self-defense." R. Owen, THE WRONG OF SLAVERY 111–12 (1864).

270. JOURNAL OF THE JOINT COMMITTEE at 85.

271. Id.

272. Id.

273. Id. at 87.

274. Id. at 88.

275. Id. at 106.
276. Id.
277. Id. at 106, 110.
278. Id. at 114–15.
279. CONG. GLOBE, 39th Cong., 1st Sess. 2286 (Apr. 30, 1866).
280. Id.
281. Ex. Doc. No. 43, U.S. Senate, 39th Cong., 1st Sess., at 8 (1866).
282. CONG. GLOBE, 39th Cong., 1st Sess. 2459 (May 8, 1866).
283. Id. at 2465 (May 8, 1866).
284. Id. at 2542.
285. Id. at 2542-43.
286. H. Flack, THE ADOPTION OF THE FOURTEENTH AMENDMENT 80 (1908).
287. CONG. GLOBE, 39th Cong., 1st Sess. 2545 (May 10, 1866).
288. *New York Evening Post*, May 11, 1866, at 2, col. 1.
289. Id., Apr. 7, 1866, at 2, col. 1.
290. CONG. GLOBE, 39th Cong., 1st Sess. 2743 (May 22, 1866).
291. Id. at 3412 (June 26, 1866).
292. Ex. Doc. No. 118, House of Representatives, 39th Cong., 1st Sess. 7 (1866).
293. Id. at 20.
294. CONG. GLOBE, 39th Cong., 1st Sess. 2765 (May 23, 1866).
295. Id.
296. Id. at 2766.
297. I. Brant, THE BILL OF RIGHTS 337 (1965).
298. CONG. GLOBE, 39th Cong., 1st Sess. 2766 (May 23, 1866).
299. Id.
300. *New York Times*, May 24, 1866, at 1, col. 6.
301. *New York Herald*, May 24, 1866, at 1, col 3.
302. *National Intelligencer*, May 24, 1866, at 3, col. 2.
303. *Philadelphia Inquirer*, May 24, 1866, at 8, col. 2.
304. *New York Times*, May 25, 1866, at 2, col. 4.
305. *Chicago Tribune*, May 29, 1866, at 2, col. 3.
306. *Baltimore Gazette*, May 24, 1866, at 4, col. 2.
307. See, for example, *Boston Daily Journal*, May 24, 1866, at 4, col. 4; *Boston Daily Advertiser*, May 24, 1866, at 1, col. 6; *Springfield Daily Republican*, May 24, 1866, at 3, col. 1. The Southern Democratic newspapers generally did not publish any speeches by Republicans, but their reactions to the Howard Amendment are insightful. The amendment's supporters, complained the *Daily Richmond Examiner*, "are first to make citizens and voters of the negroes." Yet the *Examiner* praised Senator Howard for objecting to the clause that disenfranchised ex-Confederates. The Southern newspapers never claimed that the amendment was unclear, but they objected to its breadth in guaranteeing to blacks the rights guaranteed in the first eight amendments as well as the right to vote. See *Daily Richmond Examiner*, May 25, 1866, at 2, col. 3; id., May 26, 1866, at 1,

col. 6; *Charleston Daily Courier*, May 28, 1866, at 1, col. 2, and at 4, col. 2; id., May 29, 1866, at 1, cols. 1–2 (comment on Howard's speech).

308. CONG. GLOBE, 39th Cong., 1st Sess. 2773 (May 23, 1866).

309. Id. at 3412 (June 26, 1866).

310. Id. at 2773 (May 23, 1866).

311. Id.

312. Id. at 2774.

313. Id. at 2775.

314. Id. at 2878.

315. Id.

316. *New York Evening Post*, May 30, 1866, at 2, Col. 3.

317. "The Freedmen's Bureau Bill," id. at 2, col. 1.

318. CONG. GLOBE, 39th Cong., 1st Sess. 2890 (May 30, 1866).

319. Id. at 2897.

320. Id. at 2961 (June 5, 1866).

321. Id. at 3032 (June 8, 1866).

322. Id.

323. Id.

324. Scott v. Sanford, 60 U.S. 393, 416–17 (1857).

325. CONG. GLOBE, 39th Cong., 1st Sess. 3041 (June 8, 1866).

326. Scott v. Sandford, 60 U.S. 393, 416–17 (1857). Johnson's oral argument in *Dred Scott* has not been preserved. See 3 LANDMARK BRIEFS AND ARGUMENTS OF THE SUPREME COURT OF THE UNITED STATES (1978).

327. CONG. GLOBE, 39th Cong., 1st Sess. 40 (Dec. 13, 1865).

328. Id. at 3042 (June 8, 1866).

329. Id. at 3149 (June 13, 1866).

330. Id. at 3180–81 (June 15, 1866); Id. at 3071 (June 11, 1866).

331. Id. at 3210 (June 17, 1866).

332. Id. at 3412 (June 26, 1866).

333. Id.

334. Id.

335. Id.

336. Id. at 3465 (June 28, 1866).

337. Id. at 3501 (June 29, 1866).

338. Id. at 3502.

339. Id. at 3524 (July 2, 1866).

340. Id. at 3562 (July 3, 1866).

341. Id. at 3849 (July 16, 1866).

342. Id.

343. Id. at 3850.

344. Id.

345. Id. More than 12 of the 45 members who did not vote were excused by their Republican colleagues as absent because of "indisposition." Id. at 3850–51. It is unclear whether the indisposition stemmed from spirituous liquors the night

before or political considerations.

346.   Id. at 3838.

347.   Id. at 3842 (July 16, 1866).

348.   14 STATUTES AT LARGE 173 (1866).

349.   Id. at 176–77.

350.   CONG. GLOBE, 39th Cong., 1st Sess. 943 (Feb. 20, 1866). See id. at 421 (Jan. 25, 1866) (original Senate passage of S. 60) and 748 (Feb. 8, 1866) (Senate concurs in House amendments by voice vote).

351.   Id. at 3042 (June 8, 1866).

352.   Id. at 3413 (June 26, 1866).

353.   Id. at 3842 (July 16, 1866).

354.   Raw data of each individual member's voting record was compiled by the author. All voting tabulations were compiled from id. at 943, 3042, and 3842. George Edmunds voted for H.R. 613, but could not vote for S. 60 because he was not yet a Senator, having been appointed to that office on April 3, 1866. BIOGRAPHICAL DIRECTORY OF THE UNITED STATES CONGRESS 1774–1989 at 951 (1989). James Lane of Kansas voted for S. 60, but died on July 11, just before the vote on H.R. 613. Id. at 1339. Morgan, Stewart, and Willey had voted not to override the president's veto of S. 60, but then voted to override the veto of H.R. 613. Stewart explained that he would sustain the veto of S. 60 only because the president agreed to sign the Civil Rights Bill. When Johnson reneged, Stewart became a bitter enemy. B. Kendrick, JOURNAL OF THE JOINT COMMITTEE 293 n. 3 (1914).

355.   The chief objection to the Freedmen's Bureau Bills, as set forth in debate and the president's veto messages, was that it asserted military jurisdiction in lieu of the civil courts. For example, CONG. GLOBE, 39th Cong., 1st Sess. 915–18 (Feb. 19, 1866) and 933–43 (Feb. 20, 1866). No one objected to the provisions that recognized the right to bear arms. On separate occasions, senators who voted against the Freedmen's Bureau Bills also favorably invoked the Second Amendment. For example, id. at 371 (Jan. 23, 1866) (remarks of Senator Davis).

356.   Id. at 654 (Feb. 5, 1866).

357.   Id. at 688 (Feb. 6, 1866).

358.   Id. at 2545 (May 10, 1866).

359.   Id. at 3149 (June 13, 1866).

360.   Id. at 2878 (May 29, 1866).

361.   Id. at 3850 (July 16, 1866). Colleagues excused 13 absentees who would have voted for the bill but were absent because of "indisposition." Id. at 3850–51.

362.   Eleven members who voted for either S. 60 or H.R. 613 but not both were not present for the vote on the other. Nine members voted yes on S. 60 and no on H.R. 613, no on H.R. 613 but yes on the H.R. 613 override, or otherwise voted inconsistently. Three members voted both for and against the Fourteenth Amendment on two occasions. These aberrations are statistically insignificant.

363.   14 STATUTES AT LARGE 173, 176 (1866).

2

Congress Reacts to Southern Rejection of the Fourteenth Amendment

THE CIVIL RIGHTS ACT AND THE RIGHT TO BEAR ARMS IN THE SOUTHERN COURTS

When the Fourteenth Amendment and the second Freedmen's Bureau Bill were being debated in Congress, Representative George Julian warned that Southern courts were nullifying the Civil Rights Act and the states were continuing to prohibit freedmen from keeping and bearing arms.[1] In the fall of 1866, the *New York Times* reprinted two court opinions from Mississippi, one upholding the right to keep and bear arms, the other negating that right and the Civil Rights Act of 1866.[2]

The first opinion rendered was *State* v. *Wash Lowe* and similarly captioned prosecutions against other freedmen who were charged under the 1865 law that prohibited blacks from carrying firearms. Judge R. Bullock, described as "a native citizen,"[3] pointed to the Mississippi Constitution adopted that same year, which outlawed slavery and mandated that the legislature "provide by law for the protection and security of the person and property of the freedmen of the State."[4] Mississippi passed a civil rights law reflecting the language of the 1866 federal act, yet four days later passed the firearms prohibition.[5] The court struck down the statute based on the following:

When this act was passed our State was overrun by thieves, robbers and murderers. . . . The citizen has the right to bear arms in defense of himself, secured by the

constitution. . . . Should not then, the freedmen have and enjoy the same constitutional right to bear arms in defence of themselves, that is enjoyed by the citizen?
It is a natural and personal right — the right of self-preservation. . . . The act,
therefore, prohibiting them from keeping or carrying firearms, was a violation of
that article in the Constitution which provides for and makes it incumbent upon
the Legislature to pass laws for the protection of person and property of the freedmen. . . . While, therefore, the citizens of the State and other white persons are
allowed to carry arms, the freedmen can have no adequate protection against acts
of violence unless they are allowed the same privilege.[6]

The court noted the irony that the Mississippi statute also prohibited the
sale of firearms to blacks, but the merchants who sold the firearms went
unprosecuted. The court ordered the prisoners to be discharged and their
firearms returned.[7]

The second Mississippi decision involved James Lewis, a discharged
black soldier. Hired by a Northerner to work on a plantation, Lewis hunted
there with the musket he had carried in the war. After a neighbor had him
arrested, Lewis could not pay the fine and was incarcerated. The Freedmen's Bureau filed a petition for a writ of habeas corpus and retained
"eminent counsel" on Lewis' behalf.[8]

Chief Justice A. H. Handy of Mississippi's highest court upheld the
conviction and declared the federal Civil Rights Act unconstitutional.[9]
Handy rejected arguments that the firearms prohibition violated the Thirteenth Amendment because the abolition of slavery had allegedly made
Lewis a citizen, or that it violated the state constitutional guarantee that
"every citizen has the right to bear arms in defense of himself and of the
State."[10] Like Dred Scott, Lewis was not, in Justice Handy's eyes, a citizen and thus had none of the civil rights of a citizen.[11] The court determined that the Thirteenth Amendment did not validate the Civil Rights
Act, which was unconstitutional and void.[12] The Second Amendment was
not mentioned.

The *Lewis* decision gave further impetus to the movement already
underway in Congress to require the Southern States to adopt the Fourteenth Amendment. Ratification of the Fourteenth Amendment would
remove any doubt as to the act's constitutionality, thereby safeguarding
the right to bear arms and other fundamental rights.

In his opening message to the second session of the Thirty-Ninth
Congress, President Andrew Johnson presented a rosy picture of Southern
affairs, stating that the civil laws were being enforced and that Congress
should allow the Southern States to be represented in Congress.[13] A few
days earlier, however, Congress had received the report of General U. S.

Grant and his generals. Grant asserted the continuing need to keep a military force in the South "to protect life and property against the acts of those who, as yet, will acknowledge no law but force."[14]

In the report, Brevet Major General Thomas J. Wood detailed Mississippi's most objectionable laws,[15] including prohibitions on blacks testifying in court, purchasing real estate, performing unlicensed labor, and the following: "The statute prohibiting the colored people from bearing arms, without a special license, is unjust, oppressive, and unconstitutional. One of the courts of the State has decided the law to be unconstitutional, while another has maintained its constitutionality."[16] Wood also related an earlier period involving Mississippi's firearms prohibition that had been discussed extensively in the Reconstruction committee hearings and floor debates in Congress. Wood stated:

In December last [1865], his Excellency the Governor of the State applied to me to consent to a general disarming of the negroes through the militia, in conformity with the State statute prohibiting that class of persons from bearing arms without a special license to do so. The reason assigned for the proposition to disarm the negroes was the apprehension of a negro insurrection. Believing there was no foundation in fact for the apprehension of an *émeute* of the negroes, and entertaining the sincere conviction that the State law prohibiting them from bearing arms was unjust and unconstitutional, I declined to give my assent to the proposed measure. I informed the Governor, however, that I would submit his request . . . to his Excellency the President, for his orders in the premises. The President's decision sustained the position I had taken. His orders were communicated to the Governor of the State; and the latter, at my request, issued an order to the militia of the State not to attempt to enforce the State statute prohibiting the negroes from bearing arms.[17]

Although never before mentioned in Congress, this reveals that President Johnson had ordered the protection of the right of freedmen to keep and bear arms and repudiated the disarming of blacks by state-organized militias. Moreover, the Freedmen's Bureau brought charges under the Civil Rights Act against local officers for infringing the freedmen's right to keep and bear arms and the right against unreasonable search and seizure.[18]

THE THIRTY-NINTH CONGRESS' SECOND SESSION: UNFINISHED BUSINESS

Within minutes of the invocation opening the Second Session of the Thirty-Ninth Congress, Senator Charles Sumner demanded consideration of S.B. No. 1, which would extend suffrage to blacks and women in the District of Columbia.[19] In the House, Representative Thomas Eliot submitted a resolution for a standing Committee on Freedmen.[20] Three days later, Senator Henry Wilson moved to take up Senate Resolution No. 32, which called for the disbanding of the Southern militias.[21] These events foreshadowed the session's attempt to enforce the civil rights revolution of the previous session.

On December 13, 1866, after the President's annual message to Congress, Representative Hamilton Ward asserted that the 1866 elections had endorsed the measures of the Thirty-Ninth Congress,[22] which proposed the constitutional amendment and passed the Freedmen's Bureau and Civil Rights Bills.[23] Calling for enforcement measures, Ward assumed that the Fourteenth Amendment reflected those bills and the Bill of Rights: "We have a good civil rights bill in the Constitution as it stands. The freedom of the press, of speech, and protection of life, liberty, and property are secured thereby, and yet for more than half a century none of those rights have been enjoyed by a large portion of the southern people. . . . Southern courts now defy and disobey the civil rights bill. Everything there is organized against the black man, from the judge upon the bench to the constable with his process."[24]

On January 3, 1867, the Senate received reports of Bureau commissioners and a synopsis of Southern state laws that singled out the freedmen.[25] Commissioner O. O. Howard noted that the Mississippi decisions declaring the Civil Rights Act unconstitutional "robbed the colored people of privileges intended to be secured to them by that law."[26] Assistant Commissioner J. G. Foster reported from Florida that, the federal courts not being in session, he had been unable to prosecute cases under the Civil Rights and Freedmen's Bureau Acts.[27] Foster asked Florida Governor D. S. Walker "for a decision on the illegality of the law prohibiting negroes from keeping or bearing arms," and the state attorney general found the law violative of the state constitutional guarantee that all inhabitants "shall enjoy the rights of person and property without distinction of color."[28] Thereafter officials recognized the right of blacks to possess arms, except in certain remote counties.[29]

Although not included in the above report, freedmen in Franklin County, Florida, wrote to Assistant Commissioner Thomas Osborn of the Freedmen's Bureau: "The civil authority in this county are taking away all the fire arms that is found in the hands of the Colored people. They do not only take our arms but they bring us before a Criminal Court and make us pay eight or ten dollars as cost of Court then we have to get two white men as Bail to appear in court in March. Sir we hope these are not the laws of the U.S. if they are then we are worst than Slaves, houses are searched Day and Night. Peaceful persons put in jail if a gun is found in their house."[30] In September 1866, judges and sheriffs in another Florida county were still requiring blacks to obtain licenses for firearms, but were later prosecuted in federal court for violation of the Civil Rights Act.[31]

In a message to the Florida legislature, Governor Walker stated that the law "in regard to freedmen carrying firearms does not accord with our Constitution, has not been enforced and should be repealed."[32] John Wallace, a black politician, commented:

The law prohibiting colored people handling arms of any kind without a license, was a dead letter, except in some cases where some of the freedmen would go around plantations hunting, with apparently no other occupation, such a person would be suspected of hunting something that did not belong to him and his arms would be taken away from him. We have often passed through the streets of Tallahassee with our gun upon our shoulder, without a license, and were never disturbed by any one during the time this law was in force.[33]

Nonetheless, the prohibition remained on the books in 1867 when the above report was sent to Congress.[34]

Through the Freedmen's Bureau reports, Congress was also made aware that the black code prohibitions on firearms also remained on the books in Mississippi[35] and South Carolina.[36] From Mississippi, Assistant Commissioner Wood reported "unjust and oppressive" statutes, such as one "forbidding the freed people to carry arms."[37] The Civil Rights Act nullified such statutes, and improvement in enforcing civil rights was made.[38]

The reports from Florida and Mississippi suggested that, despite great difficulties, progress was being made in the South. This progress was sufficient for President Johnson but insufficient for the Republican majority in Congress.

On January 7 Johnson vetoed S.B. No. 1 concerning suffrage in the District of Columbia.[39] An impeachment resolution was offered by Representative John A. Logan that same day.[40] Both Houses overrode the president's veto within two days.[41] Meanwhile, the Senate passed a resolution asking the president to report concerning enforcement of the Civil Rights Act.[42]

THE FOURTEENTH AMENDMENT
AND THE MILITARY BILL

By January 1, 1867, all but three of the ex-Confederate states had over-whelmingly rejected the Fourteenth Amendment, and those three states did so shortly thereafter.[43] Impatient with President Johnson's moderate Reconstruction plans, radical Republicans now sought to impose strong military rule in the South and to require ratification of the Fourteenth Amendment as a condition to reentering the Union.

The first military reconstruction proposal was H.B. No. 543, which required the Southern States to adopt the Fourteenth Amendment. A supporter,[44] Representative George F. Miller (R-Pa.) paraphrased the Fourteenth Amendment as protecting "the rights of citizens" and charac-terized it as "ingrafting the civil rights bill."[45]

Although Southern state rejections of the Fourteenth Amendment gave impetus to reconstruction based on military force, moderate Republicans from John Bingham to Henry Raymond castigated the military bill because it abrogated the right of the writ of habeas corpus and curtailed the right to petition.[46] Representative Raymond argued that the Freed-men's Bureau and Civil Rights Bills already gave the federal government authority to protect civil rights from violation by local authorities.[47] Although enforcement of those laws rested on President Johnson, Raymond conceded, so too would the proposals for military rule.[48]

Representative George Julian relied on the same statutes in support of military rule. He averred that the Southern regions "are still unprovided with any valid civil governments, and no loyal man within their limits, black or white, is safe in his person or estate. The civil rights act and the Freedmen's Bureau bill are set at open defiance, while freedom of speech and of the press are unknown."[49] Once again, the right to protect "person or estate" — words from the Civil Rights Act and the first Freedman's Bureau bill — was associated with Bill of Rights guarantees.

ENFORCEMENT OF THE BILL OF RIGHTS?

As members of Congress had been recently reminded, under Florida's black code the prohibition on keeping firearms by blacks was punishable by whipping.[50] On January 28, 1867, the House considered a bill that gave rise to a revealing debate concerning the relation of the Bill of Rights to the Fourteenth Amendment. A bill introduced by John Kasson (R-Ia.) recited the Eighth Amendment's prohibition against cruel and unusual punishments and "the barbarous practice of punishing offenses against the law with the whip and scourge."[51] It would have made it a crime for any judge, civil officer, or other state agent to punish a citizen by lashes, blows, or physical torture.[52]

The constitutional basis of the bill, Kasson asserted, was Congress's "right to enforce all provisions of the Constitution of the United States," including the Eighth Amendment.[53] Kasson saw whipping as an incident of slavery being applied to freedmen, who were now "endowed with the personal rights" that belong to citizens.[54] Representative Rufus Spalding questioned how Congress could legislate concerning slavery's incidents except in the "disloyal States," to which Kasson replied: "I do not think there can be any reasonable doubt of the power of Congress to protect personal rights guarantied by the Constitution. The Constitution says that the citizens of one State shall have all the privileges and immunities of citizens in any other State, and I think Congress has the right to protect our citizens in the enjoyment of these rights."[55]

Thomas Williams replied that the prohibition could apply only in federal courts, for "these amendments were intended only as a limitation of the powers of Congress."[56] Kasson rejoined that although procedural rights may not be enforceable against the states, substantive rights were: "Not in relation to the personal rights guarantied by the Constitution. The Constitution guaranties the right of trial by jury in civil cases described, and that has been held to apply to the practice in the Federal courts only. That relates to the form and administration of justice. The clause to which I have referred relates to the rights of persons."[57]

Bingham, author of the Fourteenth Amendment, entered the fray. Bingham instructed his colleagues that, although recent legislation had been passed to enforce the Thirteenth Amendment, Congress had no present power to enforce the Eighth Amendment against the states:

One word further as to the gentleman's statement that the provision of the eighth amendment has relation to personal rights. Admit it, sir; but the same is true of many others of the first ten articles of amendment. For example, by the fifth of the amendments it is provided that private property shall not be taken for public use without just compensation. Of this, as also of the other amendments for the protection of personal rights, it has always been decided that they are limitations upon the powers of Congress, but not such limitations upon the States as can be enforced by Congress and the judgments of the United States courts.[58]

Bingham asserted that the Supreme Court had invariably ruled that the Bill of Rights did not apply to the states.[59] He emphasized, however, that the entire Bill of Rights would apply to the states once the Fourteenth Amendment was adopted:

So far as we can constitutionally do anything to prevent the infliction of cruel punishments by State laws I wish to see it done. I trust the day is not distant when by solemn act of the Legislatures of three fourths of the States of the Union now represented in Congress *the pending constitutional amendments* will become part of the supreme law of the land, by which no State may deny to any person the equal protection of the laws, *including all the limitations for personal protection of every article and section of the Constitution*, and by which also the *Congress will be empowered by law to enforce every one of those limitations* so essential to justice and humanity.[60] (emphasis added)

After further discussion, Kasson agreed that the bill should be referred to the Judiciary Committee.[61]

THE RIGHTS OF THE CITIZEN
AND THE MILITARY BILL

After inconclusive debate, the House referred H.B. No. 543 to the Joint Committee on Reconstruction.[62] In contrast with the previous session of Congress, the Joint Committee met only two days, and its work related only to the military bill.[63] Reported back to the House by Thaddeus Stevens as H.B. No. 1143, "a Reconstruction bill to provide for the more efficient government of the rebel States," the bill now excluded adoption of the Fourteenth Amendment as the method by which the Southern States could be readmitted into the Union and military rule ended.[64]

Bingham took the floor on February 7, arguing that the bill was unduly harsh on the citizens of the South. Bingham objected to the terms "so-called States," noting that § 14 of the Freedmen's Bureau Act of 1866 had recognized the Southern States as states.[65] That provision applied "in every State" where the rebellion had interrupted ordinary judicial proceedings, Bingham noted, and guaranteed that "full and equal benefit of all laws and proceedings concerning personal liberty, personal security, and [estate], including the constitutional right to bear arms, shall be secured to and enjoyed by all the citizens of such State."[66] Bingham objected to the subjugation of all persons in the Southern States, including the "loyal citizen," to military rule.[67]

Bingham envisioned that military rule would end when the Southern States adopted constitutions in accord with the federal Constitution and ratified the Fourteenth Amendment.[68] By so doing, the states would place "into the fundamental law the sublime decree, the nation's will, that no State shall deny to any mortal man the equal protection of the laws . . . and above all, sir, of that great law, the Constitution."[69] Once again, Bingham stated that the Fourteenth Amendment would protect every right guaranteed in the Constitution.

Bingham sought to add to the military bill the condition that military rule would end when the Southern States ratified the Fourteenth Amendment and allowed universal male suffrage.[70] James G. Blaine of Maine proposed a similar amendment.[71] Thus, adoption of the Fourteenth Amendment would trigger the sunset of military rule, which in the original bill had no end. After raucous debate, the Radical Republicans and the Democrats defeated the moderate Republicans' attempt to recommit the bill to committee to add the Blaine amendment.[72] At that point, the bill provided for indefinite military rule without any sunset clause as a reward for adoption of the Fourteenth Amendment.

In the Senate, the military bill was opposed by Willard Saulsbury, who argued that "there is not a single provision in this bill that is constitutional" and that the bill would "outrage the civil rights of the people."[73] Ironically, Saulsbury had opposed the Civil Rights Bill because the states could no longer prohibit possession of firearms by blacks.[74]

Senator Wilson asserted that ratification of the Fourteenth Amendment "would settle all these questions in ninety days" by giving "equality of rights and privileges to all citizens, without distinction of color."[75] Instead, Wilson continued, it was rejected by the Southern States, and "since the passage of the civil rights law 375 murders of freedmen have been committed in the rebel States, and 556 outrages."[76]

Senator Reverdy Johnson countered that "the citizens of these States are entitled to all the guarantees of personal liberty which the Constitution secures," including trial by jury.[77] Senator Doolittle of Wisconsin alleged that the accounts of outrages were greatly exaggerated.[78] He recalled that Bingham originated the first section of the Fourteenth Amendment "for the purpose of making the civil rights bill constitutional."[79]

In perhaps the most powerful speech of the debate against the bill's provision for martial law, Saulsbury appealed to both procedural and substantive guarantees of the Bill of Rights. He argued: "Under the pretext of guarantying to these States a republican form of government you are creating over them an absolute despotism, denying them the benefit of the writ of *habeas corpus*, of trial by jury, and of every right that is guarantied and secured to the people of the whole country by the fundamental law of the land."[80] Claiming that presses had been suspended and publishers punished, Saulsbury charged that the bill "delegates to even a lieutenant the power to punish a citizen of any one of these States for freedom of speech or freedom of worship or for anything he pleases."[81] Under martial law, he continued, it was "the daily practice to search houses, seize papers, and arrest persons without warrant."[82] Although the inherent contradiction of protecting rights through military force was left unresolved, it is revealing that Saulsbury had never complained about massive searches and seizures of freedmen's houses by Southern militias to seize firearms.

Saulsbury did not ignore the Fifth Amendment privilege of indictment by a grand jury and the due process clause, and the Sixth Amendment right to a speedy trial by jury.[83] Although an opponent of the Fourteenth Amendment and its enforcement of the Bill of Rights against the states, Saulsbury now insisted: "These rights are all expressly and clearly guarantied to every citizen of the country by the Constitution; they are placed beyond the reach of legislative authority; they constitute part of our bill of rights that no power on earth can invade."[84]

Just before midnight on the sixteenth Senator John Sherman proposed a substitute that added to the military bill the Bingham-Blaine proposals providing for a sunset of military rule upon ratification of the Fourteenth Amendment.[85] Bitter debate lasted until 6:22 a.m. on Sunday, when the bill passed the Senate with no sunset provision.[86]

The military bill was sent back to the House with the Senate amendments. Representative George Boutwell argued that the military bill would have been unnecessary if President Johnson had simply enforced the Civil Rights Act.[87] Representative James Wilson of Iowa supported the military bill in order to enforce the Bill of Rights against state action, particularly the rights to assemble and petition.[88] Bingham supported the bill in its unamended form, which entrusted enforcement to the president, not to an army general, and emphasized the bill's provision for Southern representation in Congress upon adoption of the Fourteenth Amendment.[89]

Democrats attacked the bill for establishing a military despotism. Elijah Hise of Kentucky argued that no redress would exist for "the crimes of murder, rapine, and arson, crimes which have ever stained the annals of military dominion over an unarmed people, deprived of the means of resistance or of self-defense."[90] This statement again highlighted the paradox of seeking to enforce the Bill of Rights by means that were anathema to the rule of law. Under the bill, Hise argued, 8 million Southerners "may be tried and condemned and deprived of life, liberty, and property by an irresponsible military tribunal without charge, with no opportunity for defense, and without the intervention of a jury."[91]

Meanwhile, President Johnson reported to the Senate that few violations of the Civil Rights Act were known to exist, and that no violation had been reported to the Attorney General, other than one matter referred by the Secretary of War.[92] In the eyes of Radical Republicans, this report confirmed the president's unwillingness to enforce the Act.

The House disagreed with the Senate amendments to the military bill and resolved that a conference committee be appointed,[93] resulting in further Senate debate. Senator Trumbull considered the bill to be superfluous,[94] noting: "The law as it now stands confers all the power that was attempted to be conferred by that House bill. I will read the section of the statute, and it will be seen that it embraces everything that was in the original House bill as it came here. It is the fourteenth section of the act amendatory of the act creating the Freedmen's Bureau."[95] Trumbull proceeded to read that section, including its guarantee that "full and equal benefit of all laws and proceedings concerning personal liberty, personal security, and . . . estate . . . , including the constitutional right to bear arms, shall be secured to and enjoyed by all the citizens."[96]

The Freedmen's Bureau Act had divided the South into military districts, resulting in the appointment of General Howard in command as Commissioner.[97] That act made it the duty of the president as commander-in-chief, Trumbull continued, to protect the freedmen in "every right and in the enjoyment of every liberty."[98] Trumbull asked, "Will it be executed any better if you repeat the law?"[99] Again alluding to § 14 of the Freedmen's Bureau Act, Trumbull claimed that the act had not been adequately enforced because of "the bad man who sits in the executive chair."[100]

Senator Wilson endorsed the bill, particularly its requirement that the Southern States ratify the Fourteenth Amendment and adopt conforming constitutions.[101] He added: "The provisions for the security of the right of persons in the first section of the amendment . . . are of priceless value to the nation."[102] Senator Timothy Howe of Wisconsin detailed injustices against freedman, including the black codes of South Carolina and Florida,[103] and recalled the disturbances in New Orleans in July 1866, where unarmed freedmen had been shot and killed by the New Orleans police during a peaceful demonstration.[104]

After further amendments, the military bill finally passed both houses with the provision concerning the Fourteenth Amendment.[105] Thus, the Bill of Rights would be enforced by military force until the Southern States adopted the Fourteenth Amendment.

DISBANDING THE SOUTHERN MILITIAS

Meanwhile, Senator Wilson's bill to disband the Southern militias was debated. The bill provided: "That all militia forces now organized or in service in either of the States of Virginia, North Carolina, South Carolina, Georgia, Florida, Alabama, Louisiana, Mississippi, and Texas, be forthwith disarmed and disbanded, and that the further organization, arming, or calling into service of the said militia forces, or any part thereof, is hereby prohibited under any circumstances whatever until the same shall be authorized by Congress."[106]

Senator Wilson claimed that "we have evidence of great wrongs perpetrated" by the "local State militia" in the South.[107] Senator Charles Buchalew of Pennsylvania responded: "The organization of local forces for the preservation of order and for defense is one of those ordinary and common rights and privileges, which ought not to be curtailed."[108] Senator Thomas Hendricks objected that such action would amount to "repealing a clause of the Constitution,"[109] without mentioning either the militia clause of Article I, § 8 or the Second Amendment.

The bill was taken up again a week later. Senator Wilson urged abolition of the state militias because "in some localities they have been used to disarm portions of the people."[110] Disbanding of the militia was vigorously opposed by Senator Waitman Willey (R-W.Va.) inasmuch as "the militia should at least carry arms to a limited extent. . . . There may be some constitutional objection against depriving men of the right to bear arms and the total disarming of men in time of peace."[111] Senator Wilson retorted that the militia organizations "go up and down the country taking arms away from men who own arms, and committing outrages of various kinds."[112] Willey remained unsatisfied because the bill "takes the right to bear arms away from every citizen of the southern States. . . . I should be very willing to favor discriminating legislation that would regulate the use of arms by the militia in the South; but a sweeping enactment of the character that I understand this to be does not meet my approbation as at present advised."[113]

Hendricks' argument that the bill would violate the Second Amendment by disarming not only state militias, but also individuals, carried the day. Quoting the Second Amendment, he averred: "If this infringes the right of the people to bear arms we have no authority to adopt it. *This provision . . . relates to people wherever they may be under the jurisdiction of the United States.* Of course in time of war people bearing arms in hostility to the Government would not be protected by this provision of the Constitution; but . . . in a time of peace, certainly the provision of the Constitution applies now, if it ever does"[114] (emphasis added).

Wilson responded by modifying the bill "by striking out the word 'disarmed.' Then it will provide simply for disbanding these organizations."[115] This made the bill more acceptable to Willey, for whom the idea "of disarming the whole people of the South seemed to me to be so directly in the face of the Constitution."[116] The bill then passed the Senate,[117] was pushed through the House without debate,[118] and became law.[119]

As these debates demonstrate, both Republicans and Democrats agreed that the core guarantee of the Second Amendment was the personal right to keep and bear arms. The power of states to maintain militias was secondary, particularly for Republicans who voted to ban the state militias and who championed the right of freedmen to keep arms in opposition to searches and seizures of arms by state militias. Indeed, the Fourteenth Amendment was intended to protect individual firearm ownership against state infringement. Astonishingly, while still waving the bloody shirt and depriving Southerners of suffrage, Republicans were unwilling to deny the right to have arms to ex-Confederates.

Roll call votes reveal that 82 percent (18 of 22) of the senators who voted for the Fourteenth Amendment (and who were present during voting on the militia bill) also voted for the militia disbanding bill, and 18 percent (4 of 22) voted against the bill.[120] Every senator who voted against the Fourteenth Amendment also voted against disbanding the militia if present on the latter vote.

The militia provision passed as part of the army appropriations bill. This bill also required that the Freedmen's Bureau and the Army enforce the Eighth Amendment by prohibiting "whipping or maiming of the person as a punishment of any crime," albeit only "by any pretended civil authority in any State lately in rebellion."[121] That language was introduced in the Senate by Lyman Trumbull and passed Congress without comment.[122] Thus was resurrected Representative John Kasson's bill, which, because the Fourteenth Amendment had not been ratified, had been criticized because the Bill of Rights did not yet apply to the states.[123] President Johnson signed the bill mandating the disbanding of the local Southern militias and prohibiting whipping as punishment for crime.[124]

CONGRESS OVERRIDES THE PRESIDENT'S
VETO OF THE MILITARY BILL

As expected, Johnson vetoed the military bill.[125] In his March 2, 1867, message to Congress, Johnson decried military rule and the abrogation of constitutional rights,[126] asserting that the military bill sought to coerce Southerners to adopt principles they opposed.[127] Indeed, just minutes before the president laid his message before Congress, Representative Miller introduced a resolution denouncing the rejection of the Fourteenth Amendment by ten Southern states and rejecting their readmission into the Union until they ratified. [128] The House proceeded to override the president's veto by a landslide vote.[129]

On the same day the Senate override attempt was led by none other than Reverdy Johnson, a Democrat and counsel for the slaveowner in the *Dred Scott* case.[130] Johnson found the bill no "more obnoxious to constitutional objection than are the civil rights and Freedmen's Bureau bills," which also authorized the president to use military force.[131] Johnson and other moderates realized that far more punitive legislation could pass, such as military rule without the possibility of redemption via ratification of the Fourteenth Amendment. By contrast, Democrat firebrand Hendricks backed the President and rejected any compromise because "liberty and life and personal security" could not spring from military despotism.[132] The override overwhelmingly passed.[133] The Thirty-Ninth Congress then adjourned *sine die*.

The military bill was passed as "An Act to provide for the more efficient Government of the Rebel States."[134] It recited that "no legal State governments or adequate protection for life or property now exists in the rebel States," naming ten states.[135] These states were divided into five military districts, each commanded by a military officer, whose duty was "to protect all persons in their rights of person and property" as well as to suppress insurrection and punish crime.[136] Although they could not inflict "cruel or unusual punishment," military tribunals could try any offense to the exclusion of the state courts, and the death sentence could be imposed if approved by the president.[137] Thus, the basic rights of person and property would be protected, including the substantive guarantees of the Bill of Rights, with a mechanism in opposition to its explicit procedural guarantees, such as jury trial and due process of law.

The act further provided that each Southern state could be admitted to representation in Congress when it framed a constitution that conformed to the federal constitution "in all respects," and the source of this constitution was a convention of delegates elected by universal male suffrage, excluding disenfranchised ex-Confederates.[138] The Southern States were required to ratify the Fourteenth Amendment, which would have to be ratified by enough states (Southern and Northern) to make it part of the federal constitution.[139] Military rule would end when the Southern States accepted an amendment intended to enforce the Bill of Rights against the states and guarantee equal rights to all.

THE FOURTEENTH AMENDMENT IN THE STATES

The records of the states that considered adoption of the Fourteenth Amendment make clear that contemporaries believed the amendment to incorporate the Bill of Rights, especially the right to keep and bear arms. The amendment was submitted to the states in June 1866, less than a month after Senator Jacob Howard's widely published speech explaining that the amendment protected the Bill of Rights. State ratifications began the same month and were two-thirds completed by January 1867. Most Southern states initially rejected the amendment, but would ratify it later as a condition for reentry into the Union.

The messages of governors who submitted the Fourteenth Amendment to their state legislatures, legislative debates (which were recorded in only two states), and committee reports demonstrate that both proponents and opponents understood the amendment to guarantee broad rights. The governors' messages contained little rigorous scrutiny. "The people of this state are thoroughly familiar with its provisions, and with a full understanding of them in all their bearings," Wisconsin's governor stated. "I need therefore urge upon you no extended argument in support of it."[140]

The most complete discussion of the Fourteenth Amendment and its relation to the Bill of Rights came from the reports of the Committee on Federal Relations in the Massachusetts legislative body known as the General Court. That committee split between a majority that held that the Bill of Rights already bound the states, and hence that § 1 of the amendment was unnecessary, and a minority that recommended ratification to leave no doubt on the subject.

The majority cited the Constitution's guarantees of privileges and immunities and a republican form of government, and quoted four provisions in the Bill of Rights, including the Second Amendment.[141] The report stated: "Nearly every one of the amendments to the constitution grew out of a jealousy for the rights of the people, and is in the direction, more or less direct, of a guarantee of human rights . . . . These provisions cover the whole ground of section first of the proposed amendment."[142]

The report held that all native born inhabitants were already citizens, and that the privileges and immunities and due process clauses were already in the Constitution, "illustrated, as these express provisions are, by the whole tenor and spirit of the amendments."[143] Even the equal protection clause was unnecessary: "The denial by any State to any person within its jurisdiction, of the equal protection of the laws, would be a flagrant perversion of the guarantees of personal rights which we have quoted."[144]

The committee minority agreed that the proposed amendment asserted preexisting rights, but it urged ratification in a spirit of caution: "As a declaration of the true intent and meaning of American citizenship, it appeals to freemen everywhere. . . . It is an advance in the direction of establishing unrestricted popular rights."[145] No dispute existed about the nature of the guarantees recognized in both reports, which provided the clearest published discussion of § 1 of the Fourteenth Amendment that took place in any ratifying state.[146] In the minds of the Massachusetts legislators the "human rights" guaranteed in the Second Amendment included the personal right of freedmen to keep and bear arms.

Various committee reports issued in Texas — which initially rejected the amendment — present an interesting comparison with the Massachusetts reports. The Republican minority in the Texas legislature, meeting at the state constitutional convention, filed a report supportive of black suffrage that stated:

These fundamental principles of American liberty constitute the basis of the Bill of Rights, which, under various modifications, pervade all our constitutional charters. . . . The framers of the Federal Constitution were careful to confide all power to the *people*, and to provide for the protection of the *whole* people. To illustrate this, it is only necessary to refer to the constitution itself.

"Art. 2. A well regulated militia being necessary to the sucess [sic] of a free state, the right of the *people* to keep and bear arms shall not be infringed."[147]

"Those who were lately slaves," the report continued, "are now freemen, entitled to all the rights and privileges of American citizens."[148]

When the Texas legislature considered the Fourteenth Amendment, the report of the Senate Committee on Federal Relations noted that blacks had no right of suffrage, but "our Constitution guarantees to the negro every other right of citizenship."[149] Indeed, the Texas Constitution guaranteed that "every citizen shall have the right to keep and bear arms in the lawful defense of himself or the State."[150] In contrast, the House report suggested that § 1 of the Fourteenth Amendment would make blacks "entitled to all 'the privileges and immunities' of white citizens; in these privileges would be embraced the exercise of suffrage at the polls, participation in jury duty in all cases, [and] bearing arms in the militia."[151] Proponents of the amendment, of course, did not limit the right to bear arms of freedmen and others to the militia.

No committee report in any of the states suggested that the Fourteenth Amendment failed to protect from state infringement Bill of Rights guarantees. A typical objection to the amendment was that the Constitution already protected fundamental rights. For instance, the Wisconsin Senate minority report averred: "The absolute rights of personal security, personal liberty and the right to acquire and enjoy private property, descended to the people of this government as a part of the common law of England."[152] Because these rights "form a part of the bill of rights" of the state and the federal constitutions, it asked, "Why, then, is it necessary to engraft into the federal constitution that part of section one [of] the amendments which says: 'Nor shall any state deprive any person of life, liberty or property, without due process of law?'"[153]

State ratification convention debates, recorded only in Pennsylvania and Indiana, reiterated the understanding that the Fourteenth Amendment incorporated the Bill of Rights. Advocates in the Pennsylvania General Assembly averred that "the spirit of this section [1] is already in the Constitution, and that we are only reenacting it in plainer terms."[154] Section one protected "the rights to life, liberty and property; in short the inalienable rights enunciated in the Declaration of Independence."[155] The proposed amendment was said to embody the Pennsylvania Declaration of Rights guarantee that all men "have certain inherent and indefeasible rights," including those of "defending life and liberty."[156]

One opponent of the amendment argued that the issue of citizenship raised by the *Dred Scott* decision had been resolved by the Civil Rights Act.[157] Another contended that unless § 1 meant to establish black suffrage, "the whole section is mere surplusage, conveying no additional right or safeguard not already conveyed in better form."[158] In short, opponents urged, blacks were already protected in all rights of citizenship (which *Dred Scott* said included keeping and bearing arms) other than suffrage, and thus the amendment was unnecessary.

In Indiana, one opponent "considered what privileges and immunities the negro would acquire under this amendment. They were the same as those enuring to the white men."[159] These rights, such as having arms, were guaranteed under the United States and Indiana constitutions. These perceived rights of citizens prompted the assertion that "the first section assumed too much for the United States — to say who shall be citizens of a particular state."[160] That speaker objected to "the exaltation of the negro to citizenship."[161] These arguments were answered by distinguishing Bill of Rights freedoms from suffrage: "Civil rights were inherent — were of God; political rights were conferred by constitutions."[162]

Meanwhile, Congress quickly reconvened, and the struggle was renewed to use every means to obtain ratification of the Fourteenth Amendment by the states.

THE SUPPLEMENTARY RECONSTRUCTION ACT

The first session of the Fortieth Congress was devoted to passage of the Supplementary Reconstruction Act, which concerned the calling of state conventions in the South to adopt new state constitutions. Congressional approval of a constitution would admit the state to the Union and entitle it to representation in Congress.[163]

Senator Wilson explained that he introduced the bill to facilitate the restoration of the Southern States to the Union.[164] With the freeing of the slaves and the enactment of the Civil Rights Act, he stated, "these freemen were declared citizens of the United States and entitled to all the civil rights that belonged to other citizens of the Republic."[165] Wilson characterized the "no State shall" clause of the Fourteenth Amendment as a "grand, comprehensive, and all-embracing provision" that made every man free. The Reconstruction Act required the Southern States "to adopt the constitutional amendment that takes forever from them the power to abridge the privileges or immunities of their three and a half million colored men, or to deprive the humblest of them of life, liberty, or property, or to deny to them the equal protection of the laws."[166] Wilson anticipated that each state convention would adopt a constitution "guarantying and securing personal rights."[167]

Meanwhile, conflict brewed in Tennessee, which had been readmitted into the Union without passing through the purgatory of Reconstruction. In support of a bill to furnish that state with 2,500 militia arms, Representative Paine explained that Unionists there were at a disadvantage in defending themselves from attacks: "The Union soldiers who left the Federal Army were not permitted to take with them their arms unless they purchased them. . . . And the black troops, when they have purchased their arms from the Government, have been for the most part robbed of them by the rebels of Tennessee."[168] This passage provides more background to the complaints in the Thirty-Ninth Congress that the states were seizing the arms of black veterans. As Paine noted, all Union soldiers were allowed to purchase their arms on discharge, and many blacks apparently did so.

The first Reconstruction Act had empowered the military "to protect all persons in their rights of person and property." Senator Howard explained about this clause: "The rights of person and property are not created by State laws. They exist by the law of nature, and laws are made, or should be made, to protect them."[169] This comment could as well have been made about the Bill of Rights and the Fourteenth Amendment.

Unlike the Thirty-Ninth Congress, which formulated and explicated the great rights of mankind, the Fortieth Congress was devoted to working out the details of Reconstruction. The meaning of the Fourteenth Amendment and the intent to protect Bill of Rights freedoms would not be discussed at length again until the introduction of major new civil rights legislation in 1870.

FARRAR'S *MANUAL OF THE CONSTITUTION*

Senator Howard's remark that the rights of person and property derive from natural law expressed a widely held contemporary view. In 1867, Judge Timothy Farrar published his *Manual of the Constitution*, which was written the year before when the Fourteenth Amendment was "in the process of adoption by the State legislatures."[170] The *Manual* stated the following about the origin and substance of rights:

The people of the United States, in making their Constitution, do not create or confer on themselves any new right, but they expressly reserve all the rights they then held, except what were delegated for their own benefit; and they particularly and expressly recognized and perpetuate many natural and civil common-law rights, which, of course, are placed beyond the reach of any subordinate government, and even of their own. Among these are the following:

1. The right to be, what they call themselves, "the people of the United States," citizens, and component members of the body politic, the nation; and to participate in all the privileges, immunities, and benefits the Constitution was designed to obtain or secure for all the American people.

5. A right to keep and bear arms.[171]

Although the Fourteenth Amendment was not yet ratified, Farrar nonetheless contended that the Bill of Rights applied to the states, an antebellum view with strong adherents still: "The right of every person to 'life, liberty, and property,' to 'keep and bear arms,' to the 'writ of *habeas corpus*,' to 'trial by jury,' and divers other, are recognized by, and held under, the Constitution of the United States, and cannot be infringed by individuals or States, or even by the government itself."[172] Farrar argued that the Bill of Rights was actually unnecessary because Congress possessed no delegated power to infringe the rights declared therein: "The first Amendment . . . relates to the establishment and free exercise of religion, freedom of speech and of the press, peaceable assemblies of the people, and the right to petition the government. Which of the enumerated powers, as they have been insidiously called, or what other specific power mentioned in any part of the Constitution, authorizes Congress to touch any other of these subjects, for any purpose whatever? . . . So of 'the right to keep and bear arms,' and divers other valuable common-law rights."[173]

Later in his treatise, Farrar returned to the theme that the Bill of Rights enumerates natural rights on which no level of government may infringe.[174] Farrar proceeded to list these natural rights:

1. The free exercise of religion, without any legal establishment thereof.
2. The freedom of speech and of the press.
3. The right to assemble and petition the government.
4. The right to keep and bear arms.[175]

Farrar's reflections represent yet another indication of the understanding of the Bill of Rights when the Fourteenth Amendment was being considered by the states. Farrar's *Manual*, in turn, influenced legal opinions at the national level.[176]

ASSEMBLY, BEARING ARMS, AND THE BLACK MILITIAS OF THE DISTRICT OF COLUMBIA

The existence of independent black militias in the District of Columbia contributed to the already divisive controversy between supporters of civil rights and President Johnson. In November 1867 Johnson ordered the disbandment of these volunteer militias, which many Radical Republicans viewed as protected by the Constitution.

This controversy was mentioned by George W. Paschal, a prominent jurist and law professor,[177] in *The Constitution of the United States* as follows:

This clause [the Second Amendment] has reference to a free government, and is based on the idea, that the people cannot be oppressed or enslaved, who are not first disarmed.

The President, by order, disbanded the volunteer companies of the District of Columbia, in November, 1867. His right to do so has been denied.[178]

Paschal wrote that "the people" by definition "embraces all the inhabitants,"[179] and the term "militia" means "the body of arms- bearing citizens."[180] Regarding the Fourteenth Amendment, Paschal wrote: "The new feature declared is that the general principles which had been construed to apply only to the national government, are thus imposed upon the States. Most of the States, in general terms, had adopted the same bill of rights in their own constitutions."[181]

Two independent black militias had drilled in the District of Columbia since the end of the Civil War with muskets they purchased from the government.[182] Washington's *Daily Chronicle* commented: "The time may come when they may be essential in preserving the peace of the District as they were essential in preserving their liberties."[183] However, the *Daily National Intelligencer* replied that the companies were drilling "for the avowed purpose of supporting Congress in the enforcement of the laws to be enacted for the purpose of deposing the President during his impeachment."[184]

President Johnson ordered General Grant to suppress all such organizations in the District of Columbia, which the *Chronicle* saw as an order "to disarm or disband the freedman before he commences his campaign against them."[185] Although Congress was still in recess, the president's constitutional and statutory power to order the militias disbanded were vigorously debated in the press.[186] The military commander for the District reported to Grant that, in the absence of martial law, he had no authority to execute the president's order.[187] The president asked the attorney general for an opinion as to his power.[188]

District Mayor Wallach stated that "the negroes had as much right as white men to raise companies in conformity with the militia laws of the District."[189] The scope of the president's order encompassed all militia-type organizations, not just black ones, leading the *New York Times* to comment that "in attempting to snub the African [the president] has literally 'put his foot into it' with his white friends to an embarrassing degree."[190] Charles Fischer, major of one of the black militia companies, wrote to Grant that the "armed portion of the organization is made up of those members who purchased arms from the Government." Denying that "we are hostile bands of armed negroes," Fischer asserted: "Our object is to show to the world that we are worthy of the freedom obtained by the late war."[191] The freedmen militias stopped parading in the streets, but did not disband, and promised a challenge to the President's order in the courts.[192]

Although the outcome of any such challenge is unknown, the *Daily Chronicle* attacked the president's order as a violation of the First and Second Amendments: "In every State of the Union the people have claimed the right of peaceably assembling and organizing themselves into military and civic associations at will. They have asserted their right to do this in their Declaration of Rights; and, in the Constitution of the United States, the right to bear arms is expressly reserved. . . . If the President may order their disbandment, he may also disperse a religious society or a debating club. If he can take away the arms of a citizen, why may he not also take away his clothes or his Bible."[193]

The *New York Tribune* accused the president of infringing on the Second Amendment and usurping Congress' constitutional power to exercise exclusive jurisdiction over the District.[194] It commented:

> The President might, if he had the power, disband all the base-ball clubs and confiscate the bats and other apparatus; but he would have no *right* to do it. Similarly he may abolish the Militia of the District of Columbia and seize their arms; but the act would be one of the most flagrant and despotic usurpation. . . . Even Congress itself has no authority to infringe upon "the right of the people to keep and bear arms." It may "regulate" the militia, but it cannot say that there shall be no militia, nor can it, without a violation of the Constitution, take away any man's musket while he "keeps it" and "bears it" for lawful purposes.[195]

Even Johnson's strongest supporter in the press, the Baltimore *Sun*, could hardly defend the president's action: "Under the wording of the order it would seem to embrace all societies and organizations in possession of arms. . . . Upon no construction of the order has it ever been contemplated to interfere with the rights of citizens to possess arms *as individuals*"[196] (emphasis added).

The militia controversy arose on the eve of and was overshadowed by the beginning of Johnson's impeachment trial. The issue gave rise to the expression of opinion during a critical period of Reconstruction concerning the rights of individuals to bear arms and of groups to associate and to bear arms as a militia.

NOTES

1. CONG. GLOBE, 39th Cong., 1st Sess. 3210 (June 17, 1866).

2. "Mississippi . . . The Civil Rights Bill Declared Unconstitutional by a State Court," *New York Times*, Oct. 26, 1866, at 2, cols. 2–4.

3. Id., col. 3.

4. Id.

5. Id.

6. Id.

7. Id.

8. Id.

9. Id. The opinion is not printed in *Mississippi Reports*.

10. Id., col. 3.

11. Id.

12. Id.

13. CONG. GLOBE, 39th Cong., 2d Sess., App. 1 (Dec. 3, 1866).

14. Id. at 19 (Nov. 14, 1866).

15. Id. at 32.

16. Id. at 33.

17. Id. at 32.

18. Robert J. Kaczorowski, THE POLITICS OF JUDICIAL INTERPRETATION: THE FEDERAL COURTS, DEPARTMENT OF JUSTICE AND CIVIL RIGHTS, 1866–1876, at 38 (1985) (citing Freedmen's Bureau archives).

19. CONG. GLOBE, 39th Cong., 2d Sess. 2 (Dec. 3, 1866).

20. Id. at 4.

21. Id. at 27 (Dec. 6, 1866).

22. Id. at 115 (Dec. 13, 1866).

23. Id. at 116.

24. Id. at 117.

25. Ex. Doc. No. 6, 39th Cong., 2d Sess. (Jan. 3, 1867).

26. Id. at 2.

27. Id. at 44.

28. Id. at 45.

29. Id.

30. Jerrell H. Shofner, NOR IS IT OVER YET: FLORIDA IN THE ERA OF RECONSTRUCTION, 1863–1877, at 84 (1974), quoting Many Colored Citizens of Franklin County to T. W. Osborn, Feb. 23, 1866.

31. Id. at 84.

32. FLA. SEN. J. 13 (1866).

33. J. Wallace, CARPET BAG RULE IN FLORIDA 35 (1888).

34. Ex. Doc. No. 6, 39th Cong., 2d Sess., 174 (Jan. 3, 1867).

35. Id. at 195–96.

36. Id. at 204.

37. Id. at 96.

38. Id. Assistant Commissioner Wood reported as follows: "The efforts to overcome these difficulties have been strong and unceasing, and an improvement is manifest. The higher authorities of the State, executive and judicial, are doing

what even one year since was thought impossible by the most sanguine; witness the decisions of the several judicial officers herewith enclosed; and this animus is finding its way down to the lower courts, slowly, to be sure, but with that power by which all great principles are moved."

39. CONG. GLOBE, 39th Cong., 2d Sess. 303 (Jan. 7, 1867).

40. Id. at 319.

41. Id. at 313–14 (Senate), 344 (House) (Jan. 8, 1867).

42. Id. at 326.

43. J. Burgess, RECONSTRUCTION AND THE CONSTITUTION 106 (1902).

44. CONG. GLOBE, 39th Cong., 2d Sess., App., at 80–82 (Jan. 19, 1867).

45. Id. at 82.

46. Id. at 502–5 (Jan. 16, 1867) (remarks of John Bingham), 716 (Jan. 24, 1867) (remarks of Rep. Raymond).

47. Id. at 716.

48. Id.

49. Id., App., at 78.

50. Ex. Doc. No. 6, 39th Cong., 2d Sess. 174 (Jan. 3, 1867).

51. Id. at 810 (Jan. 28, 1867).

52. Id.

53. Id.

54. Id.

55. Id. at 811.

56. Id. (remarks of Rep. Williams).

57. Id.

58. Id.

59. Id. See Barron v. Baltimore, 32 U.S. 243 (1831).

60. Id.

61. Id. at 812.

62. Id. at 817 (Jan. 28, 1867).

63. B. Kendrick, THE JOURNAL OF THE JOINT COMMITTEE OF FIFTEEN ON RECONSTRUCTION 122–29 (1914).

64. CONG. GLOBE, 39th Cong., 2d Sess. 1036–37 (Feb. 6, 1867).

65. Id. at 1080 (Feb. 7, 1867).

66. Id.

67. Id. at 1080–81.

68. Id. at 1083.

69. Id.

70. Id. at 1176–77.

71. Id. at 1182.

72. Id. at 1215 (Feb. 13, 1867).

73. Id. at 1375 (Feb. 15, 1867).

74. CONG. GLOBE, 39th Cong., 1st Sess. 478 (Jan. 29, 1866).

75. CONG. GLOBE, 39th Cong., 2d Sess. 1375 (Feb. 15, 1867).

76. Id.

77. Id. at 1379.
78. Id. at 1441 (Feb. 16, 1867).
79. Id. at 1443.
80. Id. at 1451.
81. Id. at 1454.
82. Id.
83. Id. at 1455.
84. Id. at 1458.
85. Id. at 1459.
86. Id. at 1469.
87. Id. at 1316 (Feb. 18, 1867) (remarks of Reps. Boutwell and Wilson).
88. Id. at 1318.
89. Id. at 1319.
90. Id. at 1326.
91. Id. at 1327.
92. Ex. Doc. No. 29, 39th Cong., 2d Sess. 1–3 (Feb. 19, 1867).
93. CONG. GLOBE, 39th Cong., 2d Sess. 1340 (Feb. 19, 1867).
94. Id. at 1561.
95. Id.
96. Id.
97. Id.
98. Id.
99. Id.
100. Id.
101. Id. at 1626 (Feb. 20, 1867).
102. Id. at 1627.
103. Id. at 1632.
104. Id. at 1633.
105. Id. at 1400 (House), 1645 (Senate) (Feb. 20, 1867).
106. Id. at 1848 (Feb. 26, 1867).
107. Id. at 1575–76 (Feb. 19, 1867).
108. Id. at 1576.
109. Id.
110. Id. at 1848 (Feb. 26, 1867).
111. Id.
112. Id. at 1849.
113. Id.
114. Id.
115. Id.
116. Id.
117. Id.
118. Id. at 1706 (Mar. 1, 1867), 1733, 1752 (Mar. 2, 1867).
119. 14 STATUTES AT LARGE 487 (Mar. 2, 1867).
120. The voting records on the Fourteenth Amendment and the militia bill

are located respectively in CONG. GLOBE, 39th Cong., 1st Sess. 3042 (June 8, 1866) and id., 2d Sess. 1849 (Feb. 26, 1867). Of the four persons who were Fourteenth Amendment supporters but militia bill opponents, all were Republicans. The other three likely concurred, but for constitutional or policy reasons voted against the militia bill.

121. CONG. GLOBE, 39th Cong., 2d. Sess. 1705 (Mar. 1, 1867).
122. Id. at 1848 (Feb. 26, 1867).
123. Id. at 810–12 (Jan. 28, 1867).
124. 14 STATUTES AT LARGE 487 (Mar. 2, 1867).
125. CONG. GLOBE, 39th Cong., 2d Sess. 1729 (Mar. 2, 1867).
126. Id. at 1729–31.
127. Id. at 1729.
128. Id. at 1722.
129. Id. at 1733.
130. Id. at 1972–73.
131. Id. at 1973.
132. Id.
133. Id. at 1976.
134. 14 STATUTES AT LARGE 428 (Mar. 2, 1867).
135. Id.
136. Id.
137. Id. at 428–29.
138. Id. at 429.
139. Id.
140. WISC. SEN. J. 32 (1867).
141. MASS. H. R. Doc. No. 149, at 3 (Feb. 28, 1867).
142. Id.
143. Id. at 4.
144. Id.
145. Id. at 25.
146. I. Brant, THE BILL OF RIGHTS 343 (1965).
147. JOURNAL OF TEXAS STATE CONVENTION 82 (1866). The convention met between February 7 and April 2, 1866.
148. Id. at 88.
149. TEX. SEN. J. 420 (Oct. 22, 1866).
150. TEX. CONST. I, § 13 (1866).
151. TEX. H. J. 578 (Oct. 13, 1866).
152. WISC. SEN. J. 106 (1867).
153. Id.
154. PA. LEG., App., 59 (Jan. 31, 1867) (remarks of Rep. Ewing).
155. Id. at 65 (Jan. 30, 1867) (remarks of Rep. Day).
156. Id. at 94 (Feb. 6, 1867) (remarks of Rep. Allen).
157. Id. at 25 (Jan. 16, 1867) (remarks of Rep. Burnett).
158. Id. at 67 (Jan. 30, 1867) (remarks of Rep. Deise).

159.   BREVIER LEG. REPTS. 80 (Jan. 22, 1867) (remarks of Rep. Ross).

160.   Id. (Remarks of Rep. Bird).

161.   Id. at 81.

162.   Id. at 90.

163.   15 Stat. 2 (1867).

164.   CONG. GLOBE, 40th Cong., 1st Sess. 102 (Mar. 14, 1867).

165.   Id.

166.   Id.

167.   Id. at 143 (Mar. 16, 1867).

168.   Id. at 288 (Mar. 22, 1867).

169.   Id. at 551 (July 10, 1867).

170.   T. Farrar, MANUAL OF THE CONSTITUTION OF THE UNITED STATES OF
AMERICA 401 (Boston 1867).

171.   Id. at 58–59.

172.   Id. at 145.

173.   Id. at 285–86.

174.   Id. at 395.

175.   Id. at 396.

176.   R. Aynes, *On Misreading John Bingham and the Fourteenth Amendment*, 103 YALE L. J. 57, 85 (1993).

177.   Id. at 85–89.

178.   George W. Paschal, THE CONSTITUTION OF THE UNITED STATES: DEFINED
& CAREFULLY ANNOTATED 256 (Washington, D.C.: W. H. & O. H. Morrison,
Law Booksellers, 1868). Although Paschal did not elaborate, Judge Thomas
Cooley, perhaps the most widely-read constitutional scholar of the nineteenth
century, explained why the Second Amendment protected the right of the people
to form local militias:

The right of the people to bear arms in their own defence, and to form and drill military
organizations in defence of the State, . . . is reserved by the people as a possible and necessary resort for the protection of self-government against usurpation, and against any
attempt on the part of those who may for the time be in possession of State authority or
resources to set aside the constitution and substitute their own rule for that of the people.
Should the contingency ever arise when it would be necessary for the people to make use
of the arms in their hands for the protection of constitutional liberty, the proceeding, so far
from being revolutionary, would be in strict accord with popular right and duty.

Thomas M. Cooley, *The Abnegation of Self-Government*, 12 PRINCETON REVIEW
213–14 (1883).

179.   Paschal, supra note 178, at 257.

180.   Id. at 135.

181.   Id. at 86.

182.   *Daily Chronicle* (Washington, D.C.), Oct. 22, 1867, at 2.

183.   Id.

184. "Unauthorized Negro Military Organizations," *Daily National Intelligencer* (Washington, D.C.), November 5, 1867, at 2.

185. "A Panic in the White House," *Daily Chronicle* (Washington, D.C.), November 6, 1867, at 2. Johnson's order to Grant, printed in "Unauthorized Negro Military Organizations," *Daily National Intelligencer*, November 8, 1867, at 2, stated: "I am reliably advised that there are within the District of Columbia a number of armed organizations, formed without authority of law, and for purposes which have not been communicated to the Government. Being at the present time unnecessary for the preservation of order or the protection of the civil authority, they have excited serious apprehensions as to their real design. You will, therefore, take official steps for promptly disbanding and suppressing all such illegal organizations."

186. "The Militia and Regular Forces in Washington," *New York Herald*, Nov. 8, 1867, at 3 noted: "A very old act of Congress, passed late in the last century, provided that all military volunteer organizations in the District of Columbia shall be under control of the President." However, "Affairs at the National Capital," *New York Times*, Nov. 7, 1867, at 5, observed:

It remains to be seen whether the President will decide that he has any more authority over the militia of the District of Columbia than he would have over that of a State. Military organizations have always existed here with the sanction of the local authorities, and have never been prohibited, even if not specially authorized by act of Congress. With regard to disbanding the colored militia organizations at the South, . . . the President has called the attention of the Secretary of War to what he deems their dangerous character, but has not yet issued any order to suppress them, possibly for the reason that he regards the States as States, and that he has no right to interfere, as he has no constitutional power over the militia except in time of war.

187. "President Johnson Asks Advice of Binckley in the Colored Militia Case," *The Press* (Philadelphia, Pa.), Nov. 8, 1867, at 1.

188. "The Colored Militia of the District of Columbia," *New York Times*, Nov. 9, 1867, at 1.

189. "Unauthorized Military Organizations," *The Sun* (Baltimore, Md.), Nov. 9, 1867, at 1.

190. "Affairs at the National Capital," *New York Times*, Nov. 8, 1867, at 5.

191. "Our Colored Militia," *Daily Chronicle* (Washington, D.C.), November 9, 1867, at 1.

192. "Concerning the Disbandment of the Freedmen's Military Organizations," *The Press* (Philadelphia, Pa.), Nov. 7, 1867, at 1.

193. "Volunteer Military Organizations," *Daily Chronicle* (Washington, D.C.), Nov. 12, 1867, at 2.

194. "The Militia Disbandment," *New York Tribune*, Nov. 13, 1867, at 4.

195. Id. The editorial continued: "Monarchical governments have claimed and exercised the right to disarm the people, as the English Government disarmed the Highlanders, and subsequently Irishmen. It was with a full recollection of the

fantastic tricks of tyrants that our fathers framed the Constitutional provision which we have quoted. They foresaw a President desperately bent upon grasping supreme and irresponsible power, and they reserved to the people the means of defending themselves, in the last resort, against the violence of a possible usurper."

196.   "Letter from Washington," *The Sun* (Baltimore, Md.), Nov. 9, 1867, at 4.

3

The Southern State
Constitutional Conventions

In 1867 Congress required by law that the constitutions of the reconstructed states conform to the U.S. Constitution, including the Fourteenth
Amendment, even though it was not yet fully ratified.[1] Ten Southern
states held conventions in 1867–68 that drafted new state constitutions,
and eventually these states won Congressional approval to reenter the
Union. Maryland, a border state, held a convention in 1867 but was not
obliged to make its constitution conform to the Fourteenth Amendment.
In 1870 Tennessee, the only ex-Confederate state not included in the
statute, adopted a constitution consistent with the Fourteenth Amendment.

The antebellum constitutions and common law of most of these states
guaranteed the right to keep and bear arms to "the people," "citizens," or
"free white men." Blacks, not considered to be encompassed in these
classifications, were denied this right. This chapter analyzes the impact of
the Fourteenth Amendment upon these constitutions and, thus, the
extent to which that amendment was perceived as incorporating the
Second Amendment. It concludes with a summary of the status of the
right to keep and bear arms under the constitutions of all the states during
Reconstruction.

MARYLAND

A convention to revise the Maryland Constitution commenced in May 1867, several months before the Southern state conventions began. Although the Maryland convention was not called because of any federal requirements, its proceedings illustrate attitudes toward the right to keep and bear arms and whether this right should be guaranteed to blacks.

As of 1860 the Maryland Code had no firearms prohibitions applicable to whites.[2] It provided, however, that "no slave shall carry any gun, or any other offensive weapon, from off his master's land, without a license from his said master," and punished violations by whipping.[3] The code also provided that "no free negro shall be suffered to keep or carry a firelock of any kind, any military weapon, or any powder or lead, without first obtaining a license," punishable by forfeiture of the weapon and, for a subsequent offense, by up to 39 stripes.[4]

Maryland abolished slavery in 1864 and a year later repealed its slave code, including the prohibition on carrying firearms.[5] Thereafter no restrictions on having arms existed, although freedmen may have been unlawfully disarmed in specific instances.

In early 1867 the Maryland Senate rejected the Fourteenth Amendment.[6] Predictably, the delegates at the Maryland constitutional convention of 1867 drafted a constitution that did not conform to the Fourteenth Amendment. The convention considered a proposal by the Committee on a Declaration of Rights to amend article 32, which declared "that a well regulated militia is the proper and natural defense of a free government."[7] The following discussion ensued:

Mr. Giddings moved to amend by adding after the word "government" the words, "and every citizen has the right to bear arms in defence of himself and the State."

Mr. Garey moved to amend the amendment by inserting the word "white" after the word "every."

Mr. Jones hoped the gentleman from Baltimore (Mr. Garey) would withdraw his amendment. Every citizen of the State means every white citizen, and none other.

Mr. Garey withdrew his amendment.[8]

Perhaps the amendment was prompted by the mass disarmings that took place in Baltimore early in the Civil War and the suspension of habeas corpus.[9] Luther Giddings may have sought to protect freedmen who had been disarmed in Maryland as they had been generally in the former slave states. Henry Garey and Isaac Jones clearly did not want nonwhites to have a right to bear arms.

Opposition to the proposed amendment couched in idealistic terms was then expressed by delegate George Brown as follows: "If this broad declaration was put in the Bill of Rights, he did not see how you could disarm any man, drunk or sober, as he could throw himself on his reserved rights."[10] Brown did not address the situation of those who bear arms for lawful purposes or explain why an intoxicated person brandishing a weapon could not be disarmed. Brown, who minutes before condemned abolition of slavery as "a great wrong," more likely opposed the guarantee because it recognized blacks as having a right to keep and bear arms.[11] The debate then shifted to different premises:

Mr. Garey read from the constitution of the United States: "The right of the people to keep and bear arms shall not be infringed." He considered the proposed amendment entirely in accordance with the constitution of the United States, and that it should be adopted.

Mr. Jones said that for the very reason that it was in the constitution of the United States, he hoped it would not be inserted here. That was amply sufficient. We did not want any such declaration in the State of Maryland.[12]

At best, this exchange reflected the antebellum view that the Second Amendment prohibited both federal and state infringement of the individual right to keep and bear arms,[13] and thus an explicit state guarantee was perceived as unnecessary. At worst, it reflected delegate Jones' campaign to prevent recognition of the right of freed slaves to bear arms. Indeed, the day before, Jones had called emancipation "a violent, ruthless, outrageous act,"[14] and persuaded the convention to make a demand for compensation to ex-slaveowners a part of the Maryland Constitution.[15]

A proposal was then introduced to allay those who feared that a right to "bear" arms guarantee would allow blacks, drunks, or both to carry arms: "Mr. Barnes offered the following amendment, to be inserted at the end of the article: 'and the citizen shall not be deprived of the right to keep arms on his premises.' Rejected." The amendment of Giddings was then rejected.[16] Delegate John Barnes' proposal was already implicit in the Declaration of Rights, because members of the well regulated militia, which included all citizens, were entitled and required to keep arms on their premises.[17] Barnes' amendment may have been rejected to prevent former slaves in Maryland from keeping arms in their homes.

The day after the right-to-arms debate, a Baltimore newspaper charged that many of the convention delegates were pro-slavery.[18] Arguing for black suffrage, the editorial stated: "Goldsmith, in the Vicar of Wakefield, says: 'The penal laws are in the hands of the rich.' In Maryland, where a slaveocracy ruled, slaves were taxed less than any other property. But what shall be said of the laws against the free blacks? A free negro could not keep a dog or a gun. . . . This is a long series of laws touching directly upon the rights and freedom of the blacks."[19]

The right to bear arms guarantee failed to be made part of the Maryland Constitution in 1867 for the same reason that a provision calling for compensation to ex-slaveowners for loss of property succeeded. Apparently the slaveocracy still ruled in Maryland.

ALABAMA

The Alabama constitutional convention, which commenced on November 5, 1867, reenacted its antebellum guarantee that "every citizen has a right to bear arms in defense of himself and the State."[20] In upholding a prohibition on carrying concealed weapons, Alabama's high court cautioned: "A statute which, under the pretence of regulating, amounts to a destruction of the right, or which requires arms to be borne as to render them wholly useless for the purpose of defence, would be clearly unconstitutional."[21] A recommendation in the convention that would have limited this right to "the common defense" failed.[22] Because the new constitution, consistent with the Fourteenth Amendment, made all residents citizens, blacks were now protected by the Alabama Constitution in keeping and bearing arms.

LOUISIANA

Antebellum Louisiana courts held that the Second Amendment applied to the states, which is perhaps why the prewar and postwar Louisiana constitutions included no right-to-arms guarantees.[23] In upholding a prohibition on concealed weapons, Louisiana's high court held that the right to carry arms openly "is the right guaranteed by the Constitution of the United States, and which is calculated to incite men to a manly and noble defence of themselves, if necessary, and of their country."[24]

In the constitutional convention, which convened on November 23, 1867, a bill of rights was proposed and referred to committee. It provided that the military should be subordinate to the civil power, and that "every citizen has the right to keep and bear arms for the common defense, and this right shall never be questioned."[25] The committee reporting the bill of rights deleted the arms provision.[26] Neither the majority nor minority reports on the bill of rights included the provision, although it could have been intended to be protected in the unenumerated rights guarantee.[27]

When the convention debated the proposed bill of rights, racial equality was the main subject of contention, and the right to bear arms was not mentioned.[28]

Because Louisiana courts had held that the Second Amendment protected the right to keep and bear arms from state infringement, a view that would have been strengthened by the Fourteenth Amendment, the Louisiana convention may have deemed a specific right to arms provision unnecessary. In 1879 the 1868 bill of rights was strengthened by addition of the guarantee of the right to bear arms.[29]

VIRGINIA

The Virginia Declaration of Rights of 1776 provided: "That a well regulated militia, composed of the body of the people, trained to arms, is the proper, natural and safe defense of a free state."[30] Henry St. George Tucker wrote that Virginia common law recognized "the right of bearing arms — which with us is not limited and restrained by an arbitrary system of game laws as in England; but is practically enjoyed by every citizen, and is among his most valuable privileges, since it furnishes the means of resisting as a freeman ought, the inroads of usurpation."[31]

The "well regulated militia" clause of the declaration seems to have recognized private rights, because the convention that commenced on December 3, 1867, readopted it under the category "RIGHT TO BEAR ARMS,"[32] and provided for the militia in a separate article.[33] In the words of convention delegate John Hawnhurst: "The Bill of Rights . . . is a declaration of individual rights, as against the Government. It is an assertion of certain rights that the Government shall not take away from the individual."[34]

Discussion centered on the fact that the Fourteenth Amendment would confer citizenship on freedmen. As evident from the authorities upon which they relied, the delegates were clearly aware that citizenship carried with it broad rights, including keeping and bearing arms.[35] The utility of being armed to resist oppression was suggested in the following analogy by Thomas Bayne in support of the Freedmen's Bureau: "Now, as on former occasions, in every age and country of the world, the weak must always suffer when the strong oppress them. If the highway robber meets the unarmed man in the road he takes his purse away from him simply because he wants it and is able to take it."[36] The Virginia convention reaffirmed that state's traditional concept of the value of an armed populace, and recognized that the Fourteenth Amendment would confer upon the freedmen the basic rights of citizenship.

GEORGIA

Although Georgia's antebellum constitution had no right to bear arms provision, the Georgia Supreme Court held in 1846 that "the language of the second amendment is broad enough to embrace both Federal and State governments."[37] The court declared a state statute banning breast pistols violative of the Second Amendment, explaining: "The right of the whole people, old and young, men, women and boys, and not militia only, to keep and bear *arms* of every description, and not *such* as are used by the *militia*, shall not be infringed."[38] The same court, however, narrowed the right two years later in holding that "free persons of color have never been recognized as citizens of Georgia" and hence "are not entitled to bear arms."[39]

The postwar Georgia Constitution of 1865 adopted a right to arms provision with the identical wording of the Second Amendment.[40] The federally mandated Georgia convention met between December 1867 and March 1868 and amended the arms guarantee to read: "A well regulated militia being necessary to the security of a free people, the right of the people to keep and bear arms shall not be infringed, but the General Assembly shall have the power to prescribe by law the manner in which arms may be borne."[41] When proposed in convention, the last part read, "borne by private persons."[42] Deletion of this phrase made clear that the legislature could prescribe how officials, as well as private persons, may bear arms.

Georgia's adoption of the language of the Second Amendment for its postwar constitutions did not stem simply from the Congressional mandate that the Southern state constitutions conform to the Thirteenth and Fourteenth Amendments. It was also rooted in the fundamental character of the right to keep and bear arms as viewed in that state's tradition. Georgia's 1868 constitution reaffirmed the antebellum view that the federal Constitution prohibited states from infringing on the fundamental right to possess and carry either pistols or long guns.[43]

ARKANSAS

The antebellum Arkansas Constitution provided: "That the free white men of this State shall have a right to keep and bear arms for their common defence."[44] The antebellum high court assumed that the Second Amendment applied to the states. Three judges deciding a single case were divided over whether all arms or only militia arms were protected.[45] The court actually held only that neither constitution protected the carrying of concealed weapons.

When Arkansas seceded in 1861 the provision was amended to broaden the holders and purposes of the right: "That the free white men, and Indians, of this state shall have the right to keep and bear arms for their individual or common defence."[46] In 1864 the pro-Union state convention changed the guarantee back to its earlier, narrow version.[47] Two years later, Arkansas Senator William D. Snow explained the convention's action to the Joint Committee on Reconstruction: "The old constitution declares, 'that the free white men of the State shall have a right to keep and to bear arms for their common defence.' The new constitution retains the words 'free white' before the word 'men.' . . . There was also some uncertainty in the minds of timid men as to what the negro might do, if given arms, in a turbulent state of society, and in his then uneducated condition; and to allay what I was confident was an unnecessary alarm, that clause was retained."[48]

Limiting the right to "free white men" violated the Fourteenth Amendment, and the convention, which convened on January 7, 1868, reworded the guarantee as follows: "The citizens of this State shall have the right to keep and bear arms for their common defense."[49] The debates in the convention demonstrate the delegates' awareness of their obligation to adopt a constitution consistent with the Fourteenth Amendment.[50] As in other conventions, black suffrage, not Bill of Rights guarantees, was the most debated topic.

Eight years later the Arkansas Supreme Court declared invalid a state law that prohibited the carrying of pistols, holding that the Second Amendment protected the bearing of "the army and navy repeaters."[51] The court added: "The arms which [the Second Amendment] guarantees American citizens the right to keep and bear, are such as are needful to, and ordinarily used by a well regulated militia, and such as are necessary and suitable to a free people, to enable them to resist oppression."[52]

MISSISSIPPI

The antebellum Mississippi Constitution provided: "Every citizen has a right to bear arms, in defence of himself and the State."[53] Because blacks were not considered citizens, the postbellum legislature enacted a statute "that no freedman, free negro or mulatto, . . . not licensed to do so by the board of police of his or her county, shall keep or carry firearms of any kind."[54] Mississippi's gun control law was cited in Congress in support of the need for the Civil Rights Act of 1866 and the Fourteenth Amendment. One Mississippi judge invalidated the black code provision based on the Civil Rights Act and the Mississippi guarantee, but the chief justice of the Mississippi Supreme Court wrote an opinion upholding the black code and declaring the Civil Rights Act unconstitutional.[55]

The federally mandated convention commenced on January 7, 1868. The Bill of Rights committee proposed the following guarantee: "Every person shall have a right to keep and bear arms for their common defense."[56] A motion to change "person" back to "citizen" failed, and the word "common" was stricken from the clause.[57] As adopted, the provision read: "All persons shall have a right to keep and bear arms for their defense."[58] Thus, the Fourteenth Amendment and the state provision adopted to be consistent therewith invalidated Mississippi's prohibition against unlicensed firearms possession and carrying by blacks.

SOUTH CAROLINA

The antebellum South Carolina Constitution contained no bill of rights.[59] The slave code's firearms prohibition was the only interference with keeping and bearing arms. Reenacted in 1865 in the black codes, the prohibition was cited in debates in Congress in support of the Fourteenth Amendment.

A declaration of rights considered at the convention that commenced on January 14, 1868, included the following guarantee: "Every citizen has a right to keep and bear arms in defence of himself and the State, and this right shall never be questioned."[60] As reported from committee and adopted, this provision was changed to read, "The people have a right to keep and bear arms for the common defence."[61] The rights of "defending their lives and liberties" as well as unenumerated rights were retained.[62]

Extensive debate ensued on the separate part of the arms provision subjecting the military power to the civil authority.[63] That clause was controversial because South Carolina was under military occupation. C. C. Bowen, who proposed the right to arms provision in its original form, stated of the subordination of military to civil power: "I find men very zealous of the liberties of the people, now willing to put those liberties in the hands of the military. . . . If a military officer has a sufficient number of bayonets to carry out his edict [declaring martial law], he may enforce it by simple force of arms, and yet have no right to do so."[64]

B. O. Duncan, who unsuccessfully opposed the clause subordinating the military to the civil authority,[65] moved that "the Legislature shall enact such laws as it may deem proper and necessary to punish the carrying of concealed deadly weapons."[66] This too failed, although just over a decade later South Carolina's high court upheld a concealed weapon prohibition as still allowing "the right of the citizen to bear arms."[67]

NORTH CAROLINA

The North Carolina Declaration of Rights of 1776 included the guarantee "that the people have a right to bear arms, for the defense of the State."[68] "A man may carry a gun for any lawful purpose of business or amusement," held North Carolina's antebellum Supreme Court.[69] To reconcile this holding with a state statute prohibiting free persons of color from carrying firearms, the court in another case denied that free blacks were citizens,[70] and averred that the Second Amendment did not apply to the states.[71]

The 1776 provision was proposed in the convention commencing on January 15, 1868,[72] but the convention substituted language identical to that of the Second Amendment.[73] Like the Georgia convention, the North Carolina delegates responded to the requirement that they amend their constitution in strict conformity with the Fourteenth Amendment by adopting the Second Amendment's language verbatim. This overruled the precedent that free blacks could be disarmed, which had circumvented the federal Bill of Rights by holding that it did not apply to the states.

Incorporation of the Second Amendment into a state constitution verifies the understanding that the federal amendment protected the individual right to have arms, because no need existed in a state constitution to protect a power of the state to form militias from infringement by that same state. Militia provisions were treated separately by the convention.[74]

A convention held near the end of Reconstruction added to the arms guarantee the following: "Nothing herein contained shall justify the practice of carrying concealed weapons, or prevent the Legislature from enacting penal statutes against said practice."[75] This again indicated the individual nature of the main guarantee, as the North Carolina Supreme Court would recognize in upholding the right openly to carry firearms.[76]

FLORIDA

Florida's antebellum arms guarantee was identical with that of Arkansas: "That the free white men of this State shall have a right to keep and bear arms for their common defence."[77] The convention of 1865, although adopting a declaration of rights that included the right of "defending life and liberty,"[78] deleted the arms guarantee. The proposed Bill of Rights passed the convention unanimously,[79] and the deletion may have been intended to preclude recognition of the right of blacks to have arms.

Lack of a right to arms provision cleared the way for Florida's 1865 law making it "unlawful for any Negro, mulatto, or person of color to own, use, or keep in possession or under control any bowie-knife, dirk, sword, firearms or ammunition of any kind, unless by license of the county judge," under penalty of standing in the pillory one hour or being whipped not exceeding 39 stripes.[80] This statute was denounced in Congressional debate on the Fourteenth Amendment as designed "to restore slavery in fact,"[81] and Florida's governor stated: "The [law] in regard to freedmen carrying firearms does not accord with our Constitution, has not been enforced and should be repealed."[82]

Consistent with the Fourteenth Amendment, the Florida convention, which convened on January 20, 1868, provided in a new Declaration of Rights: "The people shall have the right to bear arms in defence of themselves and the lawful authority of the State."[83] "The people" — not just the "free white men" — were finally guaranteed the right to keep and bear arms in postbellum Florida.

TEXAS

The antebellum Texas Constitution provided: "Every citizen shall have the right to keep and bear arms in the lawful defence of himself or the State."[84] The Texas Supreme Court construed this provision as follows: "The right of a citizen to bear arms, in lawful defence of himself or the State, is absolute. . . . A law cannot be passed to infringe upon or impair it, because it is above the law, and independent of the law making power."[85]

Well aware that the state constitution was required to be consistent with the Fourteenth Amendment, the constitutional convention that convened on June 1, 1868, did not alter the guarantee. The 1867 Report of the Texas Attorney General, appended to the convention journal, contained an analysis of "Pretended Laws of 1866 against the Freedmen," the object of which was "the restoration of African slavery, in the modified form of peonage." One such law "makes the carrying of fire-arms on enclosed land, without consent of the land-owner, an offence. It was meant to operate against freedmen alone."[86] Another attorney general opinion asserted that the "'Vagrant,' 'Fire-Arms,' . . . & c., 'laws,' amount to a cunningly devised system, planned to prevent equality before the law, and for the restoration of African slavery in a modified form, in fact, though not in name."[87]

A committee report noted that Unionists "can hold public meetings only when supported by troops or armed men." Although freedmen were "generally as well armed as the whites,"[88] "bands of armed whites are traversing the country, forcibly robbing the freedmen of their arms, and committing other outrages upon them."[89] General J. J. Reynolds reported to Congress that Ku Klux Klan organizations sought "to disarm, rob, and in many cases murder Union men and negroes."[90]

The imperative to adopt "every safeguard contemplated by the Fourteenth Amendment to the Constitution of the United States"[91] led to suggestions for amendments perceived to be modeled after the federal Bill of Rights. One delegate introduced the following: "A well regulated militia being necessary to the safety of a free State, every citizen shall have the right to keep and bear arms for the common defence. Nevertheless this article shall not be construed as giving any countenance to the evil practice of carrying private or concealed weapons about the person."[92]

Literally adhering to the theme that the state constitution be in accord with the Fourteenth Amendment, which in turn incorporated the Bill of Rights, the Committee on General Provisions proposed the following language: "The inhibitions of power enunciated in articles from one to eight inclusive, and thirteen, of the amendments to the Constitution of the United States, deny to the States, as well as to the General Government, the exercise of the powers therein reserved to the people, and shall never be exercised by the government of this State."[93] Radical Republican M. C. Hamilton, the committee chairman, explained this provision as follows: "It will be observed that section 3 embodies the substance of ten of the sections in the Bill of Rights in the Constitution of 1845, it being the opinion of your Committee that the inhibitions enumerated in the said ten sections are fully covered by the nine articles mentioned as amendments to the Constitution of the United States, thus dispensing with a long string of sections which are deemed useless."[94] Although the committee recommendation was not adopted, the 1845 guarantees — which included the provision that "every citizen shall have the right to keep and bear arms in the lawful defence of himself or the State" — were perceived to guarantee the same protections as the federal Bill of Rights.

Four years after the 1868 convention, the Texas Supreme Court reiterated the view that the federal constitution protected the right to keep and bear arms — a "personal right" that is "inherent and inalienable to man" — from state deprivation.[95] Citing the Second Amendment, the court agreed with commentator Joel P. Bishop that "'though most of the amendments are restrictions on the general government alone, not on the States, this one seems to be of a nature to bind both the State and National legislatures,' and doubtless it does."[96]

TENNESSEE

Like the constitutional provisions of Arkansas and Florida, Tennessee's Constitution of 1834 provided: "That the free white men of this State have a right to keep and bear arms for their common defence."[97] The arms guarantee in the 1796 Constitution was identical, except that it did not contain the word "white."[98] Tennessee's antebellum Supreme Court quashed an indictment for carrying a pistol because: "By this clause of the constitution, an express power is given and secured to all the free citizens of the State to keep and bear arms for their defence, without any qualification whatever as to their kind or nature."[99] In a later case, that court held: "If the citizens have these [military] arms in their hands, they are prepared in the best possible manner to repel any encroachments upon their rights by those in authority."[100]

Having been thoroughly conquered by the Union army, Tennessee was the only ex-Confederate state not required to adopt a constitution consistent with the Fourteenth Amendment as a precondition to reentering the Union. However, when a convention was called in 1870, provisions inconsistent with the Fourteenth Amendment were stricken. One delegate moved that the arms guarantee "be so amended as to strike out the words 'the free white men' and insert the words 'all persons.'"[101] Earlier drafts sought to substitute "all citizens" or "the citizens."[102] A motion to empower the legislature to regulate the manner of carrying weapons was successful.[103] As adopted, the provision read: "That the citizens of this State have a right to keep and bear arms for their common defense. But the Legislature shall have the power, by law, to regulate the wearing of arms with a view to prevent crime."[104]

Delegate John A. Gardner, who had sponsored the provision authorizing the legislature to regulate the wearing of arms, explained that the state was beset by murder and robbery:

The members of the Legislature are impressed with the importance of this subject, but, I understand, they are restrained from providing efficient remedies, from a doubt they entertain as to the extent of their power in this direction, under the provisions of the 26th section of the Bill of Rights. This power, I consider, is secured for the common, and not for individual defense — as when the peace and safety of the people of the whole State, or of a county, or even a single neighborhood, is threatened, the people shall have arms, and a right to bear and use them to preserve the peace and good order of society. I would not, however, interfere with, or in the slightest degree abridge, the citizen's right of self-defense.[105]

Restriction of the right to whites was, of course, inconsistent with the Fourteenth Amendment. The provision empowering the legislature to regulate the wearing of arms may have been calculated to repeal the Republican-passed statute exempting discharged Union soldiers and "citizens who have always been loyal" from the concealed weapons prohibition.[106]

In response to the guarantee that all citizens, not just free white men, could keep and bear arms, the Tennessee legislature promptly declared that it was unlawful "for any person to publicly or privately carry a . . . revolver."[107] A year later, the Tennessee Supreme Court declared this statute unconstitutional. Finding that the Second Amendment and the Tennessee arms guarantee protected the same rights,[108] the court held that the right of the people to keep arms included the rights to purchase arms and "to use such arms for all the ordinary purposes, and in all the ordinary modes usual in the country."[109] "The power to regulate" the wearing of arms, the court added, "does not fairly mean the power to prohibit."[110]

SUMMARY OF STATE ARMS GUARANTEES

The right to keep and bear arms was deemed fundamental in the antebellum South, although the right was denied to blacks. The Fourteenth Amendment's protection of the right of all persons to have arms required deletion of the restriction of this right to free white men in the constitutions of Arkansas, Florida, and Tennessee. The Fourteenth Amendment also invalidated the prohibitions in Mississippi, Louisiana, Alabama, and South Carolina on freedmen keeping and carrying firearms without a license.

The constitutions of all other states were consistent with the Fourteenth Amendment's incorporation of the right to keep and bear arms both before and after the amendment's adoption. Of the state constitutions in existence through the end of Reconstruction, 23 had specific right to bear arms provisions, but 12 either had no bill of rights or, if so, no arms provision.[111] Of the 23 states with arms guarantees, the right is described as being held by one of the following entities: "every citizen," "the citizen," "every person," "the people," or "all persons." The following are stated as objectives of the right:

Stated Objective	Number of States
"defense of himself [or themselves] and the State"[112]	10
"common defence"[113]	5
"their defense [and security]"[114]	3
"[defense of his] home, person, or property"[115]	2
[language equivalent to the Second Amendment][116]	2
[no specific purpose stated][117]	1

The state bills of rights that did not specifically mention a right to have arms invariably did so by implication, guaranteeing the right to defend and protect life, liberty, and property, protecting unenumerated rights, or by declaring the necessity of a well-regulated militia, which presupposes an armed populace. The existence of the Second Amendment led some to believe that an equivalent state guarantee was unnecessary.

It has been argued that because some states failed to guarantee a right to indictment (Fifth Amendment) or jury trial in civil cases where more than $20 is in controversy (Seventh Amendment), the Bill of Rights could not have been intended to apply to the states through the Fourteenth Amendment.[118] Unlike violations of rights such as assembly and bearing arms, few, if any, complaints about violations of these merely procedural rights were heard in the Reconstruction debates.

As in Congress, the state ratification debates focused on powderkeg issues such as black suffrage and open-ended federal authority to define and enforce rights, and nonemotional issues such as the grand jury system and jury trial in civil cases stirred little, if any, debate.[119] Unlike the countless violations of the right to keep and bear arms that were brought to Congress's attention during ratification, these minor discrepancies between the Bill of Rights and some state constitutions were brushed aside.

The fact that some Northern state constitutions lacked some of the substantive rights of the federal Bill of Rights during Reconstruction does not reveal an intent *not* to incorporate these rights into the Fourteenth Amendment. Many of these states had no occasion to call a constitutional convention after the Fourteenth Amendment was adopted. Moreover, if the Fourteenth Amendment was an ideal that the defeated Southerners should be forced meticulously to follow, the Northern victors perceived no need to reconstruct themselves. Further, the enumeration in the federal Bill of Rights of basic freedoms may have been deemed sufficient.

Even ignoring that everyone during Reconstruction who mentioned the subject at all agreed that incorporation was intended, the most important substantive rights, such as the right to keep and bear arms and freedom from unreasonable search and seizure, were very much on the minds of the Fourteenth Amendment's supporters. At a minimum, selective incorporation of these more significant rights follows from the test of consistency between Bill of Rights provisions and comparable state provisions.

During the Fourteenth Amendment's ratification process, most state constitutions already protected, and three were amended to protect, the right of all citizens or persons to keep and bear arms. Given its nearly universal protection under the state and federal constitutions, the right to have arms was considered as a fundamental right that was guaranteed from both state and federal infringement.

NOTES

1. 14 Stat. 428 (1867).

2. Carrying concealed weapons was not regulated. The only marginally relevant prohibitions were on dueling and "gunning," that is, hunting on another's land without permission. THE MARYLAND CODE 216, 220–21 (Baltimore 1860).

3. Id. at 454.

4. Id. at 464. This law prohibited the unlicensed *keeping* of firearms, whereas its predecessor only regulated the carrying of firearms by free blacks. THE MARYLAND CODE 298–99 (Baltimore 1806).

5. 3 SUPPLEMENT TO THE CODE OF MARYLAND 52 (Baltimore 1865).

6. Maryland did not ratify the Fourteenth Amendment until 1959. WE THE STATES 91 (Richmond 1964).

7. Perlman, DEBATES OF THE MARYLAND CONVENTION OF 1867 at 79, 151 (Baltimore 1867). The debates were compiled from accounts in the *Baltimore Sun*.

8. Id. at 150–151.

9. For example, Ex Parte Merryman, 17 Fed. Cas. 144, 145 (1861); E. Pollard, THE LOST CAUSE, 117, 125 (1867).

10. Perlman, DEBATES OF THE MARYLAND CONVENTION, at 151.

11. *The Baltimore Gazette*, May 29, 1867, at 4, col. 3.

12. Perlman, DEBATES OF THE MARYLAND CONVENTION at 151; *The Baltimore Gazette*, May 30, 1867, at 4, col. 2.

13. S. Halbrook, THAT EVERY MAN BE ARMED 92, 95–96, 102–3, and 107 (1994).

14. *The Baltimore Gazette*, May 29, 1867, at 4, col. 3.

15. Md. Const., Art. III, Sec. 37 (1867). Jones was well known for his authorship of the "emancipation compensation" amendment. For example, *Maryland Journal* (Towson), May 30, 1867, at 2, col. 1; *The Sun* (Baltimore), May 30, 1867, at 1, col. 2.

16. Perlman, DEBATES OF THE MARYLAND CONVENTION, at 151.

17. In 1774, the Maryland provincial committee resolved that "a well regulated Militia, composed of the gentlemen, freeholders, and other freemen, is the natural strength and stable security of a free Government," and recommended that all able-bodied Marylanders "associate and enroll themselves into [militia] Companies." 1 P. Force, AMERICAN ARCHIVES 1032 (1837–53). See W. Rawle, A VIEW OF THE CONSTITUTION 153 (2d ed. 1829) ("In a people permitted and accustomed to bear arms, we have the rudiments of a militia.").

18. *American and Commercial Advertiser* (Baltimore, Md.), May 30, 1867, at 1, col. 4.

19. Id.

20. Ala. Const., Art. I, § 23 (1819, 1865), § 28 (1867), § 27 (1875).

21. State v. Reid, 1 Ala. 612, 616–17 (1840).

22. OFFICIAL JOURNAL OF THE CONSTITUTIONAL CONVENTION OF THE STATE OF ALABAMA . . . COMMENCING NOV. 5, 1867, at 144 (1868).

23. The antebellum constitution of Louisiana, however, included a provision making the bearing of arms a duty: "The free white men of the State shall be armed and disciplined, for its defence." La. Const., III, § 22 (1812), § 60 (1845), § 59 (1852). Despite the reference to white men, free men of color volunteered and provided their own arms for defense of New Orleans in the War of 1812 and again in 1861 for Confederate service. R. McConnell, NEGRO TROOPS OF ANTE-BELLUM LOUISIANA (1968). In 1864, the reference to race was stricken: "All able-bodied men in the State shall be armed and disciplined for its defence. " La. Const., IV, § 67 (1864).

24. State v. Chandler, 5 La. Ann. 489, 490 (1850). *Accord*, State v. Jumel, 13 La. Ann. 399 (1858) (holding that a concealed carry prohibition was consistent with the Second Amendment).

25. OFFICIAL JOURNAL OF PROCEEDINGS OF THE CONVENTION (La.) 37 (1867–1868).

26. Id. at 41.

27. Id. at 84. The unenumerated rights guarantee became La. Const., I § 14 (1868).

28. Id. at 263, 275–79, 290–93. For an account of the convention of 1867–68, see W. Billings and E. Haas eds., IN SEARCH OF FUNDAMENTAL LAW: LOUISIANA'S CONSTITUTIONS, 1812–1974, at 69–80 (1993).

29. W. Billings and E. Haas eds., IN SEARCH OF FUNDAMENTAL LAW at 88. "When we see a man with a musket to shoulder, or carbine slung on back, or pistol belted to his side, or such like, he is bearing arms in the constitutional sense." State v. Bias, 37 La. Ann. 259, 260 (1885).

30. Va. Const., I, § 13 (1776, 1870).

31. Henry St. Geo. Tucker, COMMENTARIES ON THE LAWS OF VIRGINIA 43 (1831).

32. 1 VIRGINIA CONVENTION OF 1867–1868, DEBATES AND PROCEEDINGS 350 (1868).

33. Id. at 519; ADDRESS OF CONSERVATIVE MEMBERS at 5–6; Va. Const. IX (1870).

34. 1 VIRGINIA CONVENTION OF 1867–1868 at 421. And see id. at 634: "the rights declared in the Bill of Rights are natural and inherent rights, rights which previously existed." (remarks of Edward K. Snead).

35. For instance, Radical delegate Snead read extensively from St. George Tucker's essay on slavery, id. at 535–40, and the *Dred Scott* decision was discussed. Id. at 622.

36. Id. at 166. Advocates of the right of revolution undoubtedly recognized the same utility of an armed people. See id. at 356, 403 ff.

37. Nunn v. State, 1 Ga. 243, 250 (1846).

38. Id. at 251.

39. Cooper v. Savannah, 4 Ga. 72 (1848).

40. Ga. Const., I, § 4 (1865); JOURNAL OF THE PROCEEDINGS OF THE CONVENTION (Ga.) 182, 366 (1910).

41. Ga. Const., I, § 14 (1868).

42. JOURNAL OF THE PROCEEDINGS OF THE CONSTITUTIONAL CONVENTION (Ga.) 168 (1868).

43. Hill v. State, 53 Ga. 472 (1874); Strickland v. State, 137 Ga. 1, 72 S.E. 260, 267 (1911).

44. Ark. Const., I, § 21 (1836). See JOURNAL OF PROCEEDINGS (Ark.) 16 (1836).

45. State v. Buzzard, 4 Ark. 18 (1842). "Again, the term 'arms' . . . includes guns or firearms of every description." Id. at 21.

46. Ark. Const., I, § 21 (1861). See JOURNAL OF BOTH SESSIONS OF THE CONVENTION OF THE STATE OF ARKANSAS 430 (1861). This wording was consistent with the governor's urging of an alliance with the Indians "because of the utter incapacity on the part of the Indians to resist alone the occupation of their country by federal troops or federal agents." Id. at 156.

47. Ark. Const., 1, § 21 (1864). JOURNAL OF THE CONVENTION OF DELEGATES OF THE PEOPLE OF ARKANSAS OF 1864 (1870), is unenlightening on this matter.

48. REPORT OF THE JOINT COMMITTEE ON RECONSTRUCTION, 39th Cong., 1st Sess., pt. 3, 81 (1866). See also Id. at 86.

49. Ark. Const., I, § 5 (1868).

50. DEBATES AND PROCEEDINGS OF THE CONVENTION (Ark.) (1868). For example, id. at 128 ("When the present proposed Amendments to the Constitution of the United States shall have been adopted, then, under that Constitution, these colored friends will be citizens") (remarks of Delegate Duvall); id. at 377 (Delegate Langley observed that the Fourteenth Amendment "is part of the condition precedent to our admission into the Union."); see also id. at 502 (remarks of Delegate Hodges).

For the progress of the arms provision in Committee Reports, see id. at 354, 584.

51. Fife v. State, 31 Ark. 455, 460–1 (1876).

52. Id. at 458. See also Wilson v. State, 33 Ark. 557, 34 Am. Rep. 52, 54–55 (1878), reversing a conviction for carrying a revolver:

But to prohibit the citizen from wearing or carrying a war arm . . . is an unwarranted restriction upon his constitutional right to keep and bear arms.

　　If cowardly and dishonorable men sometimes shoot unarmed men with army pistols or guns, the evil must be prevented by the penitentiary and gallows, and not by a general deprivation of a constitutional privilege.

53. Miss. Const., I, § 23 (1817, 1832). Abolitionist William Goodell cited this provision to show the illegality of slavery under the state constitutions. Goodell, VIEWS OF AMERICAN CONSTITUTIONAL LAW 132 (1845).

54. Laws of Miss. 165 (1865).

55. The decisions were reprinted in the *New York Times*, Oct. 26, 1866, at 2, cols. 2–4.

56. JOURNAL OF PROCEEDINGS IN THE CONSTITUTIONAL CONVENTION (Miss.) 84, 156 (1868).

57. Id. at 231.

58. Miss. Const., I, § 15 (1868).

59. S.C. Const. (1776, 1778, 1790, 1865).

60. PROCEEDINGS OF THE CONSTITUTIONAL CONVENTION OF SOUTH CAROLINA 85 (1868).

61. Id. at 258; S.C. Const., I, § 28 (1868).

62. Id. at 257, 259.

63. Id. at 341–49.

64. Id. at 346–47.

65. Id. at 343.

66. Id. at 357.

67. See State v. Johnson, 16 S.C. 187 (1881).

68. N.C. Const., Declaration of Rights, XVII (1776).

69. State v. Huntley, 25 N.C. 418, 422–23 (1843).

70. State v. Newsom, 27 N.C. 203, 204 (1844).

71. Id. at 207 ("In the second article of the amended Constitution, the States are neither mentioned nor referred to. It is therefore only restrictive of the powers of the Federal Government.").

72. JOURNAL OF THE CONSTITUTIONAL CONVENTION (N.C.) 165, 212, 215, 229 (1868).

73. N.C. Const., I, § 24 (1868).

74. For example, JOURNAL at 175, 485 (controversy on whether whites and blacks to be enrolled in the same militia companies).

75. JOURNAL OF CONVENTION OF STATE OF NORTH CAROLINA 261 (1875).

76. State v. Speller, 86 N.C. (11 Kenan) 697, 700 (1882); State v. Kerner, 181 N.C. 574, 107 S.E. 222, 223–25 (1921).

77.   Fla. Const. I, § 21 (1838, 1861). See JOURNAL OF PROCEEDINGS OF A CONVENTION (Fla.) 1838–1839 at 17 (1839).

78.   Fla. Const., I, § 1 (1865); JOURNAL OF PROCEEDINGS OF THE CONVENTION OF FLORIDA 30, 135 (1865).

79.   Id. at 99.

80.   Ex. Doc. No. 118, House of Representatives, 39th Cong., 1st Sess. 20 (1866). See W.E.B. DuBois, BLACK RECONSTRUCTION IN AMERICA 172 (1962).

81.   CONG. GLOBE, 39th Cong., 1st Sess., pt. 4, 3210 (June 16, 1866) (remarks of George W. Julian).

82.   FLA. SEN. J. 13 (1866).

83.   Fla. Const., Dec. of Rights, § 22 (1868). See JOURNAL OF PROCEEDINGS OF THE CONSTITUTIONAL CONVENTION (Fla.) 5, 73 (1868).

84.   Tex. Const., I, § 13 (1845, 1866, 1868), § 23 (1876). For a history of the Texas guarantee, see S. Halbrook, *The Right to Bear Arms in Texas: the Intent of the Framers of the Bills of Rights*, 41 BAYLOR LAW REVIEW 629 (1989).

85.   Cockrum v. State, 24 Tex. 394, 401–2 (1859). The premise of the Second Amendment is that "the people cannot be effectually oppressed and enslaved, who are not first disarmed." Id.

86.   1 JOURNAL OF THE RECONSTRUCTION CONVENTION, WHICH MET AT AUSTIN, TEXAS 953–55 (1870).

87.   Id. at 975.

88.   Id. at 195.

89.   Id. at 195–97.

90.   Id., 2, at 111. This situation led to a resolution that the law-abiding "will be compelled, in the exercise of the sacred right of self defence, to organize for their own protection." Id., 1, at 111.

91.   Id., 2, at 387.

92.   Id., 1, at 152.

93.   Id. at 235. See also id. at 236 ("]e declare that everything in this 'Bill of Rights' is excepted out of the general powers of government, and shall forever remain inviolate").

94.   Id. at 233.

95.   English v. State, 35 Tex. 473, 477 (1872).

96.   Id. at 475, citing 2 Bishop, CRIMINAL LAW § 124 (holding that the Second Amendment protects the private possession of militia-type arms).

97.   Tenn. Const., I, § 26 (1834).

98.   Tenn. Const., XI, § 26 (1796).

99.   Simpson v. State, 13 Tenn. (5 Yerg.) 356, 360 (1833).

100.   Aymette v. State, 21 Tenn. (2 Hump.) 154, 158 (1840). Nearly a century later, the United States Supreme Court cited *Aymette* in holding that the Second Amendment protects the possession of military weapons by private citizens. United States v. Miller, 307 U.S. 177, 178 (1939).

Smith v. Ishenhour, 43 Tenn. (3 Cold.) 214, 217 (1866) held of a Civil War firearms confiscation measure: "This is the first attempt, in the history of the

Anglo-Saxon race, of which we are apprised, to disarm the people by legislation."

101. JOURNAL OF PROCEEDINGS OF CONVENTION (Tenn.) 72 (1870).

102. Id. at 20, 63.

103. Id. at 106.

104. Tenn. Const., 1, § 26 (1870). "That the sure and certain defense of a free people is a well-regulated militia" was provided in § 24.

105. *Nashville Union and American*, Jan. 21, 1870, at 1, col. 5, quoted in G. Reynolds, *The Right to Keep and Bear Arms Under the Tennessee Constitution*, 61 TENN. LAW REV. 647, 660 (1994).

106. REPORT OF THE JOINT COMMITTEE ON RECONSTRUCTION, pt. 1, at 34 (1866). That legislation provided: "That all discharged Union soldiers, who have served either as State or Federal soldiers, and have been honorably discharged [from] the service, and all citizens who have always been loyal, shall be permitted to carry any and all necessary side-arms, being their own private property, for their personal protection and common defence."

107. An Act to Preserve the Peace and Prevent Homicide, June 11, 1870, Tenn. Laws 28–29 (2d Sess. 1869–1870). This was apparently the same legislature that, complained Republican Representative Horace Maynard of Tennessee, "repealed the Ku Klux law, . . . the law allowing Union soldiers to go armed, to say nothing of . . . the laws for the protection of the poor laborer." CONG. GLOBE, 42nd Cong., 1st Sess. 309 (Mar. 30, 1871).

108. Andrews v. State, 3 Heisk. 165, 8 Am. Repts. 8, 13 (1871).

109. Id. The use of arms "will properly train and render [the citizen] efficient in defense of his own liberties as well as of the State." 8 Am. Repts. at 14.

110. Id. at 15.

111. See THE FEDERAL AND STATE CONSTITUTIONS (B. Poore compl. 1877).

112. Ala., I, § 28 (1867); Conn., I, § 17 (1818); Fla., I, § 22 (1868); Ind., I § 32 (1851); Ky., XIII (1850); Mich., XVIII, § 7 (1850); Ore., I, § 28 (1857); Penn., I, § 21 (1838, 1873); Tex., I, § 13 (1868); Vt., I, § 16 (1796).

113. Ark., I, § 5 (1868); Me., I, § 16 (1820); Mass., I, § 17 (1780); S.C., I, § 28 (1868); Tenn., I, § 26 (1870).

114. Kan., I, § 4 (1859); Miss., I, § 15 (1868); Ohio, I, § 4 (1851).

115. Colo., I, § 13 (1876); Mo., II, § 17 (1875).

116. Ga., I, § 14 (1868); N.C., I, § 24 (1868).

117. R.I., I, § 22 (1842).

118. Fairman, *Does the Fourteenth Amendment Incorporate the Bill of Rights?*, 2 STAN. L. REV. 5 (1949).

119. Earl M. Maltz, CIVIL RIGHTS, THE CONSTITUTION, AND CONGRESS, 1863–1869, at 116–17 (Univ. Kansas Press 1990).

4

The Freedmen's Bureau Act Reenacted and the Fourteenth Amendment Ratified

POMEROY'S TREATISE ON CONSTITUTIONAL LAW

In 1868 John N. Pomeroy, dean of the Law School at the University of New York, published his treatise *An Introduction to the Constitutional Law of the United States*. In a review of the book, *The Nation* endorsed Pomeroy's view that the Fourteenth Amendment would make the Bill of Rights applicable to the states.[1] The work was favorably cited in Congressional debates and was used as a textbook at various law schools.[2]

Pomeroy discussed at length "the privileges and immunities" of citizenship, including the Second Amendment's "right of the people to keep and bear arms."[3] He lamented that although the United States may not "deprive a person of any of the immunities and privileges guarded by the Bill of Rights," the states may "infringe upon them all."[4] Although a state was bound by its own bill of rights, the U.S. Supreme Court, Pomeroy noted, could not decide whether a state statute violated the state bill of rights.[5] Pomeroy illustrated this dilemma with an insightful hypothetical question:

Let it be supposed that the constitution of a certain state contains clauses securing to the people the right of keeping and bearing arms; and declaring that no person shall be deprived of life, liberty, and property without due process of law. Let it also be supposed that the legislature of the same state passes statutes by which certain classes of the inhabitants — say negroes — are required to surrender their arms, and are forbidden to keep and bear them under certain penalties. . . . An individual of the class mentioned in these statutes incurs some or all of their penalties; is proceeded against. He insists that the statutes in question are opposed to the Bill of Rights in the state constitution; the local courts settle the law against him. . . . Now, this person could obtain no redress from the national courts under the amendments to the United States Constitution which we are considering [the Bill of Rights].[6]

However, § 1 of the pending Fourteenth Amendment, Pomeroy wrote, was designed to remedy this problem. "It would give the nation complete power to protect its citizens against local injustice and oppression."[7]

Pomeroy proceeded to explore the Bill of Rights, which protected "the liberties of the citizen" from government encroachment.[8] Pomeroy discussed the Second Amendment at length: "The right of the people to keep and bear arms. The object of this clause is to secure a well-armed militia. . . . But a militia would be useless unless the citizens were enabled to exercise themselves in the use of warlike weapons. To preserve this privilege, and to secure to the people the ability to oppose themselves in military force against the usurpations of government, as well as against enemies from without, that government is forbidden by any law or proceeding to invade or destroy the right to keep and bear arms."[9] The Second Amendment was not violated by laws forbidding the carrying of concealed weapons or accumulating arms for use in riot or sedition.[10] "The clause," wrote Pomeroy, "is analogous to the one securing freedom of speech and of the press. Freedom, not license, is secured; the fair use, not the libellous abuse, is protected."[11]

FROM REENACTMENT OF THE FREEDMEN'S BUREAU ACT TO RATIFICATION OF THE FOURTEENTH AMENDMENT

The 1866 Freedmen's Bureau Act, which had a two-year life, was renewed in 1868 for an additional year.[12] Enacted on July 6, 1868, the second Freedmen's Bureau Act reenacted and provided for continuation of the 1866 act, adding a requirement that the Secretary of War reestablish the bureau in areas where it had been discontinued, and where "the personal safety of freedmen shall require it."[13] The act also provided that bureau operations would be discontinued in states that were restored to the Union, unless the Secretary of War found that the bureau's continuation was necessary.[14] Thus, states that had ratified the Fourteenth Amendment

— the price of readmission — had the opportunity to rid themselves of the Freedmen's Bureau.

By passing the 1868 act, Congress reaffirmed, during the same period in which the states would complete ratification of the Fourteenth Amendment, that the rights of personal security and personal liberty included "the constitutional right to bear arms." This was clearly related to the terms of the 1868 Act concerning "the personal safety of freedmen," because the bureau protected the right of freedmen to keep and bear arms.

The second session of the Fortieth Congress was devoted primarily to Reconstruction measures. The states were still considering ratification of the Fourteenth Amendment and Southern states were holding conventions to draft new constitutions, but there was little discussion in Congress about the Bill of Rights or the amendment's meaning. There were, however, several references to the right to keep and bear arms and the Klan's disarming of freedmen.

Senator Willard Saulsbury railed against military dictatorship in the South, charging that during the late war the Republicans violated freedom of speech, "infringed the people's right to keep and bear arms," and otherwise waged war against the Constitution.[15] Supporting readmission of Southern states on moderate terms, Representative James Beck (D-Ky.) stated that "these people of the South are unarmed and defenseless, and are imploring protection for life, liberty, and property at your hands."[16]

Thaddeus Stevens, arguing for the extension of the ballot to blacks, suggested that the rights to have firearms and self-defense are among "those great rights, privileges, and immunities" set forth in the Declaration of Independence:

What are those rights, privileges, and immunities? Without excluding others, three are specifically enumerated — life, liberty, and the pursuit of happiness. . . . It follows that everything necessary for their establishment and defense is within those rights. . . . Disarm a community and you rob them of the means of defending life. Take away their weapons of defense and you take away the inalienable right of defending liberty.

The fourteenth amendment, now so happily adopted, settles the whole question.[17]

Representative Thomas Eliot offered a bill to protect blacks on behalf of the Committee on Freedmen's Affairs,[18] which reported that blacks continued to be oppressed in the South and could not obtain justice from the courts or law enforcement.[19] The Freedmen's Bureau, he averred, "protected loyal men, whether white or black,"[20] but unarmed freedmen continued to be murdered.[21]

Representative George Adams (D-Ky.), a member of the Committee on Freedmen's Affairs, quoted from the 1866 act to illustrate what was being reenacted, including the reference in § 14 to "full and equal benefit of all laws and proceedings concerning personal liberty, personal security, and [estate], including the constitutional right to bear arms."[22] Adams commented "here Congress undertakes to confer upon the negro population of these States all the civil rights and immunities that are enjoyed by white persons."[23] He argued that the states, not Congress, should determine who should or should not testify, contract, and marry, adding that his state had decided that "there should be some limitation to both the civil and political rights of these colored persons."[24] Adams then quoted § 1 of the Civil Rights Act, including its reference to "full and equal benefit of all laws and proceedings for the security of person and property."[25] He added that "this civil rights bill confers or attempts to confer upon the freedmen all the rights proposed to be conferred by the bill under consideration."[26] Once again, the Civil Rights Act was perceived as protecting the same rights as the Freedmen's Bureau Act, which recognized "the constitutional right to bear arms."

Representative Samuel Arnell of Tennessee asked whether the Committee on Freedmen's Affairs had investigated the Ku Klux Klan in his state.[27] Eliot replied that the Committee had discussed the matter with the bureau, which supplied information concerning Klan murders. In one incident documented by the bureau, a group of whites attacked eight freedmen who "attempted to defend themselves, a few of them having pistols."[28] Such incidents were sufficient for the House, which passed the bill by a veto-proof vote of 97 to 38 (72 percent).[29]

Representative John Bingham remarked that the state constitutions, consistent with the Fourteenth Amendment, now served to "secure equal political and civil rights and equal privileges to all citizens."[30] He proposed the following prerequisite for readmission of Southern states: "That civil and political rights and privileges shall be forever equally secured in said States to all citizens."[31] By thus enforcing the Fourteenth Amendment, the people of a state could not amend their constitution to delete rights, but leaving the privilege of "enlarging, if they choose, the liberties of the people, or removing restrictions."[32]

In the Senate, Henry Wilson noted that the bureau had at little cost soundly promoted "the security of person, liberty, and property."[33] The bureau had decided more than 100,000 cases. "To this tribunal," Wilson concluded, "the freedman has turned for protection, for justice, for security."[34] The Senate passed the bill without a recorded vote.[35]

On June 12 the Senate amended the bill and sent it back to the House.[36] On June 18 the House overwhelmingly passed the Senate version by a vote of 98 to 20 (83 percent).[37] This impressive margin persuaded President Johnson of the futility of vetoing the reenactment of the 1866 Freedmen's Bureau Act. He refused to sign or return the bill to Congress, so it became law without his approval.[38]

The day the bill became law, Bureau Commissioner O. O. Howard filed with the House a report on freedmen in Kentucky and Tennessee.[39] Howard's report documented numerous firearms seizures and attacks on blacks.[40] One bureau official stated: "No Union man or negro who attempts to take any active part in politics, or the improvement of his race, is safe a single day; and nearly all sleep upon their arms at night, and carry concealed weapons during the day. . . . But to the poor, superstitious, unarmed negroes, the organization [the Klan] is of incalculable injury, as they are in daily terror of them."[41]

In debate on a related bill (S. 567) to keep the Freedmen's Bureau functioning, Representative Arnell demonstrated the need for the bureau by reference to newspaper accounts of Klan outrages. In one incident, five intruders were told that their intended victim was not at home; the Klansmen "proceeded to search the premises, took what arms they could find, and such other articles as they chose to appropriate."[42] They then found the man and murdered him.[43] In another incident, 50 Klansman broke into the house of a carpetbagger teacher who educated freedmen. The Klansmen fired a shot in the house, whipped the teacher, and "disarmed him of his pistol."[44] Arnell concluded that the Freedmen's Bureau was "the only guardian for these colored persons that is capable of ferreting out these outrages and bringing them to public notice."[45]

President Johnson vetoed S. 567, but the Senate and House overrode his veto by votes of 42 to 5 and 115 to 23 respectively.[46,47] Once again, Congress overwhelmingly supported continued operation of a government agency that had as one of its objectives the protection of "the constitutional right to bear arms."

On July 28, 1868, just days after enactment of the Freedmen's Bureau legislation, it was officially proclaimed that the Fourteenth Amendment had been ratified by three-fourths of the states and was now a part of the Constitution.[48]

In the Third Session of the Fortieth Congress, Senator Wilson presented "a memorial of a convention of the colored citizens of Georgia" assembled in October 1868. The memorial protested the expulsion of 29 black members of the state legislature, contrary to the new Georgia Constitution. That constitution was devoid of the words "white" and "colored," defined "citizen" in the same way as the Fourteenth Amendment did, and provided: "No laws shall be made or enforced which shall abridge the privileges or immunities of citizens of the United States, or of this State, or deny to any person within its jurisdiction the equal protection of its laws."[49]

Because of the Civil Rights Act of 1866 and the Fourteenth Amendment, the memorial reasoned, "we became citizens of the State of Georgia, and as such entitled to the same 'rights,' privileges, and immunities belonging to other citizens."[50] Under the new state constitution, the memorial continued, "it shall be the duty of the General Assembly, by appropriate legislation, to protect every person in the due enjoyment of the rights, privileges, and immunities guaranteed in this section."[51] Accordingly, the memorial stated as follows:

The eleventh article of the constitution adopted, as a part of the general laws in force in this State, the new code called "Irwin's code." This code contains the following definition of the rights of citizens:

"Sec. 1648. *Among the rights of citizens are the enjoyment of personal security, of personal liberty*, private property and the disposition thereof, the elective franchise, the right to hold office, to appeal to the courts, to testify as a witness, to perform any civil function, *and to keep and bear arms*."[52] (emphasis added)

The right of the citizen to keep and bear arms as a right of personal security and personal liberty is the same Blackstonian language that Congress used in the Freedmen's Bureau Act and that was now being used as the particularized expression of rights guaranteed by the Fourteenth Amendment. The Southern States were required to adopt constitutions and laws consistent with the Fourteenth Amendment, and the above formalization of rights again clarifies that contemporaries believed that the Fourteenth Amendment protected the right to keep and bear arms.

THE WASHINGTON TARGET-SHOOTING ASSOCIATION

The same Congress that reenacted the Freedmen's Bureau Act also passed a noncontroversial bill incorporating the Washington Target-Shooting Association in the District of Columbia. That organization established "the 'Washington Schutzen-Park,' the object of which shall be moral and social, and to acquire proficiency and skill as marksmen."[53]

Although the two bills were obviously not related, they both illustrate the contemporary view that firearms ownership was a social good.

Debate on the bill in the House reflected Reconstruction issues in an interesting way. The following exchange took place:

> Mr. Ross. I desire to know whether this corporation is to be confined to loyal persons or not? I should object to it unless there is that proviso in the bill.
>
> Mr. Higby. And without distinction of race or color.
>
> Mr. Ross. Yes sir; and without distinction of race or color, and also requiring the test-oath to be taken.[54]

Representative James Mullins — whose home state of Tennessee had just recently been allowed representation in Congress — responded that "I hope the majority of this House will make that bill so comprehensive in its provisions and so little sectional that even the gentleman can come in and shoot if he desires. [Laughter.]"[55] The exchange continued:

> Mr. Ross. Do you think it will let Tennessee in then?
>
> Mr. Mullins. I am now in. [Laughter.][56]

Representative Charles Van Wyck (R-N.Y.) was bewildered as to why the bill was even being considered: "Is it not possible for these men to enjoy all the advantages of mark-shooting under the Constitution without an act of Congress?"[57] After an explanation that acquisition of a large tract of land required incorporation, the bill passed.[58] Taking the test oath would not be a requirement to go target shooting.

RESTORATION OF THE
SOUTHERN STATE MILITIAS

Advocating the supplying of his state's militia with its federal quota of arms, Representative Isaac Jones of North Carolina noted: "The constitution of North Carolina provides for organizing and arming the militia . . . . Washington taught that a 'free people ought not only to be armed, but disciplined for the national security and the preservation of order.'"[59] Jones quoted North Carolina Governor William Holden concerning the need for arms "in order to provide for self-protection."[60] Although Holden's use of the militia would generate controversy, he was quoted in a newspaper recognizing "the constitutional right of all citizens to the possession of arms for proper purposes."[61]

At the end of 1868 the Senate considered S. Res. 665, an act to repeal the 1867 abolition of Southern state militias.[62] Senator Wilson noted that the president recommended repeal and no one opposed it in the last session. Senator George Edmunds of Vermont asked why Congress should permit Virginia, Texas, and Mississippi, "which are yet in a state of rebellion and who are held under the authority of military law, to set up a local militia of their own."[63] Senator Thomas Hendricks countered that there were "no serious outrages" by local militias when the bill passed, but that carpetbagger militias in Arkansas and Tennessee had committed "great wrongs and outrages."[64]

Senator William Fessenden of Maine replied that the act had originally passed because of "a general distrust of the loyal character of the provisional governments formerly existing in those States, and that it would be dangerous to put an armed militia within their control."[65] As for Texas, "the militia of that State, if you call it a State, should be organized in order that there may be some force adequate to the suppression of these outrages."[66] Edmunds was willing to allow a militia force of "loyal men" (that is, Republicans) in Texas, but feared repeal because "it will authorize anybody and everybody in the State of Texas, under what they call its ancient militia laws . . . to organize a militia hostile to the Government."[67] Thus Edmunds advocated "a selected militia" approved by the Texas government and Congress.

Noting that the president in his annual message had denounced the militia disbanding law as unconstitutional, Senator Charles Buchalew of Pennsylvania explained:

One of the amendments to our fundamental law expressly provides that "the right of the people to keep and bear arms shall not be infringed" — of course by this Government; and it gives the reason that a well-regulated militia in the several divisions of the country is necessary for the protection and for the interests of the people. . . . The party in power in Congress passed this law in order to weaken the then existing political governments in the South which were not in accord with them . . . in a political sense — and they now propose to restore to that section of the country all power over local militia and to furnish arms for their organizations, because the political power which now exists is politically friendly to them. . . . It will influence elections.[68]

Senator Wilson responded that the act had been originally passed because Southern militias were going "up and down the country disarming Union men, black and white, and committing outrages upon the people."[69]

The Senate voted to repeal the ban on state militias, and the next day the House did the same with little debate. Representative Halbert Paine of Wisconsin argued that several of the affected states had been readmitted to the Union and were thus entitled to maintain militias.[70] John Farnsworth (R-Ill.) asserted that Congress had no power to "prevent States from organizing militia."[71] In the end, Congress passed two separate yet virtually identical statutes repealing the 1867 statute that prohibited the organization of militias in six Southern states.[72]

The debates on the militia controversy during the years 1866 to 1869 contributed to the understanding of the intention of the Congress that proposed the Fourteenth Amendment to the states. Supporters of the Fourteenth Amendment considered the right to keep and bear arms so fundamental that they were ready to abolish the state militias to protect freedmen from deprivation of this right. The state power to raise militia organizations might be temporarily abated by Congress, which would take care not to infringe on the right of the people to keep and bear arms, in order to protect against state infringement of that very same right of freedmen and all other persons to keep and bear arms. Despite all the bitterness of the period, no law would ever be passed making it unlawful for ex-Confederates to keep and bear arms like all other Americans. The rights to vote and to trial by jury were taken away, but Southern whites continued to enjoy a right that freedmen now exercised under Congressional sponsorship: "the constitutional right to bear arms."

NOTES

1. *Pomeroy's Constitutional Law*, NATION, July 16, 1868, at 53–54, cited in R. Aynes, *On Misreading John Bingham and the Fourteenth Amendment*, 103 YALE LAW JOURNAL 57, 90 n. 218 (1993).
2. Id. at 90.
3. J. Pomeroy, AN INTRODUCTION TO THE CONSTITUTIONAL LAW OF THE UNITED STATES 144 (1868).
4. Id. at 147.
5. Id. at 149–50.
6. Id. at 150–51.
7. Id. at 151.
8. Id.
9. Id. at 152.
10. Id. at 152–53.
11. Id. at 153.
12. At least four Southern state constitutional conventions petitioned Congress to extend the life of the Freedmen's Bureau. House Misc. Doc. No. 44,

40th Cong., 2d Sess., at 1 (Jan. 29, 1868).

13. 15 STATUTES AT LARGE 83 (1868).

14. Id.

15. CONG. GLOBE, 40th Cong., 2d Sess. 1438 (Feb. 26, 1868).

16. Id. at 1826 (Mar. 11, 1868).

17. Id. at 1967 (Mar. 18, 1868).

18. Id. at 1793 (Mar. 10, 1868).

19. House Rept. No. 30, 40th Cong., 2d Sess. *passim* (Mar. 10, 1868).

20. CONG. GLOBE, 40th Cong., 2nd Sess. 1813, 1815 (Mar. 11, 1868).

21. Id. at 1816–17.

22. Id., App., at 292 (Mar. 17, 1868).

23. Id.

24. Id. at 293.

25. Id.

26. Id.

27. CONG. GLOBE, 40th Cong., 2d Sess. 1996 (Mar. 19, 1868).

28. Id.

29. Id. at 1998.

30. CONG. GLOBE, 40th Cong., 2d Sess. 2462 (May 14, 1868).

31. Id.

32. Id. at 2463.

33. Id. at 3057 (June 11, 1868).

34. Id.

35. Id. at 3058.

36. Id. at 3089 (June 12, 1868). Just minutes before the House took action on the bill, that body had appointed a committee to represent the Congress at a great festival to be held in New York City by the National Association of American Sharpshooters. Id. The Fortieth Congress, many members of which voted for the Fourteenth Amendment, perceived the possession and use of firearms in a positive manner.

37. Id. at 3310 (June 19, 1868).

38. 15 STATUTES AT LARGE 83, 84 (July 6, 1868).

39. House Ex. Doc. 329, 40th Cong., 2d Sess. (1868).

40. Id. at 29, 42, 45.

41. Id. at 40.

42. CONG. GLOBE, 40th Cong., 2d. Sess. 4006 (July 13, 1868).

43. Id.

44. Id.

45. Id. Representative Horace Maynard (R-Tn.) described the condition of the freedmen in the following terms: "Everything likely to alleviate their hard condition has been resisted bitterly as leading to 'negro equality,' their freedom, their right to control their own labor, to own property, to testify in court, no less than their right to vote and to hold office. . . . Murdered, shot at, whipped, robbed, disarmed." Id., App., 456 (July 16, 1868).

46. Id. at 4451 (July 25, 1868).

47. Id. at 4479.

48. 15 STATUTES AT LARGE, 708, 709–11 (1868).

49. CONG. GLOBE, 40th Cong., 3rd Sess. 3 (Dec. 7, 1868).

50. Id.

51. Id.

52. Id.

53. 15 STATUTES AT LARGE, 170.

54. CONG. GLOBE, 40th Cong., 2d Sess. 830 (Jan. 29, 1868).

55. Id.

56. Id.

57. Id.

58. Id.

59. CONG. GLOBE, 40th Cong., 3rd Sess., App., 493 (July 25, 1868).

60. Id.

61. *Weekly Journal* (Wilmington, N.C.), Sept. 25, 1868.

62. CONG. GLOBE, 40th Cong., 3rd Sess., pt. 1, 80 (Dec. 15, 1868).

63. Id.

64. Id.

65. Id.

66. Id. at 81.

67. Id.

68. Id. at 83–84.

69. Id. at 84.

70. Id. at 115 (Dec. 16, 1868).

71. Id.

72. 15 STATUTES AT LARGE, 266, 337 (1869). A final repeal provision was passed in 1870. 16 STATUTES AT LARGE, 364 (1870).

5

Toward Adoption of the Civil Rights Act of 1871

THE ENFORCEMENT ACT OF 1870

The relationship between the Bill of Rights and the Fourteenth Amendment was overshadowed in the next few sessions of Congress by the push to pass the Fifteenth Amendment, which guarantees that the right to vote shall not be denied on account of race, color, or previous condition of servitude. Congress' authority to enforce the Fifteenth Amendment together with numerous reports of Klan attacks in the Southern States inspired the Forty-First Congress to enact the Enforcement Act of 1870,[1] which criminalized civil rights violations by private parties. The Enforcement Act reopened the debate on the meaning of the Fourteenth Amendment.[2]

Besides enforcing the voting guarantees of the Fifteenth Amendment, the Enforcement Act provided that "all persons within the jurisdiction of the United States shall have the same right . . . to the full and equal benefit of all laws and proceedings for the security of person and property as is enjoyed by white citizens," essentially reenacting the Civil Rights Act of 1866.[3] The act made it a felony to conspire "to injure, oppress, threaten, or intimidate any citizen with intent to prevent or hinder his free exercise and enjoyment of any right or privilege granted or secured to him by the Constitution or laws of the United States."[4]

Violence in the South was a frequent topic in debates on the Enforcement Act. Because every community has "a constitutional right to protect itself against illegal violence," Senator George Edmunds of Vermont argued, when an aggressor attacks with deadly force, "the law would justify me, in slaying him before he did slay me."[5] Senator John Pool of North Carolina argued that individuals must at times use force to protect their civil rights, because "you cannot put a policeman to walk with every citizen through the streets."[6] Noting that Klan members dared not attack white Republicans who were armed, Pool added that Klansmen would "order the colored men to give up their arms; saying that everybody would be Kukluxed in whose house fire-arms were found."[7]

Senator Charles Drake of Missouri pointed out that "the negro . . . has no arms to defend himself."[8] "If you discover a burglar coming into your house at night to rob you, and you have a pistol in your hand," Drake asked, "do you throw a pillow at him instead of a bullet?"[9] Senator John Thayer of Nebraska made the same point: "The rights of citizenship, of self-defense, of life itself were denied to the colored race before the war [and] are denied to them now."[10]

Two questions were raised in the Enforcement Act debates that would eventually have to be settled by the Supreme Court. First, the Fourteenth and Fifteenth Amendments protected certain rights, privileges, and immunities from violation by the states. Did Congress have constitutional authority to punish private citizens for violating these constitutional protections? Secondly, as Thomas Bayard (D-Del.) asked, "What are the 'rights or privileges secured to citizens by the Constitution and laws of the United States?' If you mean to make it an offense to invade these rights, it is your duty as legislators to point out the precise offense intended."[11] These two issues would become the Achilles' heel of the Enforcement Act in the Supreme Court.

THE CIVIL RIGHTS ACT OF 1871

Aside from the Fourteenth Amendment, the Civil Rights Act of 1871 was the most important and lasting accomplishment of the Reconstruction Congress in support of civil rights and the liberation of the freedmen. Its purpose was to remedy infringement of rights under color of state law and to suppress Ku Klux Klan violence. The entitlement of freedmen to all the rights of citizenship, including the right to keep and bear arms, was clear enough. The difficult question was how these rights might be protected by statute and in the courts.

Early in the third session of the Forty-First Congress, Representative John Bingham reported for the majority of the House Judiciary Committee that the Fourteenth Amendment did not protect women's suffrage.[12]

The Committee made clear, however, that the Fourteenth Amendment incorporated the Bill of Rights:

The fourteenth amendment . . . did not add to the privileges or immunities before mentioned [in Article 4, § 2], but was deemed necessary for their enforcement as an express limitation upon the powers of the States. It had been judicially determined that the first eight articles of amendment of the Constitution were not limitations on the power of the States.
    To remedy this defect of the Constitution, the express limitations upon the States contained in the first section of the fourteenth amendment . . . were incorporated in the Constitution.[13]

Representatives William Loughridge (Iowa) and Benjamin F. Butler (Massachusetts), a former Union army general, issued a minority report arguing that the Fourteenth Amendment protected women's suffrage. The report quoted from Justice Bushrod Washington's opinion in *Corfield* v. *Coryell* (1823) that the privileges and immunities protected by the Constitution are "those which are in their nature fundamental, and belong to the citizens of all free governments. Such are the rights of protection of life and liberty."[14] The report also quoted from an 1848 Georgia decision holding that free blacks were not citizens because "they are not entitled to bear arms, vote for members of the legislature, or hold any civil office."[15] The report commented that "all such fallacious theories as this are swept away by the fourteenth amendment, which abolishes the theory of different grades of citizenship, . . . guaranteeing to all citizens the rights and privileges of citizens of the republic."[16]

Klan terrorism in Tennessee's 1868 elections was the subject of a speech on February 14, 1871, by Representative Horace Maynard of that state, who cited accounts of firearms seizures and intimidation of black voters. Klansmen threatened and seized firearms from black Republicans.[17] One black man testified that Klansmen came to "my house, inquiring for guns and pistols."[18] Klansmen threatened a black who admitted that he would vote for Grant, and ransacked his house after he refused to surrender his pistols.[19] Blacks frequently defended themselves with their pistols.[20]

Meanwhile Butler introduced H.R. No. 3011, a bill to protect the loyal and peaceable citizens of the United States in the full enjoyment of their rights, persons, liberties, and property, and it was referred to the Committee on Reconstruction. On February 20 on behalf of the committee Butler submitted a report to the House on the bill.[21] The bill, which would become the basis of the Civil Rights Act passed in the next session, was then recommitted to the committee.[22] Noting instances of terrorism against the freedman, the report that accompanied the bill warned: "The negro may be pressed too far, and be compelled to take up arms in his own defense. These men who oppress him in the manner before mentioned seem to dread this, for in many counties they have preceded their outrages upon him by disarming him, in violation of his right as a citizen to 'keep and bear arms,' which the Constitution expressly says shall never be infringed."[23]

The bill would have punished private violence, whereas the Fourteenth Amendment only provided that "no State shall" abridge, deprive, or deny persons of rights. The report argued that the bill was nonetheless constitutional:

The Constitution, in the fifth article of amendment, as well as in the fourteenth article of amendment, . . . provides that "no person shall be deprived of life, liberty, or property without due process of law;" and by the second article "the right of the people to keep and bear arms shall not be infringed." . . . The fourteenth amendment of the Constitution also has vested in the Congress of the United States the power, by proper legislation, to prevent any State from depriving any citizen of the United States of the enjoyment of life, liberty, and property.[24]

The state action requirement of the Fourteenth Amendment was met, according to the report, because a state that does not punish terrorism "has, by its neglect or want of power, deprived the citizens of the United States of protection in the enjoyment of life, liberty, and property as fully and completely as if it had passed a legislative act to the same effect."[25]

A section-by-section analysis of Butler's bill reveals that, like the Freedmen's Bureau Act of 1866, the Second Amendment guarantee was the only provision in the Bill of Rights to be mentioned by name:

Section eight is intended to enforce the well-known constitutional provision guaranteeing the right in the citizen to "keep and bear arms," and provides that whoever shall take away, by force or violence, or by threats and intimidation, the arms and weapons which any person may have for his defense, shall be deemed guilty of larceny of the same. . . . Before these midnight marauders made attacks upon peaceful citizens, there were very many instances in the South where the sheriff of the county had preceded them and taken away the arms of their victims. This was specially noticeable in Union County [South Carolina], where all the negro population were disarmed by the sheriff only a few months ago under the order of the judge who resigned lest he should be impeached by the legislature; and then, the sheriff having disarmed the citizens, the five hundred masked men rode at night and murdered and otherwise maltreated the ten persons who were in jail in that county.[26]

On February 28 Butler reported the bill with amendments back from the Committee on Reconstruction.[27] The third session of the Forty-First Congress adjourned shortly thereafter. Within a matter of days, however, the Forty-Second Congress convened, and the civil rights revolution continued with full force. This Congress would enact the anti–Ku Klux Klan Act, also known as the Civil Rights Act of 1871.[28]

At the beginning of the session, the report and evidence of the special Senate committee to investigate Southern outrages was ordered to be printed.[29] The 423-page document had been laid before the Senate on March 10,[30] and would be relied on frequently in the upcoming debates on the Civil Rights Bill.[31]

On March 20 Butler introduced H.R. No. 189, a bill to protect loyal and peaceable citizens in the South, which was substantially the same as the Civil Rights Bill Butler introduced in the previous session. The preamble recited that lawless persons were depriving persons of their constitutional rights, and that the states had failed to suppress these violations.[32] Although the bill provided remedies for violations of "any right guaranteed" by the Constitution,[33] the only specific substantive right in the Bill of Rights singled out for special mention and protection was the right to keep and bear arms. Section 8 of the bill provided: "That whoever shall, without due process of law, by violence, intimidation, or threats, take away or deprive any citizen of the United States of any arms or weapons he may have in his house or possession for the defense of his person, family, or property, shall be deemed guilty of a larceny thereof, and be punished as provided in this act for a felony."[34] The bill was referred to the Committee on the Judiciary.[35] Butler would later explain that the bill was supported by a two-thirds majority in a joint committee of the two Houses, and that the committee agreed that every provision of the bill was "within the constitutional power of Congress."[36]

On March 23 Congress received a message from President Grant noting that life and property were insecure in some states and urging the passage of only one bill for the session: "legislation as . . . shall effectually secure life, liberty, and property, and the enforcement of law in all parts of the United States."[37] The president's message, urged Butler, stressed the need for the House to take up his bill, which "does meet the approval of a majority of the Republicans on this floor."[38] The president's message was then referred to a select committee of nine.[39]

Instead of Butler's lengthy bill, on March 28 the House considered a condensed bill, H. R. No. 320, reported by the select committee to which was referred the president's message.[40] Section 1 of the bill, taken partly from the Civil Rights Act of 1866, survives today as 42 U.S.C. § 1983. It enforced the Fourteenth Amendment by establishing a remedy for depriving all persons — not only former slaves — of their federal constitutional rights under color of state law. This portion of the bill also provided civil remedies against state agents who deprived any person . . . of "any rights, privileges, or immunities" to which the person is "entitled under the Constitution or laws of the United States."[41] Section 2 punished a conspiracy "to do any act in violation of the rights, privileges, or immunities of another person,"[42] and was intended to protect the "fundamental" rights of citizens.[43] Section 3 provided that where domestic violence deprived a class of people of "any of the rights, privileges, or immunities named in and secured by this act," and the state failed to provide protection, such facts shall be deemed a denial of equal protection of the laws.[44]

The bill was attacked as unconstitutional because it punished private conduct.[45] Representative Michael Kerr (D-Ind.) conceded that the Bill of Rights "guaranties to the people certain great personal rights," and that the Fourteenth Amendment was "a limitation on the power of the States as against any infringement of the rights of the citizens of the United States."[46]

George Morgan (D-Ohio) charged that Grant's message urging emergency legislation was an attempt to sidestep an investigatory committee, and that Butler had met with the president to accomplish the goal.[47] Although Butler may have engineered the unusually fast introduction and consideration of H.R. No. 320, that bill did not include some of the specific provisions of Butler's own bill, H.R. No. 189. Dropped from the current bill, for example, was a provision making simple larceny of a firearm a federal crime, an offense of dubious federal jurisdiction. State infringement on the right to keep and bear arms was another matter, and was recognized as being within the scope of H.R. No. 320.

Representative Washington Whitthorne of Tennessee complained that "in having organized a negro militia, in having disarmed the white man," the Republicans had "plundered and robbed" the whites of South Carolina through "unequal laws." A member of the committee that reported the bill, Whitthorne objected that § 1 protected the right to keep and bear arms from state infringement:

By the first section suits may be instituted without regard to amount or character of claim by any person within the limits of the United States who conceives that he has been deprived of any right, privilege, or immunity secured him by the Constitution of the United States, under color of any law, statute, ordinance, regulation, custom, or usage of any State. This is to say, that if a police officer of the city of Richmond or New York should find a drunken negro or white man upon the streets with a loaded pistol flourishing it, & c., and by virtue of any ordinance, law, or usage, either of city or State, he takes it away, the officer may be sued, because the right to bear arms is secured by the Constitution.[48]

Supporters of the bill did not agree with Whitthorne's exaggeration that the right to keep and bear arms protected a drunken person brandishing or committing assault with a pistol. Proponents were concerned that a police officer would seize the arms of a law-abiding person of the wrong race or political party, perhaps to ensure the success of an extremist group's attack. However, no one in the lengthy ensuing debate disputed Whitthorne's premise that state agents could be sued under the predecessor to today's 42 U.S.C. § 1983 for deprivation of the right to keep and bear arms.[49]

Although the bill being debated did not include the provision on larceny of a firearm from Butler's original bill, Representative James Beck of Kentucky complained that "General Butler of course obtains practically by this bill all and more than all that his own bill proposed."[50] This is yet another indication that the Civil Rights Bill was intended, like Butler's bill, to protect Second Amendment rights.

Debate over the constitutionality of the bill naturally required exposition of § 1 of the Fourteenth Amendment, and none was better qualified to explain that section than its draftsman, Bingham. Bingham explained that he framed § 1 "as it now stands, letter for letter and syllable for syllable," except for "the introductory clause defining citizens."[51] Bingham added that he wrote the final draft of the provision with *Barron v. Baltimore*, which held that the Bill of Rights was inapplicable to the states, in mind.[52] The first eight amendments "secured the citizens against any deprivation of any essential rights of person by any act of Congress,"[53] and the Fourteenth Amendment secured them against state infringement:

Mr. Speaker, that the scope and meaning of the limitations imposed by the first section, fourteenth amendment of the Constitution may be more fully understood, permit me to say that the privileges and immunities of citizens of a State, are chiefly defined in the first eight amendments to the Constitution of the United States. Those eight amendments are as follows:

Article I
Congress shall make no law respecting an establishment of religion, or prohibiting the free exercise thereof, or abridging the freedom of speech, or of the

press, or the right of the people peaceably to assemble, and to petition the
Government for a redress of grievances.

Article II

A well-regulated militia being necessary to the security of a free State, the
right of the people to keep and bear arms shall not be infringed. [The Third
through the Eighth Amendments, also listed by Bingham, are here omitted.]

These eight articles I have shown never were limitations upon the power of the
States, until made so by the fourteenth amendment. The words of that amendment, "no State shall make or enforce any law which shall abridge the privileges
or immunities of citizens of the United States," are an express prohibition upon
every State of the Union.[54]

Referring to the bill at hand, Bingham urged that Congress should
follow the example of the Constitution's framers, "by passing laws for
enforcing all the privileges and immunities of citizens of the United
States, as guarantied by the amended Constitution and expressly enumerated in the Constitution."[55] To Bingham, the bill to enforce the Fourteenth
Amendment would protect the personal right to keep and bear arms from
state infringement. Not one member of the House contradicted Bingham's
explanations.[56]

Maynard pointed out that few had objected to § 1 of the bill, which
"embraces all privileges and immunities secured by the Constitution; . . .
it would include any of the personal rights the Constitution guarantees to
the citizen."[57] "Freedom of speech" and "personal security" were among
those rights.[58] Maynard cited an incident in which an elderly black man
had killed a Klan attacker who turned out to be a law enforcement officer:
"The [home] owner, under these circumstances of menace and terror, from
his humble 'castle of defense' fired and killed one of the party and drove
off the rest. The man killed was found to be the constable of the district,
and one of the others was the sheriff of the county."[59] Representative John
M. Bright of Tennessee pointed out that the deceased was also a federal
soldier.[60] Bright also noted that the black man who protected his family
was arrested, tried, and acquitted.[61]

Although Republicans deplored the disarming of Southern blacks,
Democrats argued that Southern whites were disarmed and endangered by
armed carpetbaggers and black militia. Representative Boyd Winchester
of Kentucky claimed that the South Carolina governor armed black militias but refused arms to whites, and that black militiamen had murdered
whites.[62]

Representative George McKee of Mississippi argued the bill was necessary because Southern legislatures could not be trusted. He reminded his colleagues of the reenactment of the black codes in Mississippi in the 1865–1866 period, which sanctioned peonage labor contracts, prohibited the freedmen's right to assemble, and violated the Second Amendment:

They passed a law that no freedman should keep any gun, or pistol, or bowie-knife unless he had a written permission to do so, obtained from the county board of police.

Under the ordnance regulations, in 1865, a soldier honorably mustered out of the United States Army was entitled to keep his musket or rifle by having the sum of eight dollars stopped from his pay. . . . Most of the colored soldiers availed themselves of this privilege. Yet, in a few months after they were mustered out and became citizens of the United States and of Mississippi, I have seen those muskets taken from them and confiscated under this Democratic law. The United States did not even protect the soldier in retaining the musket which it had given him, and which he had borne in its defense.[63]

Southern Democrats, McKee continued, "would, if they had their own way, untrammeled by law or constitutional amendment, enact laws against the colored men of a similar import today."[64] Clearly the Fourteenth Amendment and the pending bill were understood to preclude state infringement on the right to have arms.

In continuing debate, Representative Butler quoted a letter from Tennessee that exemplified the utility of firearms for protection against violent state agents who were members of secret extremist organizations: "Then the Ku Klux fired on them through the window one of the bullets striking a colored woman . . . and wounding her through the knee badly. The colored men then fired on the Ku Klux, and killed their leader or captain right there on the steps of the colored men's house. . . . There he remained until morning when he was identified, and proved to be 'Pat Inman,' a constable and deputy sheriff."[65] Butler commented that "I thank God for the courage of that negro, who, in defending his own roof-tree and hearthstone, shot down the sheriff and constable who, as a leader of the Ku Klux, invaded both!"[66] In the same speech, Butler traced the bill at hand to the "Butler bill," which he had introduced in the last session and reintroduced in this session.[67] The Butler Bill, as previously noted, explicitly protected the right to keep and bear arms.

Representative Samuel Cox of Ohio assailed those who "arm negro militia and create a situation of terror," exclaiming that South Carolinians "actually clamored for United States troops to save them from the rapacity and murder of the negro bands and their white allies," and saw the Klan as their only defense.[68] Although deploring the powers of the president under the bill to use military force, Cox quoted Bingham's statement that the Fourteenth Amendment made the first eight amendments binding on the states, adding that the constitutional amendments, which protected such rights as "personal liberty" and trial by jury, had become restrictions on the States.[69] Cox argued that the Fourteenth Amendment prohibited state deprivation of constitutional rights, but that the bill unconstitutionally operated upon private individuals.[70]

John Coburn of Indiana responded that Congress could legislate against violation of rights or denial of equal protection of the laws by both states and private individuals:

A State may by positive enactment cut off from some the right to vote, . . . to bear arms, and many other things. This positive denial of protection is no more flagrant or odious or dangerous than to allow certain persons to be outraged as to their property, safety, liberty, or life . . . . *How much more oppressive is the passage of a law that they shall not bear arms than the practical seizure of all arms from the hands of the colored men?* . . .

It may be safely said, then, that there is a denial of the equal protection of the law by many of these States. It is therefore the plain duty of Congress to enforce by appropriate legislation the rights secured by this clause of the fourteenth amendment of the Constitution.[71] (emphasis added)

Representative Job Stevenson of Ohio detailed how Klan threats and firearms seizures dissuaded men from voting the Republican ticket.[72] Stevenson noted that a teacher at a school for young blacks was disarmed of his revolver, beaten, and ordered to leave the area.[73] Many freedmen, he added, were armed with shotguns and muskets, which could be used against the onslaught of Klan violence.[74] Citing instances where armed blacks defended themselves against Klan violence, Stevenson surmised: "Seldom do they [the Klan] attack a man until they have disarmed him."[75]

Representative Henry Dawes of Massachusetts, a member of the committee that drafted the bill, explained that the Civil Rights Bill would protect Bill of Rights guarantees, including the Second Amendment:

The rights, privileges, and immunities of the American citizen, secured to him under the Constitution of the United States, are the subject-matter of this bill. . . . The purpose of this bill is . . . to render the American Citizen more safe in the enjoyment of those rights, privileges, and immunities.

In addition to the original rights secured to him in the first article of amendments he had secured the free exercise of his religious belief, and freedom of speech and of the press. *Then again he has secured to him the right to keep and bear arms in his defense.* [Dawes then summarized the remainder of the first eight amendments.]

It is all these, Mr. Speaker, which are comprehended in the words "American citizen," and it is to protect and secure to him in these rights, privileges, and immunities this bill is before the House.[76] (emphasis added)

Dawes argued that Congress had authority to provide for the enforcement — either criminally or civilly — of the Bill of Rights.[77]

Representative Horatio Burchard of Illinois had no objection to § 1 of the bill, but rejected the view of Dawes and Bingham that "privileges and immunities" included the first eight amendments.[78] Burchard felt that those amendments contained "rights," but that only the Fourth, Fifth, and Sixth Amendments contained "privileges and immunities."[79] Although conceding that the first eight amendments applied to the states, Burchard found nothing in the Fourteenth Amendment to empower Congress to punish private action.[80]

The bill passed the House on April 6, 1871, along partisan lines by a vote of 118 to 91.[81] The Senate took up the House bill on April 11. Senator Edmunds, floor manager of the bill, thought that no one objected to § 1, which defined "the rights secured by the Constitution of the United States when they are assailed by any State law."[82] Senator Allen Thurman quickly corrected Edmunds by noting his opposition to all sections of the bill.[83]

Senator John Stockton argued that the bill, because it authorized military rule, would "subordinate the whole Bill of Rights to the absolute and uncontrolled will of one man," the commander-in-chief.[84] Senator Willard Saulsbury found it refreshing to hear the Republicans speak of constitutional guarantees, because "almost every guarantee of that sacred instrument for personal liberty has been stricken down in their hands."[85]

Senator Pool focused on the Citizenship Clause of the Fourteenth Amendment as a guarantee of fundamental rights. Observing that the U.S. system is based on English common law, Pool explained: "By the common law, the absolute rights of individuals are the right to personal liberty, personal security, and private property. Certainly the rights incident to citizenship cannot be less than the three absolute rights recognized by the common law."[86]

Senator Bayard, an opponent of the bill, identified the rights of an American by quoting the First through the Fifth Amendments, arguing that "the fourteenth amendment gave to citizens of the United States no privileges or immunities, no rights that they had not before its adoption. The only effect of that amendment was to enlarge the class of those who should be considered citizens."[87]

Senator Thurman suggested the following relation between the privileges and immunities and due process clauses of the Fourteenth Amendment: "that privilege and that immunity is the very same thing that is mentioned in other language in the next clause — the privilege of life, the privilege of liberty, the privilege of the acquirement of property."[88] Senator James Garfield of Ohio, the future president, explained the bill as providing protection by the federal courts of "the right of every citizen to enjoy all the privileges and immunities secured to him by the Constitution."[89]

The final version of the bill as signed by the president was called "An Act to Enforce the Provisions of the Fourteenth Amendment."[90] Section 1, which survives today as 42 U.S.C. § 1983, provided: "That any person who, under color of any law, statute, ordinance, regulation, custom, or usage of any State, shall subject, or cause to be subjected, any person within the jurisdiction of the United States to the deprivation of any rights, privileges, or immunities secured by the Constitution of the United States, shall . . . be liable to the party injured in any action at law, suit in equity, or other proper proceeding for redress."[91]

Section 2, which survives today as 18 U.S.C. § 1985, made it a crime, among other things, for two or more persons to "conspire together, or go in disguise . . . for the purpose . . . of depriving any person or class of persons of the equal protection of the laws, or of equal privileges or immunities under the laws."[92]

Section 3 empowered the president to suppress domestic violence and insurrections where a state fails to protect "the rights, privilege, or immunities" of its citizens.[93] This section was controversial because it ignored the requirement in the domestic violence clause of the Constitution that federal assistance be only at the request of state authorities. Equally controversial was § 4, which authorized the president to suspend the writ of habeas corpus if he decided that unlawful combinations defied the constituted authorities of the state.[94]

Despite the broad reach of certain parts of the Civil Rights Act, other parts do not seem to have been seriously questioned. In particular, actions for civil rights violations under § 1 pertained to state action, not private action, and thus were fully encompassed within the Fourteenth Amendment.

The right to keep and bear arms was identified as protected by the Fourteenth Amendment not only in the halls of Congress, but also in public speeches. In September 1871, none other than Representative Bingham said in a speech to constituents in Ohio:

Under the Constitution as it was, no State of this Union ever had the right to make or enforce any law which abridged the privileges or immunities of citizens of the United States, as guaranteed by the Constitution of the United States. Yet in nearly half the States of the Union these privileges and immunities of the citizen were abridged by State legislation and State administration. The freedom of speech was abridged . . . and, finally, *the right to bear arms for the Union and the Constitution was abridged and prohibited by State laws*, and all this without remedy upon the Democratic construction of the Constitution as it was.[95] (emphasis added)

The Fourteenth Amendment, Bingham added, remedied this defect.[96]

The Enforcement Act of 1870 and the Civil Rights Act of 1871 were enacted to enforce the rights declared in the Fourteenth Amendment. The drama would now shift from the halls of Congress to the federal courts.

NOTES

1. 16 STATUTES AT LARGE, 140 (1870).
2. Portions of the Enforcement Act survive today as 18 U.S.C. §§ 241, 242.
3. 16 STATUTES AT LARGE, 144.
4. Id. at 141.
5. CONG. GLOBE, 41st Cong., 2d Sess. 2673 (Apr. 14, 1870).
6. Id. at 2719 (Apr. 15, 1870).
7. Id. Senator Pool observed that "the right to life, the right to security in one's own house, the right to protection against outrage and wrong, are all higher rights than the mere right to vote, . . . and yet they are violated." When the higher rights are protected by law and yet are violated, he asked, how could the right to vote be enforced? Id. at 2722.
8. Id. at 2744 (Apr. 18, 1870).
9. Id. at 2745.
10. Id. App., 322 (Apr. 19, 1870).
11. Id. at 3803 (May 25, 1870).
12. H. R. Report No. 22 on Memorial of Victoria C. Woodhull, 41st Cong., 3rd Sess. 4 (Jan. 30, 1871).
13. Id. at 1.
14. Corfield v. Coryell, 4 Wash. C.C. 380, 6 Fed. Cas. 546 (No. 3230) (C.C. E.D.Pa. 1823), quoted in H. R. Report No. 22 on Memorial of Victoria C.

Woodhull, 41st Cong., 3rd Sess., pt. 2, at 6 (Feb. 1, 1871).

15. H. R. Report No. 22, at 7–8 (Feb. 1, 1871), quoting Cooper v. Savannah, 4 Ga. 72 (1848). The report also refers to definitions of "citizenship" in Aristotle's *Politics* and in *Dred Scott*. Id. at 8. Both of these sources included the right to keep and bear arms in the term "citizenship."

16. Id. at 7–8.

17. Id., App., 218 (Feb. 14, 1871).

18. Id.

19. Id.

20. Id. at 219. One black man recounted: "They tried to take my person. I prevented him by my pistol, which I cocked, and he jumped back. . . . I told them . . . I would hurt them before they got away. They did not burn nor steal anything, nor hurt me." Id. Another man testified that Klansmen "threatened to break my door open, and I told them the first man who broke my door open I would shoot him." Id. at 222.

21. CONG. GLOBE, 41st Cong., 3rd Sess. 1457 (Feb. 20, 1871).

22. Id.

23. H. R. Rep. No. 37, 41st Cong., 3rd Sess. 3 (Feb. 20, 1871).

24. Id. at 4.

25. Id.

26. Id. at 7–8.

27. CONG. GLOBE, 41st Cong., 3rd Sess. 1761 (Feb. 28, 1871); see id., 42 Cong., 1st Sess., at 449 (Apr. 4, 1871) (explanation by Butler).

28. The act survives today as 42 U.S.C. §§ 1983, 1985, and 1986.

29. CONG. GLOBE, 42nd Cong., 1st Sess. 113 (Mar. 15, 1871).

30. Id. at 503 (Apr. 6, 1871).

31. Relying on this evidence, Senator John Sherman of Ohio observed that Klansmen "carry terror" among blacks who were "without arms." Id. at 154 (Mar. 18, 1871). Because lawless men were "overthrowing the safety of person and property, and all those rights . . . which are expressly guarantied by the Constitution of the United States to all its citizens," Sherman moved that the Judiciary Committee report a bill to "secure to all citizens the rights so guarantied to them." Id. at 163.

32. Id. at 173 (Mar. 20, 1871).

33. Id.

34. Id. at 174. Although the bill did not mention free speech or assembly, those rights were protected often by the right to bear arms. Senator Adelbert Ames of Mississippi noted about conditions in the South: "Uniformly peaceable and unobtrusive, . . . Republicans were compelled to arm in self-defense. . . . In some counties it was impossible to advocate Republican principles, those attempting it being hunted like wild beasts; in others, the speakers had to be armed and supported by not a few friends." Id. at 196 (Mar. 21, 1871).

35. Id. at 175.

36. Id. at 449 (Apr. 4, 1871).

37. Id. at 236 (Mar. 23, 1871).

38. Id. at 247.

39. Id. at 249. Republican committee members included Butler, Samuel Shellabarger of Ohio, Glenn Scofield of Pennsylvania, Dawes, Austin Blair of Michigan, and Charles Thomas of North Carolina. Democrat members were Morgan, Kerr, and Whitthorne.

40. Id. at 317 (Mar. 28, 1871).

41. Id., App., at 68 (Mar. 28, 1871). Passed as the Enforcement Act, 17 Stat. 13 (1871), § 1 survives as 42 U.S.C. § 1983: "Every person who, under color of any statute, ordinance, regulation, custom, or usage, of any State or Territory, subjects, or causes to be subjected, any citizen of the United States or other person within the jurisdiction thereof to the deprivation of any rights, privileges, or immunities secured by the Constitution and laws, shall be liable to the party injured in an action at law, suit in equity, or other proper proceedings for redress."

The present-day action for conspiracy to deprive persons of rights or privileges under 42 U.S.C. § 1985 derives from the same act.

42. Id.

43. Id. at 69.

44. Id. at 70–71.

45. Id. at 46–47.

46. Id.

47. Id. at 330 (Mar. 29, 1871) (remarks of Rep. Morgan).

48. Id. at 337.

49. William Kelley of Pennsylvania made a lengthy reply to Whitthorne, but did not deny that § 1 allowed suit for deprivation of the right to have arms. Id. at 338–41.

50. Id. at 353 (Mar. 30, 1871).

51. Id., App., at 83 (Mar. 31, 1871).

52. Id. at 84.

53. Id.

54. Id.

55. Id.

56. Id. at 86–87. The real issues were whether Congress could punish private conduct and the limits of federal power to make criminal laws. See id. (remarks of Rep. Storm).

57. Id., App., at 310.

58. Id. at 311.

59. Id., App., at 309.

60. Id.

61. Id. at 310.

62. Id. at 422 (Apr. 3, 1871). Similar claims were made by Rep. F. P. Blair of Missouri. Id., App., at 123–25.

63. Id. at 426.

64. Id.

65. Id. at 445 (Apr. 4, 1871).

66. Id.

67. Id. at 448–49.

68. Id. at 453.

69. Id. at 454.

70. Id. at 455.

71. Id. at 459.

72. Id., App., at 286.

73. Id. at 288.

74. Id. at 292.

75. Id. at 299.

76. Id. at 475–76 (Apr. 5, 1871).

77. Id. at 476. A critic of the bill, Rep. J. H. Slater of Oregon argued that "all the important and valued rights of the citizen were secured and guarded by [the Bill of Rights]," which would be destroyed by the "pretended enforcement of the fourteenth amendment." Id., App., at 304.

78. Id., App., at 314–15 (Apr. 6, 1871).

79. Id. at 314.

80. Id. at 314–15.

81. Id. at 522.

82. Id. at 568 (Apr. 11, 1871).

82. Id. at 569.

84. Id. at 572.

85. Id. at 603 (Apr. 12, 1871).

86. Id. at 607.

87. Id., App., at 242–43.

88. Id. at 697 (Apr. 14, 1871).

89. Id. at 807 (Apr. 19, 1871).

90. 17 Stat. 13 (1871).

91. Id.

92. Id.

93. Id. at 14.

94. Id. at 14–15. That provision, however, expired after the following session of Congress.

95. *Speech of Hon. John A. Bingham at Belpre, Ohio, September 14, 1871*, CADIZ REPUBLICAN, Sept. 28, 1871, at 1, col. 2.

96. Id.

6

From the Klan Trials and Hearings through the End of the Civil Rights Revolution

INDICTMENTS BASED ON THE
FIRST AND FOURTH AMENDMENTS

After passage of the 1870 Enforcement Act,[1] which protected rights "granted or secured" by the Constitution, federal prosecutors began bringing indictments alleging interference with the right to vote on account of race and violations of Bill of Rights freedoms. After federal courts in Alabama and Mississippi upheld such indictments, a concerted effort was made to bring similar indictments against members of the Ku Klux Klan in South Carolina.

In May 1871 Circuit Judge William Woods of the Southern District of Alabama upheld an indictment charging that the defendants conspired to injure persons "with intent to prevent and hinder their free exercise and enjoyment of the right of freedom of speech, the same being a right and privilege granted and secured to them by the constitution of the United States."[2] Another count alleged interference with "the right and privilege to peaceably assemble."[3] The government conceded that these rights preexisted the Constitution's adoption and hence were not "granted' by the Constitution, but contended that the rights to free speech and assembly were "secured" by the Constitution and thus were protected by the Enforcement Act.

Observing that the Bill of Rights originally only limited federal action, Judge Woods explained that the Fourteenth Amendment was intended to enforce the Bill against the states.[4] The privileges and immunities protected by the Fourteenth Amendment, he wrote, include "those which in the constitution are expressly secured to the people," such as the rights to free speech and assembly.[5] Judge Woods found Bill of Rights guarantees secured by the Constitution because: "They are expressly recognized, and both congress and the states are forbidden to abridge them. Before the fourteenth amendment, congress could not impair them, but the states might. Since the fourteenth amendment, . . . the states are positively inhibited from impairing or abridging them."[6]

Judge Woods did not limit his remarks to the First Amendment, but added that "the other rights enumerated in the first eight articles of amendment to the constitution of the United States, are the privileges and immunities of citizens."[7] Accordingly, Congress could enforce them by appropriate legislation.[8]

Another Enforcement Act prosecution took place in June 1871 before Judge Robert A. Hill in the U.S. District Court for the Northern District of Mississippi.[9] The indictments alleged that disguised men hanged Alexander Page, a freedman, with intent to hinder him "in the protection of his life and liberty so secured to him by the said Constitution of the United States," and contrary to his right of "personal security."[10] Defense counsel argued that the indictment really charged murder, a state offense, which could not be sustained under the Reconstruction amendments or the Enforcement Act, and that Congress had no power to secure the rights of life and liberty to citizens.[11]

In Judge Hill's opinion, "before the adoption of the fourteenth amendment," the protection of life and liberty was left to the states, "the Federal Government being prohibited from restricting [these rights]."[12] To secure equal rights and protection under the law, however, "the fourteenth amendment was adopted, thus placing the restriction upon the States."[13] The proscriptions of the Fourth Amendment on seizure of the person and of the Fifth Amendment on deprivation of life or liberty without due process were "inestimable rights and immunities" protected by the Fourteenth Amendment.[14]

If the Fourteenth Amendment protected the Fourth Amendment and other Bill of Rights guarantees from state deprivation, did it also protect these guarantees from private violation? This question went unanswered in the above opinions by Judges Woods and Hill, which upheld the indictments, but would later become the Achilles' heel of such prosecutions.

THE SOUTH CAROLINA INDICTMENTS
BASED ON THE FOURTH AMENDMENT

In late 1871 numerous South Carolina Klansmen were indicted under the Enforcement Act for conspiring to violate the rights of blacks to assemble, to keep and bear arms, to vote, and to be free from unreasonable searches and seizures. The trial proceedings were published in book form as *Proceedings in the Ku Klux Trials*[15] and reprinted by the Joint Select Committee on the Condition of Affairs in the Late Insurrectionary States.[16] The trial proceedings are significant both as an interpretation of the Second, Fourth, and Fourteenth Amendments, and because they documented the Klan's systematic efforts to disarm blacks.[17]

Six months before the indictments were brought the federal prosecutor in the case, David Corbin, testified before the Joint Select Committee about the volatile situation in South Carolina. Corbin told the committee that he had previously sought indictments against the Klan for deprivation of "rights secured by the Constitution and laws of the United States," but that the grand jury was not convinced that the whippings and murders that occurred had been committed with that intent.[18] Corbin acknowledged that friction resulted when the governor armed black militias and refused arms to whites.[19]

Later Corbin sought U.S. Attorney General Amos T. Akerman's advice about drafting new indictments. Because Klan attacks typically involved breaking into houses to seize firearms, Corbin planned to prosecute for Second and Fourth Amendment violations.[20] Corbin acknowledged the novelty of alleging violations of constitutional guarantees in an indictment, but felt that the recent constitutional amendments protected deprivations of these rights from both state and private action.[21] Akerman, although unsure whether "an irregular and unofficial" seizure was a Fourth Amendment violation, advised Corbin that "upon the right to bear arms, I think you are impregnable."[22]

Proceedings in the South Carolina prosecutions began on December 4, 1871, before Circuit Judge Hugh Bond of Maryland, presiding, and District Judge George Bryan of Charleston.[23] The prosecution was represented by U.S. Attorney Corbin and, by special appointment, South Carolina Attorney General Henry Chamberlain. U.S. Senator Reverdy Johnson of Maryland and former U.S. Attorney General Henry Stanbery of Ohio, both leading constitutional lawyers, represented the defendants.[24]

Stanbery argued for the dismissal of all counts against Allen Crosby and other defendants, including "the eighth, which charges an interference with rights secured by the Constitution to exemption from unreasonable searches and seizures of persons, papers and effects."[25] More precisely, the eighth count charged that the defendants conspired to interfere with Amzi Rainey's Fourth Amendment right to be free from unreasonable searches and seizures, a right and privilege granted and secured by the Constitution.[26] Stanbery argued:

There is no Act of Congress to secure a man against searches and seizures. It is declared to be a right in the Constitution; so is the right of personal liberty, and a thousand other rights, that are sacred rights, recognized by the Constitution of the United States. But I cannot go to a Federal tribunal to vindicate them.

The well established doctrine is, that the recognition of these rights in the Constitution is a restriction upon the Federal authority.[27]

In reply, Chamberlain argued that Congress had the power under the Fourteenth Amendment to enforce rights, including the Fourth Amendment, guaranteed by the Constitution.[28] Corbin chimed in, arguing that Congress as well as the states could protect constitutional rights.[29] Quoting *Barron* v. *Baltimore*, Corbin conceded that the Bill of Rights previously was a restriction upon the federal government only,[30] but argued that the Fourteenth Amendment made it applicable to the states:

The States are disposed to encroach upon the rights of the newly enfranchised citizens; and how are they to be protected? Why, manifestly, that was the object of the fourteenth amendment, the same as nearly one hundred years ago, to protect from the National Government. We have now, under the fourteenth amendment, gone further, and said this immunity and right shall be secured, as against the State Governments, and Congress shall enforce this provision, this new amendment of the Constitution, by appropriate legislation.[31]

Corbin argued that Congress had power to enforce Bill of Rights guarantees by making conspiracy to violate them a crime and need not restrict its enforcement power to violations by the states.[32]

In his opinion issued December 7, 1871, Judge Bond dismissed the eighth count, which alleged a conspiracy to prevent Rainey from exercising his right to be secure against unreasonable searches and seizures, reasoning that this right was not granted or secured by the Constitution because it antedated the Constitution: "The right to be secure in one's house is not a right derived from the Constitution, but it existed long before the adoption of the Constitution at common law, and cannot be said to come within the meaning of the words of the Act 'right, privilege or immunity granted or secured by the Constitution of the United States.'"[33]

Meanwhile, prosecutors brought new indictments, seeking to craft them consistent with the court's rulings. Chamberlain explained an indictment against James William Avery and others that charged conspiracy to intimidate to prevent the free exercise of the right to keep and bear arms.[34] There was immediate discussion of the issue being taken to the Supreme Court for resolution because Judges Bond and Bryan were divided on the sufficiency of this and other counts.[35]

THE SOUTH CAROLINA INDICTMENTS
BASED ON THE SECOND AMENDMENT

Two days later the same court heard arguments on indictments against Robert Hayes Mitchell and others for infringement of the right to bear arms. After prosecutor Corbin said that he would "fight for it [the right to bear arms] to the last," defense counsel Stanbery moved to quash that count of the indictment: "Your Honors have held that the right to be secure from searches and the right to the free enjoyment of all the privileges secured by the Constitution of the United States do not make any offense under these laws; and the right to bear arms . . . is not secured by the Constitution of the United States, but stands in the nature of a bill of rights. It is a restriction upon Congress against interfering with that right."[36]

Corbin countered that the Fourteenth Amendment guarantees the right to keep and bear arms to the citizen and that private individuals could be indicted for violation of this right. "If there is any right that is dear to the citizen," Corbin argued, "it is the right to keep and bear arms; and it was secured to the citizen of the United States on the adoption of the amendments to the Constitution."[37] Although the antebellum Supreme Court held the Bill of Rights applicable only to Congress, he continued: "The fourteenth amendment changes all that theory, and lays the same restriction upon the States that before lay upon the Congress of the United States — that, as Congress heretofore could not interfere with the right of the citizen to keep and bear arms, now, after the adoption of the fourteenth amendment, the State cannot interfere with the right of the citizen to keep and bear arms. The right to keep and bear arms is included in the fourteenth amendment, under 'privileges and immunities.'"[38]

Corbin's argument that the Fourteenth Amendment protected Bill of Rights guarantees was not disputed. However, § 6 of the Enforcement Act required a showing that the right was "granted or secured" by the Constitution or laws. Corbin continued:

The right to keep and bear arms is a privilege of a citizen of the United States — was before the adoption of the fourteenth amendment; after the adoption of the fourteenth amendment, that privilege was secured as to the citizen as against the State. . . . The Court has said that the right to be secure from unreasonable searches and seizures was a right at common law. Consequently, the Constitution of the United States did not secure it — it existed before. Now, will this Court say . . . that the right to keep and bear arms was a right secured at common law? Certainly not. Such a right never existed at common law, modified common law, or anything else.[39]

Corbin noted that the English Declaration of Rights of 1689 guaranteed the right to have arms exclusively to Protestants.[40] The Second Amendment, by contrast, secured the right to keep and bear arms to "the people," Corbin argued, and thus was "a distinct right" not found in the common law.[41] The right to bear arms was thus "granted or secured" for the first time by the Constitution, and was protected by the Enforcement Act.[42]

Defense counsel Johnson argued that because the court had decided that making it a crime to conspire to violate the right against unreasonable searches and seizures is not authorized by the Fourteenth Amendment, private violation of the Second Amendment could not be a crime either.[43] Johnson, a member of the Senate when Congress passed the Fourteenth Amendment, readily conceded: "Has he [the citizen] a right to bear arms? He has. It is an absolute right, secured by the Constitution."[44]

The Corbin-Johnson debate also got bogged down in the controversy over black militias. Corbin used as an example a Klan conspiracy in York County, South Carolina "to rob the people of their arms, and to prevent them from keeping and bearing arms."[45] Johnson asked whether "it would have been in the power of the State Government to deny to the white citizens the right to bear arms?"[46] Corbin replied that "the State of South Carolina cannot do it."[47] Although the state could disarm militia companies, Johnson rejoined, the right to bear arms is not "given by" the Constitution "but exists under the local law of the State."[48] In other words, private theft of arms was the proper subject of state, not federal, law.

Although arguing that the states could disarm persons who terrorized the people, Johnson continued:

To permit one class of citizens to bear arms, and to practically deny them to the other, is to place that other in subjection to the former. And that would be tyranny unbearable and utterly abhorrent to every principle upon which our institutions rest, and in conflict with the best considered rights of the other citizens; the right of the freeman to protect himself against aggression. . . . The black man, it is conceded, is a freeman. . . . You cannot subject the white man to the absolute and uncontrolled dominion of an armed force of the colored race.[49]

With that statement, Bond declared that the court was not ready to determine the Second Amendment issue.[50] He asked whether the prosecution was ready to proceed with another indictment, to which U.S. Attorney Corbin replied: "There are other indictments here, but they all have counts charging conspiracy to deprive citizens of the right to bear arms. That is one of the principal things in connection with this conspiracy; it was systematically done, and was one of the main objects of the conspiracy — to deprive citizens of the right to bear arms, as well as to prevent them from voting. All of the cases returned by the grand jury have that count, and we will never abandon it until we are obliged to."[51]

Corbin pressed the court to rule on "one of the vital grounds of this prosecution," the counts involving the right to bear arms, a "right [that] has been trampled on again and again in this State, in the most flagrant and systematic manner."[52] Bond repeated that he was still not prepared to rule on that count.[53] After Bond refused to rule the next day on that issue, Corbin asked the court to enter a *nolle prosequi* on the right to bear arms counts in the indictments against Mitchell and others, in order that the prosecution could proceed.[54]

THE TRIAL: WAS WILLIAMS MURDERED
TO INTIMIDATE VOTERS OR TO DISARM
AND NEUTRALIZE A THREAT?

The prosecution proceeded to try the Mitchell case on the other Enforcement Act counts, particularly the count alleging conspiracy to prevent black citizens from voting. Corbin argued in his opening statement that in York County some 50 Klansmen, led by Avery, murdered Jim Williams and "visited divers other houses of colored people, threatened them, took them out, robbed them of their arms, and informed them that, if they should vote again, they would be killed."[55]

Trial testimony substantiated that black Republicans were whipped and disarmed as part of this intimidation.[56] Andy Tims described the Klan's nighttime raid upon his residence: "They said: 'Here we come — we are the Ku Klux. Here we come, right from hell,' and two rode up on one side of my house, and one to the other. . . . Before I got the door they bursted the latch off, and two came in, and one got me by the arms and says, 'we want your guns.' . . . They got the gun, . . . and after they got these things they asked for a pistol; I told them I didn't have any pistol at that time."[57]

After asking where Williams, who was captain of the black militia, lived, the Ku Klux members left on horses. Tims and two other black men went looking for Williams and found him hanging from a tree.[58]

Tims, a clerk in Williams' militia company, testified on cross-examination that they were armed with Enfield breechloading rifles, which they frequently fired just before the election in October 1870.[59] Many carried their arms to the elections.[60] The company began arming and drilling in response to the Klan threat.[61] The night of the murder, a Klansman claimed that Williams threatened "that if his party failed he expected to kill from the cradle to the grave."[62] Tims testified that the company had 90 members and had received its arms from the governor. Other black militia companies also received arms, but their white counterparts received none.[63] The defense sought to use Tims' testimony to show that Williams' murder had nothing to do with preventing voting, but rather was meant to prevent Williams' militia company from killing whites.[64]

Gadsen Steel testified that the Klan had come to his house looking for guns the night of the murder. He denied having any and was beaten. A Klansman threatened, "we are going on to kill Williams, and are going to kill all these damned niggers that vote the Radical ticket."[65]

Rosy Williams, the victim's wife, testified that disguised men came to their house and that Williams gave them two guns. When Williams told them he had no more guns, they took him away, and that was the last time she saw him alive.[66] Mrs. Williams testified that her husband had previously been warned by the Klan to return the guns, but he refused to do so unless Governor Scott gave the order.[67]

Hiram Littlejohn testified that the Klan visited his house on the night of the murder and recalled the following conversation:

When they came up they said: "Have you any guns here."

Said I: "We have got a double-barrel shot gun."

"Hand it down here," said they; "we hung Jim Williams tonight; we intend to rule this country or die."

Said he: "You are a Radical man. Next time you go to vote, you vote the Democratic ticket, you hear."[68]

John Caldwell, a witness for the prosecution and a Klan member, testified that on the date of the murder, his associates said they were going to McConnellsville to seize firearms from blacks.[69] They searched a house for arms and were told by a black man that Williams had at least 12 firearms. Caldwell stayed with the horses when they got to Williams's residence, and was later informed that other Klan members hanged Williams.[70] Once again, the defense elicited testimony that the raiding party's alleged intent was to take Williams' guns to prevent a massacre of whites, not to prevent voting.[71]

Stanbery argued that "arms were put into the hands of the colored people — not of colored people generally — but of colored Radicals," and that they themselves were the only ones to interfere with the right of voting.[72] Williams "came to be regarded in the community as an outlaw and a dangerous man, and that his threats, becoming so violent and intimidating, the people saw there was nothing left but to disarm him."[73]

Accordingly, Bill Lindsay testified for the defense that he heard Williams say he would kill "from the cradle up," and his reason was that "they said he was to give up his arms."[74] John Lowry testified that "there was a state of alarm from the time that [Governor] Scott armed the blacks."[75] Unarmed white people then armed themselves but "only for defense, mind you."[76] After apparent acts of arson, Lowry advised Williams to return the arms to Governor Scott, because people were alarmed as a result of Williams' threats, but Williams refused.[77]

CLOSING ARGUMENTS AND VERDICT

The firearms issue figured prominently in closing arguments. Chamberlain ridiculed the defense claim that the events had nothing to do with interference with voting but were caused by the need to disarm threatening blacks. Quoting a statement that "we'll kill you" for "vot[ing] the Radical ticket," Chamberlain exclaimed: "Not political! Only a search for guns! All because of a panic among the white people!"[78] Chamberlain continued that "the purpose of the [Klan] was to control or affect elections," and not to "disarm individual Negroes" or the negro militia.[79] Klan members were "moved by their constant and controlling purpose, through the intimidation of this negro militia company, the disarming of these negro Radicals and the killing of their captain, to put down Radicalism itself."[80]

For the defense, Stanbery argued that his client, Mitchell, was guilty of only one count in the indictment — the Second Amendment count — which the court had dismissed: "To prevent and hinder his free exercise and enjoyment of a right and privilege granted and secured to him by the Constitution of the United States, to wit, the keeping and bearing of arms. That is the particular conspiracy stated there, gentlemen; that was precisely what my client was after. . . . That was an unlawful thing, as the law does not authorize him to break into another man's house to get his arms."[81] Stanbery contended that Mitchell was not guilty of conspiracy to interfere with the right to vote.[82] The governor had armed black militia companies with Winchester repeating rifles and denied them to whites,[83] Stanbery reminded the jury, and Williams' militia was arming and preparing for aggression.[84]

Johnson pleaded with the jury not to convict the defendants of the remaining charges simply because they were guilty of "conspiracy to deny James Williams the right to bear arms," as the judge dismissed that count of the indictment.[85] The government's evidence showed that "the object of the raid, on that night, was to get the guns from the hands of the blacks."[86] The conspiracy was not to deny Williams the right to vote but was to deny him "the right, which he had, to bear arms."[87]

In rebuttal, Corbin waxed eloquently on the history of slavery under the Constitution, alluding to the statement of the Supreme Court in *Dred Scott* "that the black man had no rights that the white man was bound to respect."[88] Corbin concluded with more of a political speech than a closing argument — he admonished every member of the Klan, "in the name of God, *disband!*"[89]

The jury found the defendant not guilty of conspiring to hinder the future exercise of the right to vote, but guilty of conspiring to injure Williams because of his color and because he had exercised the right to vote previously.[90] Bond, apparently believing the defendant's explanation that he had only held the horses at the raid and had no knowledge that Williams would be killed, sentenced Mitchell to 18 months imprisonment and a $100 fine.[91] There followed several other trials and a number of guilty pleas, but the pattern was invariably the same: black Radicals were targeted, disarmed, whipped, and murdered.[92]

APPEAL TO THE SUPREME COURT

Meanwhile, the government appealed the refusal of the trial court to allow the Second Amendment count to be tried to the U.S. Supreme Court. Procedurally, the appeal was made possible by the issuance by Judges Bond and Bryan of a certificate of division in the indictment against Avery and others over the questions of whether the court had jurisdiction over murder, and "whether the right to keep and bear arms is a right granted and secured by the Constitution of the United States."[93] The record filed with the U.S. Supreme Court included the indictment, which alleged a conspiracy to murder Williams "with intent to prevent and hinder his free exercise and enjoyment of a right and privilege granted and secured to him by the Constitution of the United States, to wit, the right to keep and bear arms, contrary to the Act of Congress."[94]

Although both the prosecution and defense wanted the Supreme Court to resolve the issue, U.S. Attorney General George Williams argued that the Supreme Court lacked jurisdiction to hear the case.[95] Williams, whose commitment to civil rights was considered weak, had recently replaced civil rights proponent Akerman as Attorney General.[96] In March 1872 Chief Justice Samuel Chase dismissed the Avery appeal for lack of jurisdiction. He based his decision on precedent that a motion to quash an indictment was determinable by the trial court as a matter of pure discretion.[97] By side-stepping the issue, the Supreme Court left unclear whether blacks had federal protection from Klan searches and firearm seizures.[98]

Nonetheless, in 1872 Corbin continued to bring indictments in cases where firearms seizure precipitated murder for violation of the right to keep and bear arms, and Judges Bond and Bryan accepted the charges with the hope that the Supreme Court would resolve the issue.[99] The issue was not brought before the Supreme Court, however, and the Second Amendment count eventually would be no longer alleged in indictments.[100]

HEARINGS ON THE KLAN BY THE JOINT SELECT COMMITTEE

With the passage of the Civil Rights Act of 1871, Congress created the Joint Select Committee to Inquire into the Condition of Affairs in the Late Insurrectionary States. From April 1871 through February 1872 the committee held hearings, deliberated, and issued a 13-volume hearing transcript that included majority and minority reports. The Senate Chairman was John Scott of Pennsylvania, and the House Chairman was Luke Poland of Vermont.

The committee focused on Ku Klux Klan activities. Reviewing the Klan's history, the majority report recalled an 1868 report from Texas that concluded that Klan objectives were "to disarm, rob, and, in many cases, murder Union men and negroes."[101] An ex-Klan member from South Carolina testified that "it was part of their business to disarm negroes."[102] The testimony of several witnesses exposed the distinctly political object of Klan activity: "negroes who were whipped testified that those who beat them told them that they did so because they had voted the radical ticket, . . . and wherever they had guns took them from them."[103]

In a typical incident, a black Georgia man testified how Klansmen broke into his house and shot him three times. The black man returned fire and shot one of the Klansmen, causing the whole group to flee.[104] In other instances, Klansmen "were indicted and convicted for having robbed some negroes of their guns and pistols."[105]

A subcommittee report appended to the majority report analyzed "the spirit of the constitutions and laws passed by the old rulers of the South in 1865–66," such as the continuation of the old South Carolina codes whereby "a free person of color was only a little lower than a slave. . . . [and hence] forbidden to carry or have arms."[106] The subcommittee report recalled an 1866 Senate report that castigated the disarming of discharged black soldiers returning home after the Civil War: "Their arms were taken from them by the civil authorities, and confiscated for the benefit of the commonwealth. The Union solider is *fined* for bearing arms. Thus the right of the people to keep and bear arms as provided in the Constitution is *infringed*."[107] The report documented firearms seizures in Alabama, where Klansmen broke into negro homes and "searched their trunks, boxes, &c., under the pretense of taking away fire-arms, fearing, as they said, an insurrection."[108]

The minority report of the Joint Select Committee painted a quite different picture. In South Carolina, the governor had furnished black militias with "arms of the most improved pattern, and ammunition in abundance; and they never had any political gatherings or any celebrations, except these companies appeared with their arms."[109] White companies were denied arms.[110] According to the minority report, black militias were disarmed in Alabama because they had marched to the polls on election day with muskets in hand and instigated violence.[111]

The minority report accused the majority of refusing to allow any investigation of conditions in Texas, which was under Radical rule.[112] It quoted extensively from the 1871 report of a subcommittee in the Texas constitutional convention appointed to consider violations of the state and federal constitutions by the state government:

The people have been disarmed throughout the State, notwithstanding their constitutional right "to keep and bear arms."

The police and State guards are armed . . . while the citizen dare not, under heavy pain and penalties, bear arms to defend himself. . . . The citizen is at the mercy of the policeman and the men of the State Guard.

By orders executed through his armed bodies of police, the executive has taken control of peaceable assemblies of the people . . . and there suppressed free speech.[113]

Based on the evidence amassed, the minority report concluded about the situation: "To-day, in South Carolina, Texas, and Arkansas, (and in

1866–'68 it was so in Tennessee and elsewhere,) the emancipated-slave regiments parade in State or Federal uniform, armed cap-a-pie with the most improved weapons, paid for by taxation imposed on their former masters; while the white men are denied the right to bear arms or to organize, even as militia, for the protection of their homes, their property, or the persons of their wives and their children."[114]

The minority report quoted the testimony of ex-Confederate General Nathan Bedford Forrest that the Klan was organized in 1866 in response to the Union Leagues and to Tennessee Governor William G. Brownlow's proclamation that his militia would kill rebels at will.[115] Forrest testified that Klan organizations were necessary for self-defense against "impudent colored people constantly toting about arms, firing in the night-time."[116] At the same time, "the white people [were] disarmed by Brownlow's orders, and forbidden, in organized bodies, to carry arms."[117] Forrest claimed that he had supported the Fourteenth Amendment.[118] In 1869, Forrest allegedly denounced the Klan because it was used "to disarm harmless negroes having no thought of insurrectionary movements, and to whip both whites and blacks."[119]

The majority and minority reports compose the first volume of the *Report of the Joint Committee*. The remaining 12 volumes consist of testimony from hearings in selected Southern states. Two interrelated themes dominated these hearings: the arming of black militias supportive of the Republican Party and the disarming of blacks at large by Klansmen. The evidence of these events is so extensive that only a sampling can be set forth here.

The index to volumes eight and nine of the hearings, which concerned Alabama, refers to more than 20 pages under the topic "Arms, colored people deprived of." There were widespread seizures of firearms by Klansmen from blacks[120] and also from whites who did not vote the Democratic ticket.[121] Although one witness testified that blacks deprived of arms never obtained redress in the courts,[122] an Alabama prosecutor noted that he had charged whites with assault for taking guns from blacks.[123]

Some white Southerners expressed resentment that blacks had acquired all the rights of the citizen. For instance, a North Carolina law officer testified that certain Indians known as the Lowry gang had resisted capture because "the use of fire-arms has been allowed to that class of people; their right to use fire-arms did not exist before the war." The congressman asking the questions responded rhetorically, "Does the fact that colored men have been permitted, since the war, to testify in the courts, affect your ability to have this gang of men arrested?"[124] Again in North Carolina, a single black man successfully defended his house with firearms from a dozen Klansmen.[125] Even blacks who publicly supported the Democrats were disarmed.[126] In Georgia, whites were routinely convicted of offenses for seizing guns.[127] The following exchange was typical regarding incidents in various states:

Q: Did you ever hear of the Ku-Klux visiting the colored people's houses for the purposes of taking their arms of defense?

A: They took the weapons from mighty near all the colored people in the neighborhood.

Q: They just came in and got their guns and pistols, and took them and left?

A: Yes, sir.[128]

One of the most compelling statements was: "They then asked me if I had a pistol. . . . One of the other men said, 'where is the rope? Hang him."[129]

The hearings documented extensively cases of blacks who had been whipped, killed, disarmed, and otherwise mistreated.[130] On the other side, although not brought out much by the Republican-controlled Committee, carpetbagger-controlled militias were deeply involved in political violence to influence elections and were blamed for infringing their opponents' constitutional rights to free speech and to keep and bear arms, among numerous other abuses.[131] In any event, the hearings confirmed that Klansmen disarmed blacks in order to intimidate, repress, and murder them.

CONGRESS' LAST EFFORTS TO PROTECT CIVIL RIGHTS

At the second session of the Forty-Second Congress in late 1871 Senator Charles Sumner attached an amendment to a bill to grant amnesty to ex-Confederates. Sumner's amendment would have prohibited discrimination in places of public accommodation and elsewhere.[132] Debate over this bill and later versions, which became the Civil Rights Act of 1875,[133] included undisputed explanations that the Fourteenth Amendment protects the right to keep and bear arms from infringement by the states.

Senator Matthew Carpenter (R-Wisc.) listed the rights of the American citizen in part with reference to *Cummings* v. *Missouri* (1866),[134] where the U.S. Supreme Court contrasted the French legal system, which allowed deprivation of civil rights, including "the right of voting, . . . [and] of bearing arms," with the U.S. legal system. The Fourteenth Amendment, argued Carpenter, prevented states from taking away these privileges of American citizens.[135]

Senator Allen Thurman (D-Ohio) argued that the "rights, privileges, and immunities of a citizen of the United States" were included in part in the first eight amendments. As to the Second Amendment, he stated: "Here is another right of a citizen of the United States, expressly declared to be his right — the right to bear arms; and this right, says the Constitution, shall not be infringed."[136] After prodding from Republican John Sherman, Thurman added the Ninth Amendment to the list of privileges and immunities.[137]

In early 1872 the House of Representatives resolved that the president report all information concerning his enforcement of the Civil Rights Act of 1871, better known to contemporaries as "An act to enforce the provisions of the fourteenth amendment."[138] In response in April 1872 President Grant sent a message to the House on the condition of affairs in the Southern States.[139] The president noted that Attorney General Akerman, the Joint Select Committee on Southern Outrages, state officials, military sources, U.S. attorneys, and repentant Klansmen had informed him that nine counties in South Carolina and other places throughout the South "were under the sway of powerful combinations popularly known as 'Ku-Klux Klans,' the objects of which were, by force and terror, to prevent all political action not in accord with the views of the members, *to deprive colored citizens of the right to bear arms* and of the right to a free ballot, to suppress schools in which colored citizens were taught, and to reduce the colored people to a condition closely akin to that of slavery"[140] (emphasis added). The president's message was referred to the joint select Committee on the Condition of the Southern States.[141]

The deprivation of the right to bear arms was mentioned in debate on a bill to extend the portion of the Civil Rights Act of 1871 allowing the president to suspend the writ of habeas corpus in states where violence had overwhelmed the authorities. Senator John Scott of Pennsylvania, the bill's sponsor and chairman of the committee that held the Klan hearings, quoted examples from South Carolina, where Klansmen seized the firearms of their victims before lynching them.[142]

Senator Daniel Pratt of Indiana observed that the Klansman "fears the gun" of a man in his "humble fortress."[143] The Klan targeted blacks who would "tell his fellow blacks of their legal rights, as for instance their right to carry arms and defend their persons and homes."[144] Even the bill's opponents did not deny that blacks had been systematically disarmed by the Klan.[145]

Meanwhile the Civil Rights Bill regarding public accommodations continued to be debated in the aftermath of the Supreme Court's 1873 *Slaughter-House* opinion, which held that a Louisiana state-granted monopoly in New Orleans that favored certain butchers did not violate privileges and immunities protected by the Fourteenth Amendment.[146] Representative James Beck (D-Ky.) argued that the bill was unconstitutional under *Slaughter-House* because it regulated private entities rather than states.[147] Beck quoted the court's reference to the privileges and immunities clause of the Fourteenth Amendment and its holding that it protects "the privileges and immunities of the citizen of the *United States*," not "the privileges and immunities of the citizens of the *State*."[148] In Beck's view, the *Slaughter-House* court agreed with the understanding that the Fourteenth Amendment protected Bill of Rights guarantees from state action, but provided no protection from private action:

The first ten amendments to the Constitution . . . assert what the rights of citizens of the United States shall be; and it is there declared that no State shall deprive them of any of these rights. They are laid down explicitly, and I will quote them at length:

Article II. A well regulated militia being necessary to the security of a free state, the right of the people to keep and bear arms shall not be infringed.

These are the rights of a citizen of the United States which the fourteenth amendment declares no State shall abridge. The Supreme Court recognizes them.[149]

Likewise, Representative Robert Mills (D-Tex.) argued that the Fourteenth Amendment was adopted because "it had been judicially determined that the first eight articles of amendment of the Constitution was not a limitation on the powers of the States."[150]

In one of the final debates over the Civil Rights Bill, Senator Thomas Norwood (D-Ga.) exposed the rights of U.S. citizenship by reference to a citizen residing in a territory of the United States:

His right to bear arms, to freedom of religious opinion, freedom of speech, and all others enumerated in the Constitution would still remain indefeasibly his, whether he remained in the Territory or removed to a State.

And those and certain others are the privileges and immunities which belong to him in common with every citizen of the United States, and which no State can take away or abridge, and they are given and protected by the Constitution.

The following are most, if not all the privileges and immunities of a citizen of the *United States*:

The right . . . of peaceable assembly and of petition; . . . to keep and bear arms.[151]

Observing that the Fourteenth Amendment created no new rights but rather declared that "certain existing rights should not be abridged by States," Norwood explained:

Before its [Fourteenth Amendment] adoption any State might have . . . restricted freedom of speech and of the press, or the right to bear arms. . . . A State could have deprived its citizens of any of the privileges and immunities contained in those eight articles, but the *Federal Government* could not.

And the instant the fourteenth amendment became a part of the Constitution, every State was at that moment disabled from making or enforcing any law which would deprive any citizen of a State of the benefits enjoyed by citizens of the United States under the first eight amendments to the Federal Constitution.[152]

Arguing in favor of the Civil Rights Bill, Senator Timothy Howe of Wisconsin did not dispute Norwood's analysis, but instead argued that Georgia, Norwood's state, failed to recognize the Fourteenth Amendment because its code allegedly guaranteed the rights to vote and to bear arms to "citizens," but not to "persons of color":

Sir, to Georgia you may look for the provisions which . . . call upon you to put in motion the latent powers with which you are clothed under the fourteenth amendment. . . . White men govern in Georgia. . . . Georgia — I read from the code of 1873 — makes rather minute divisions of persons.

"Natural persons are distinguished . . . according to their rights and status into: first, citizens; second residents not citizens; third, aliens; fourth, *persons of color*." Pretty accurate that! Says Georgia:

"Among the rights of *citizens* are the enjoyment of personal security," — Very necessary — "of personal liberty" — A convenient thing to have — "private property and the disposition thereof, the elective franchise, the right to hold office . . . , and to keep and bear arms."

It is a good thing to be a citizen in Georgia, provided Georgia recognizes you as a citizen. It is of no account to be a citizen of Georgia if you are a colored person.[153]

The Civil Rights Act of 1875 was the last Reconstruction law passed by Congress. This act contained several anti-discrimination prohibitions on private entities, such as cemeteries and theaters. Because it prohibited private conduct rather than state action, the Supreme Court less than a decade later would declare it unconstitutional.[154]

In any event, by the end of Reconstruction, both Democrats and Republicans agreed that the Fourteenth Amendment made the right to keep and bear arms, like other Bill of Rights freedoms, applicable to the states. The issue still left unresolved, however, was whether the Fourteenth Amendment protected the rights of blacks to assemble and to bear arms for protection from private violence.

NOTES

1.   Portions of the Enforcement Act of 1870, 16 Stat. 140, survive today as 18 U.S.C. § § 241, 242.

2.   United States v. Hall, 26 Fed. Cas. 79 (C.C.S.D.Ala. 1871). When later appointed to the Supreme Court, Justice Woods authored Presser v. Illinois, 116 U.S. 252 (1886), which held that an armed march in a city without a permit was not protected by the rights to assemble or bear arms.

3.   Id. at 80.

4.   Id. at 80–81.

5.   Id. at 81.

6.   Id.

7.   Id. at 82.

8.   Id.

9.   The Joint Select Committee on the Condition of Affairs in the Late Insurrectionary States reprinted the proceedings of this case. See 12 REPORT OF THE JOINT SELECT COMMITTEE 936 (1872).

10.   Id. at 938–39.

11.   Id. at 985.

12.   Id.

13.   Id.

13.   Id.

15.   PROCEEDINGS IN THE KU KLUX TRIALS AT COLUMBIA, S.C. IN THE UNITED STATES CIRCUIT COURT (Republican Printing Co. 1872).

16.   5 REPORT OF THE JOINT SELECT COMMITTEE (1872).

17.   Kermit L. Hall, *Political Power and Constitutional Legitimacy: The South Carolina Ku Klux Klan Trials, 1871-1872*, 33 EMORY L. J. 921, 928 (1984) observes: "The [Klan] riots posed fundamental questions involving the rights of blacks to keep and bear arms, to be secure from unlawful search and seizure, and to continue through their militia organizations to exercise an important voice in South Carolina politics."

Professor Hall also notes: "The blacks' guns and rifles were one of the Klan's principal targets, in part because such weapons secured to blacks an important means of sustaining their individual rights." Id. at 945. "In the heat of racial strife and lawlessness, the second amendment issue was politically and socially more important than the first amendment rights Judge Woods had sustained in United States v. Hall." Id. at 946 n. 102.

For a comprehensive study, see Lou Falkner Williams, THE GREAT SOUTH CAROLINA KU KLUX KLAN TRIALS, 1871–1872 (Ph.D. dissertation, University of Florida, 1991). A more concise analysis is included in Robert J. Kaczorowski, THE POLITICS OF JUDICIAL INTERPRETATION: THE FEDERAL COURTS, DEPARTMENT OF JUSTICE AND CIVIL RIGHTS, 1866–1876 at 122–32 (1985).

18. 3 TESTIMONY TAKEN BY THE JOINT SELECT COMMITTEE TO INQUIRE INTO THE CONDITION OF AFFAIRS IN THE LATE INSURRECTIONARY STATES 68, 70 (1872).

19. Id. at 77.

20. Corbin to Akerman, Nov. 13, 1871, in Williams, THE GREAT SOUTH CAROLINA KU KLUX KLAN TRIALS at 128.

21. Corbin to Akerman, Nov. 17, 1871, in id. at 125.

22. Akerman to Corbin, Nov. 16, 1871, in id. at 129.

23. PROCEEDINGS IN THE KU KLUX TRIALS 5 (1872).

24. Id. at 13.

25. Id.

26. Id. at 30.

27. Id. at 30–31.

28. Id. at 56–57.

29. Id. at 61.

30. Id. at 61–62.

31. Id. at 62.

32. Id. at 62–63, 66. Corbin also cited a decision from the U.S. District Court for the Southern District of Alabama, which held that the Enforcement Act's protection of "any right or privilege secured by the Constitution" included free speech and assembly. Id. at 64, citing United States v. John Maul, Jr., 5 AMERICAN LAW REVIEW 752.

33. PROCEEDINGS IN THE KU KLUX TRIALS 91–92; United States v. Crosby, 25 Fed.Cas. 701, 704 (C.C.D.S.C. 1871).

34. Id. at 142.

35. Id. at 142–43.

36. Id. at 146–47.

37. Id. at 147.

38. Id.

39. Id. at 147–48.

40. The English Declaration of Rights, § 7 (1689) provided: "That the Subjects which are Protestants, may have Arms for their Defence suitable to their Condition, and as allowed by Law." On the background of this provision and the common law origins of the right to bear arms, see Joyce L. Malcolm, TO KEEP AND BEAR ARMS: THE ORIGINS OF AN ANGLO-AMERICAN RIGHT (1994); S. Halbrook, THAT EVERY MAN BE ARMED 37–54 (1994).

41. PROCEEDINGS IN THE KU KLUX TRIALS at 148.

42. Id.

43. Id. at 149.

44.   Id. at 150.
45.   Id. at 148.
46.   Id. at 150.
47.   Id.
48.   Id.
49.   Id. at 151.
50.   Id.
51.   Id.
52.   Id. at 152.
53.   Id.
54.   Id. at 153.
55.   Id. at 164.
56.   Id. at 206.
57.   Id. at 222.
58.   Id. at 222–23.
59.   Id. at 224.
60.   Id. at 225–26.
61.   Id. at 228.
62.   Id.
63.   Id. at 230.
64.   Id. at 231.
65.   Id. at 233–34.
66.   Id. at 236–37.
67.   Id. at 340.
68.   Id. at 242.
69.   Id. at 245.
70.   Id. at 247–48.
71.   Id. at 250–51.
72.   Id. at 296.
73.   Id.
74.   Id. at 306.
75.   Id. at 330.
76.   Id.
77.   Id. at 332.
78.   Id. at 390.
79.   Id. at 393.
80.   Id.
81.   Id. at 402.
82.   Id. at 402–3.
83.   Id. at 405 ("When he armed the blacks to defend themselves, did he arm the white men to defend themselves? No; he armed the blacks and left the whites defenseless.").
84.   Id. at 406.
85.   Id. at 420–21.

86.   Id. at 426.

87.   Id. at 427.

88.   Id. at 432.

89.   Id. at 449.

90.   Id. at 449–51. See also United States v. Mitchell, 26 Fed. Cas. 1283, 1284 (C.C.D.S.C. 1871) (reciting the fact that the conspirators "robbed them [blacks] of their arms" and quoting jury charge).

91.   PROCEEDINGS IN THE KU KLUX TRIALS 457–59.

92.   Id. *passim.*

93.   United States v. Avery, 80 U.S. (13 Wall.) 251 (1872).

94.   Id.

95.   Id. at 252.

96.   Williams, THE GREAT SOUTH CAROLINA KU KLUX KLAN TRIALS at 196–99.

97.   80 U.S. at 253.

98.   See Kermit L. Hall, *Political Power and Constitutional Legitimacy: The Ku Klux Klan Trials, 1871–1872,* 33 EMORY LAW JOURNAL 921, 946–49 (1984) (concluding that the Supreme Court's avoidance of the private conduct issue influenced federal prosecutors to cease issuing indictments in South Carolina for violation of the rights to bear arms and against unreasonable search and seizure).

99.   Williams, THE GREAT SOUTH CAROLINA KU KLUX KLAN TRIALS at 209–17.

100. Id. at 217–18. According to Williams: "The goal of bringing all black citizens of South Carolina, women as well as men, under the protection of the federal government through the Second Amendment died . . . ; confusion remained on the incorporation issue." Id.

101. 1 REPORT OF THE JOINT SELECT COMMITTEE TO INQUIRE INTO THE CONDITION OF AFFAIRS IN THE LATE INSURRECTIONARY STATES 19 (Feb. 19, 1872).

102. Id. at 31.

103. Id. at 35.

104. Id. at 57–58.

105. Id. at 58.

106. Id. at 261–62.

107. Id. at 263 (quoting Freedmen's Bureau Commissioner Clinton B. Fisk).

108. Id. at 267.

109. Id. at 304.

110. Id.

111. Id. at 308.

112. Id. at 422.

113. Id. at 426.

114. Id. at 439.

115. Id. at 449–50.

116. Id.

117. Id.

118. Id., 13, at 20.

119. C. Bowers, THE TRAGIC ERA 311 (1929). Klan outrages in turn furnished "a plausible pretext for the organization of State militias to serve the purpose of Radical politics." Id.

120. 9 REPORT OF THE JOINT SELECT COMMITTEE at 683, 723–24, 1166–67.

121. Id. at 743.

122. Id. at 1166–67.

123. Id. at 667.

124. Id., 2, at 301. The war between the white Home Guards and the Lowrys, who had resisted conscription into forced labor camps during the Civil War, is related in W. Evans, TO DIE GAME: THE STORY OF THE LOWRY BAND, INDIAN GUERRILLAS OF RECONSTRUCTION (1971). Evans notes the following background:

In 1835 the North Carolina legislature had designated the Indians along the Lumber River as "free persons of color," and had taken away their right to bear arms, as well as their right to vote. From time to time the substantial planters who sat on the Robeson County Court would grant a permit to some Negro or Indian to own a firearm for such a legitimate purpose as shooting crows. But no permit had ever been issued to Calvin Lowry. Furthermore the whites would not have been pleased to learn that on his father's place, buried beneath the peas in the corncrib, was the stock of another unregistered gun, and hidden at various places about the farm were the remaining parts, not to mention a gourd of powder.

Id. at 5, citing U.S. War Dept., Records of the Army Commands (Record Group 393, National Archives), Hearings, 7–8.

125. REPORT OF THE JOINT COMMITTEE, 2, at 15, 90.

126. Id. at 392. One witness testified as follows: "I had a very respectable old colored man on my place . . . who voted the conservative ticket. He was about the first man raided in Lincoln County. On the morning afterwards I gave him a double-barreled shot gun, and told him he had a right to shoot any man who assaulted him, and assured that I would assist him and would prosecute them if I could find them out."

127. Id., 6, at 22.

128. Id., 9, at 683. For other exchanges involving firearms seizures, see id. at 689, 723, 743, 862–63, 1233.

129. Id. at 1233.

130. For example, id. at 928–31, 1162, 1165. See also id. at 779, 813, 914–15, 917, 927, and 1195.

131. For example, C. Bowers, THE TRAGIC ERA 439 and *passim* (1929); 0. Singletary, NEGRO MILITIA AND RECONSTRUCTION 35–41, 74–75 (1963).

132. CONG. GLOBE, 42nd Cong., 2d Sess. 244 (Dec. 20, 1871).

133. Portions of the Act survive today as 42 U.S.C. § 1984.

134. 71 U.S. 277, 321.

135. CONG. GLOBE, 42nd Cong., 2d Sess. 762 (Feb. 1, 1872).

136. Id., Appendix, 25–26 (Feb. 6, 1872).

137. Id.

138.	Ex. Doc. No. 268, 42nd Cong., 2d Sess. 2 (Apr. 19, 1872).
139.	Id. at 1.
140.	Id. at 2.
141.	CONG. GLOBE, 42nd Cong., 2d Sess. 2593 (Apr. 19, 1872).
142.	Id. at 3584 (May 17, 1872).
143.	Id. at 3587.
144.	Id. at 3589.
145.	See, for example, id., Appendix, 374–75 (May 20, 1872) (remarks of Senator Francis Blair).
146.	*Slaughter-House Cases*, 83 U.S. (16 Wall.) 36 (1873). See Robert C. Palmer, "The Parameters of Constitutional Reconstruction: Slaughter-House, Cruikshank, and the Fourteenth Amendment," UNIVERSITY OF ILLINOIS LAW REVIEW, No. 3, 739 (1984) (arguing that *Slaughter-House* considered the rights to assemble and to bear arms to be privileges and immunities protected from state action under the Fourteenth Amendment).
147.	CONG. GLOBE, 43rd Cong., 1st Sess. 342 (Dec. 19, 1873).
148.	Id.
149.	Id. at 342–43.
150.	CONG. GLOBE, 43rd Cong., 1st Sess. 384 (Jan. 5, 1874).
151.	Id., Appendix, 241–42 (May 4, 1874).
152.	Id. at 242.
153.	Id. at 4150 (May 22, 1874).
154.	*Civil Rights Cases*, 109 U.S. 3 (1883).

7

The *Cruikshank* Case, from Trial to the Supreme Court

GRANT PARISH, LOUISIANA: FROM RIOT TO MASSACRE

A tragic racial conflict in Louisiana in 1873 led to the last major federal prosecution against private individuals for conspiring to violate Bill of Rights freedoms, including the rights to assemble and bear arms. Known as either the "Colfax Riot" or the "Grant Parish Massacre," this tragedy led to the Supreme Court's decision in *United States* v. *Cruikshank*, which held that private individuals, unlike the states, cannot violate the Bill of Rights, and hence persons cannot be prosecuted for such conduct under the Enforcement Act.[1] The events and proceedings leading up to the *Cruikshank* decision reflected and shaped attitudes toward enforcement of the Bill of Rights at the end of the Reconstruction era. Contemporary accounts of the incident and ensuing criminal trials, including testimony concerning the facts and legal arguments about the constitutional issues raised, were recorded in New Orleans newspapers of the time.[2]

Competing Republican and Democrat factions claimed to have won the offices of judge and sheriff in Grant Parish, Louisiana, in the chaotic elections of 1872. In March 1873, a Republican faction, led by black militia leader William Ward, seized the courthouse in Colfax, the parish seat, and began arming and drilling within the city limits.[3] A party of whites led by Democrat political leader James Hadnot was repulsed by the black militia, most members of which were armed with the Enfield rifles they had carried in the Union army.[4]

Three miles east of Colfax, witnesses said an armed body of whites "shot and killed one Jesse McKinny in presence of his wife and children, he being unarmed in his own yard."[5] The murder of McKinny, a black, created panic, and blacks fled their homes in terror and flocked to the courthouse in Colfax for mutual protection.[6] Commented the *New Orleans Republican*: "The colored people appear to be roused to a high pitch of exasperation, and resolved to obtain redress for what wrongs they have suffered, or believe themselves to have suffered, and not to disband until they have also obtained security for the future. According to the most reliable reports they are well armed and disciplined, and confident of success."[7] The newspaper extolled the superior arms of the blacks: "In Grant parish, it seems there is a local majority of colored men not only trained in actual warfare, but armed with the most improved weapons."[8]

The pro-Democrat *Daily Picayune* reported that moderate whites sought the help of the governor to restore order, but the governor refused.[9] Led by carpetbaggers, the blacks who seized Colfax instituted a "reign of terror," committing robbery and murder.[10]

More than 400 blacks, "armed and equipped thoroughly," entrenched themselves in breastworks around the courthouse. A body of 150 whites led by Hadnot attacked, driving the blacks into the courthouse. Hadnot and other whites were later shot while approaching the courthouse under a flag of truce, after which the whites dislodged the blacks by setting fire to the courthouse. More than 100 blacks were shot and killed as they fled the burning building, and those who escaped were pursued.[11] On Easter Sunday, April 13, 1873, the whites had retaken Colfax.[12]

The *Republican* reported that "the courthouse at Colfax had been burned, and a large number of colored men massacred by a party under the leadership of Mr. Hadnot, who was himself wounded severely in the abdomen."[13] The official report to the Adjutant General explained that after the fight, 34 black prisoners, who had been taken before the burning of the courthouse, were taken to the river bank, two by two, executed and hurled in the river.[14] The report concluded that "not a single colored man was killed or wounded until after their surrender, and that then they were shot down without mercy."[15]

When first notified, U.S. Attorney General George H. Williams thought the Grant Parish reports were exaggerated.[16] The Attorney General's opinion changed, however, when the U.S. Attorney at New Orleans, G. R. Beckwith, wrote to him describing the incident as a massacre in which "the negroes were slaughtered" in cold blood.[17] The Attorney General instructed Beckwith to make a thorough investigation and to prosecute the perpetrators.[18]

THE FIRST *CRUIKSHANK* TRIAL

A total of 97 persons were indicted on June 16, 1873, but only a handful, including William J. Cruikshank, were apprehended. As later summarized in the Supreme Court decision, the indictment alleged a conspiracy under the Enforcement Act of 1870 as follows:

The *first* count was for banding together, with intent "unlawfully and feloniously to injure, oppress, threaten, and intimidate" two citizens of the United States, "of African descent and persons of color," "with the unlawful and felonious intent thereby" them "to hinder and prevent in their respective free exercise and enjoyment of their lawful right and privilege to peaceably assemble together with each other and with other citizens of the said United States for a peaceable and lawful purpose."

The *second* avers an intent to hinder and prevent the exercise by the same persons of the "right to keep and bear arms for a lawful purpose."

The *third* avers an intent to deprive the same persons "of their respective several lives and liberty of person, without due process of law."

The *fourth* avers an intent to deprive the same persons of the "free exercise and enjoyment of the right and privilege to the full and equal benefit of all laws and proceedings for the security of persons and property" enjoyed by white citizens.[19]

Besides several other counts, the above counts were duplicated in yet more counts except that, instead of "band together," the words "combine, conspire, and confederate together" were used.[20] The victims alleged in the indictments were Levi Nelson and Alexander Tillman.[21]

Day-to-day accounts of the Cruikshank trial were published in the *New Orleans Republican* and the *Daily Picayune*. Although expressing strong editorial opinions — the former for the prosecution, the latter in favor of the defendants — both newspapers contain valuable accounts of the testimony, arguments, and court proceedings. The prosecution's theory and the defense's objections respecting the Bill of Rights counts were well recorded.

The trial began on February 24, 1874, with Circuit Judge William B. Woods presiding over a crowded courtroom filled with witnesses, attorneys, and reporters.[22] Woods had upheld a federal indictment charging a conspiracy to violate the right of free speech in an Enforcement Act prosecution in Alabama three years earlier.[23] With an eye on getting to the Supreme Court, the defense successfully moved that Judge Edward H.

Durrell also sit in order to obtain a diversity of opinion on the case.[24] Woods denied demurrers to the indictment and proceeded to jury selection.[25]

The next day after jury selection was completed three hours were consumed by reading the indictment, which charged the defendants with "preventing one Levi Nelson and Alexander Tillman, two American citizens of African descent, from assembling in a peaceful manner, in accordance with the privilege granted them by the constitution, etc., and with killing and murdering Alexander Tillman."[26] In the coming days, scores of witnesses testified.

Nelson's testimony was particularly interesting, because he was one of the only two victims mentioned in the indictment, and one of the few survivors of the massacre. Nelson's testimony was summarized in the *Republican* as follows:

There were 300 colored men at the courthouse; one-half of the colored men had no arms; they assembled at the courthouse because they were too frightened to remain home; . . . shooting began at 6 A.M.; bullets struck where I was lying; one hit my hat, and one my shoulder; . . . they [the whites] kept up the fight all day; they told us to stack our arms and they wouldn't hurt us, and for us to march out; . . . then the[y] set the courthouse on fire; I was inside then; when I got a chance to run off I made an attempt, but a man was about to shoot me, when another man saved me, telling me to save a burning building; I did as directed, and when through I asked if I might go; he cursed me, saying he did not come 400 miles to kill niggers for nothing; . . . they made me go among the prisoners; . . . they kept me prisoner until midnight; they took me and another man out to shoot us; one bullet struck me in my neck, stunning and dropping me; the other man was killed; . . . they did not shoot me again; laid on the ground until morning; fearing to move.[27]

Nelson then identified all but one of the defendants. On cross examination, the defense sought to impeach his testimony.[28]

After the prosecution rested, the defense called Sheriff G. W. Shaw, who had been commissioned by Governor William Pitt Kellogg, to the witness stand. Shaw testified that 100 armed blacks in Colfax deposed and imprisoned him. He escaped, only to be captured and then released by whites led by the competing Sheriff Christopher Columbus Nash, who led the posse that attacked the blacks barricaded at the courthouse.[29]

The evidence closed after 14 days of testimony.[30] There followed two days of argument on the law and the facts.[31] Woods then summarized the indictment, including the counts that the defendants banded together "to intimidate them in the free exercise of their right peaceably to assemble together" and "to prevent Nelson and Tillman from bearing arms, etc."[32] The judge then instructed the jury. The *Republican* published the jury charge, which took up the entire front page. Woods charged the jury with great detail. Concerning the First Amendment, he declared:

The right of peaceable assembly is one of the rights secured by the constitution and laws of the United States. . . . The fact that they assemble with arms, provided these arms are to be used not for aggression, but for their protection, does not make the assemblage any the less a peaceable one.

If you find that the assemblage at Colfax on the thirteenth of April last, Levi Nelson and Alexander Tillman constituting a part thereof, was for a peaceable and lawful purpose, notwithstanding the members of the assembly were armed, if their arms were merely for protection, and the persons against whom the indictment is presented combined to injure, oppress, threaten or intimidate Nelson and Tillman with the purpose to prevent their peaceable assembling, or to break up a peaceable assembly of which they were members; or if the intent was so to intimidate Nelson and Tillman that they would fear to unite with this [*sic*] fellow-citizens in peaceable assemblies on future occasions, then you would be justified in the conclusion that the intent laid in this count is true.[33]

Notably, Woods emphasized that the First Amendment protected a peaceful assembly from private violation, adding that being armed for self-defense was consistent with the peaceableness of the assembly. He then proceeded to the Second Amendment count:

Next consider the intent of the banding and conspiring laid in the second count, which is alleged to be intimidate, etc., Nelson and Tillman, with the purpose to prevent their exercise of the right to keep and bear arms for a lawful purpose.

The right to bear arms is also a right secured by the constitution and laws of the United States. Every citizen of the United States has the right to bear arms, provided it is done for a lawful purpose and in a lawful manner. A man who carries his arms openly, and for his own protection, or for any other lawful purpose, has as clear a right to do so as to carry his own watch or wear his own hat. If the meeting at Colfax on April 13, of which Nelson and Tillman formed a part, was assembled, and was bearing arms for its own protection, and the banding charged in the indictment was with the intent to intimidate Nelson and Tillman so as to prevent their bearing arms on that occasion, or if the purpose of the banding together was so to intimidate them as to prevent or hinder them from lawfully bearing arms in the future, then the intent charged in this count is made out.[34]

The Second Amendment, according to Woods, protected the right of every citizen to carry arms for any lawful purpose. Recognizing that

Louisiana prohibited the bearing of concealed weapons, he stated that arms must be borne openly. Exercising the right of assembly did not limit the right to bear arms simultaneously. Woods did not mention the Fourteenth Amendment as being pertinent to the First and Second Amendments.[35]

After two days of deliberations, the jury informed the judge that, except for acquitting one defendant, it could not agree on a verdict.[36] Beckwith agreed that a mistrial should be entered, after which all of the defendants were remanded to prison on additional charges.[37] A second trial was scheduled, and the defendants remained incarcerated without bail.[38]

THE SECOND *CRUIKSHANK* TRIAL

The retrial began on May 18, 1874. Presiding over the case were U.S. Supreme Court Justice J. S. Bradley, sitting on circuit, and Circuit Judge Woods. The names of 200 witnesses were called. Defense objections to the jury were denied.[39] The *Picayune* claimed that the jury had nine whites and three blacks,[40] but the *Republican* asserted that there was only one black juror.[41]

Defense counsel R. H. Marr moved to dismiss the first 24 counts of the indictment, which included the counts relating to the rights to assemble and bear arms. Marr attacked the constitutionality of the Enforcement Act. Under the Bill of Rights, he said, "the United States shall not interfere with these inherent rights to carry arms" and "did not pretend to have any power or jurisdiction over these rights."[42] The Fourteenth Amendment, Marr continued, made the Bill of Rights applicable to state infringement, but not to private violation: "The fourteenth amendment was the first change in this power of the General Government, and that amendment provides that no State shall pass any law depriving any citizen of his right to bear arms. . . . It does not provide against personal aggression; the infringement of these inherent rights by individuals, this is left to the State; but it merely protects the citizen against the aggression of the State, of organized power."[43]

Marr and Bradley then argued over the holding in the *Slaughter-House* case. According to the *Daily Picayune*: "Justice Bradley thought that the decision of the Supreme Court in the Slaughter-House case merely meant that the rights claimed in that case were not rights mentioned in the constitution, and that the only rights that the fourteenth amendment affected were those therein mentioned."[44] Bradley's comment on *Slaughter-House* is revealing: he presumed that the Fourteenth Amendment incorporated the Bill of Rights. Bradley proceeded to note that "this same question of the constitutionality of the Ku-Klux act has come before the Supreme Court of the United States," referring to the *Avery* case from South Carolina, which the Supreme Court would dispose of without resolving the merits.[45] Bradley ended by promising a quick decision on the Enforcement Act's constitutionality.[46]

The testimony concluded on the sixteenth day of the trial.[47] Closing arguments by counsel addressed the prosecution's and the defense's views of the counts alleging violation of the rights to assemble and bear arms as applied to the facts in the case.[48] Beckwith argued that the trouble in Grant Parish started with the murder of Jesse McKinney: "It was then, and then only, that the negroes flocked into Colfax, to protect their lives and those of their wives and children." Beckwith argued that the whites had no right to break up a constitutionally protected peaceful assembly. Even if the assembly were not peaceful, Beckwith concluded, the participants should have been dispersed lawfully, not massacred.[49]

Marr assumed, for purposes of his closing argument, the validity of the indictment, and insisted that the defendants did not violate the rights alleged. Marr asserted that the troubles began weeks before McKinney was killed, when a lawless "negro army" seized the courthouse and terrorized the whites. Asserting that this was a conspiracy, not a peaceful assembly, Marr argued that "no attempt had ever been made to prevent the negroes peaceably assembling, or to take away their arms or right of voting; yet the prisoners were charged with this merely because they tried to open the Court-House to business to all the people of the parish, black or white."[50]

The next day, defense counsel W. S. Bryan, who was also a judge, continued the same theme, arguing both the facts and the law.[51] According to a possibly garbled newspaper account, he contended that, under the Bill of Rights, "the Federal Government shall in no wise interfere with the right of citizens to bear arms peaceably to assemble."[52] He curiously referred to "these natural rights" as "applicable only to the United States, not to the individual States," but did not mention the Fourteenth Amendment.[53]

Defense counsel William R. Whitaker focused on the murder counts, which were matters exclusively within the jurisdiction of the state courts.[54] Besides, Whitaker argued, the "mob" at Colfax was not a peaceable assembly, and its members were not bearing arms for a lawful purpose.[55]

The crowded court heard defense counsel John Ellis argue that the defendants were serving as a posse under the sheriff and could not be liable.[56] "Mr. Ellis wound up with a vivid picture of the peaceful assemblage of the negroes at Colfax, engaged in peacefully robbing, threatening and murdering: being frequently interrupted in his speech by bursts of subdued applause."[57] Woods ordered the deputy sheriffs to arrest anyone disrupting the proceedings, after which Beckwith made his rebuttal argument. Woods then instructed the jury almost identically as in the previous trial.[58]

Two days later, the jury returned a verdict.[59] All defendants were acquitted of murder, and five defendants were acquitted of all other charges as well. Cruikshank and two others were acquitted of 16 counts, but found guilty of 16 counts of conspiracy "to prevent the peaceable assemblage of the negroes, to prevent their voting, bearing arms and generally taking away their rights."[60]

Anticipating the sentencing phase, counsel conceded that two defendants were in the fight, but incredulously asserted that Cruikshank "had entered Colfax after the court house was burnt to save a negro's life and had left immediately."[61] The *Picayune* recalled that Bradley had promised to return to hear the motion in arrest of judgment concerning "the constitutionality of the Ku-Klux act, so that this question can reach the Supreme Court."[62] Meanwhile, the prosecution announced that it would bring identical indictments against all the defendants with the substitution of William Williams for Tillman as the victim.[63]

Marr made a post-verdict motion based on jury irregularities, extolling the virtues of the jury system by "the framers of the great palladium of our liberties."[64] The *Republican* responded with an editorial arguing that the jury system had "fallen through," and arguing that "the colored folks will hereafter depend to some extent upon the same weapons for defense that their enemies use for attack. A jury is really no match for a firearm."[65] The editorial continued: "If it be generally known that in each negro cabin in the country there is a lively weapon of defense, there will not be such a constant recurrence of homicides as have disgraced the annuals of this State for many years. We expect these shotguns to prove famous peacemakers."[66]

JUSTICE BRADLEY'S OPINION

On June 27, 1874, Woods denied the defendants' motion for a new trial.[67] However, Bradley ordered an arrest of judgment and released the prisoners on bail.[68] Bradley gave an oral rendition of his decision from the bench, subjecting each count to a "critical analysis."[69] As to the count charging conspiracy to prevent the exercise of the right to bear arms, Bradley ruled: "The United States courts have no jurisdiction over a violation by an individual of the right of another to bear arms."[70] He made the same ruling on the count charging private interference with a lawful assembly.[71]

Woods announced that he differed from Bradley's opinion and that their certificate of division would send the case to the Supreme Court. Bail was set in the amount of $5,000 for Cruikshank and his two co-defendants.[72]

The *Picayune* opined that Bradley's opinion doomed any further prosecutions on the same theories.[73] "As Judge Bradley consulted with his brethren of the Supreme Court on his recent visit to Washington, we are justified in assuming that this is the authentic exposition of the act of Congress known as the Ku-Klux law."[74]

The *Republican* was as disappointed as the *Picayune* was exhilarant. Although Bradley's views were counterbalanced by those of Judge Woods, further reforms would be necessary if Bradley's holding prevailed: "under this modern interpretation of the law, Congress is the only thing that is forbidden to break up a peaceable assembly of citizens or to take their arms from them. Anybody else may violate these wise regulations with impunity, and the army and judiciary of the United States be compelled to stand idly by."[75]

Bradley began his formal, written opinion by summarizing the indictment and the pertinent provisions of the Enforcement Act.[76] The issue was whether legislation enforcing the Fourteenth Amendment could encompass a private conspiracy to disperse an assembly, seize arms, and murder the participants. To Bradley, the answer was obvious: "When it is declared that no state shall deprive any person of life, liberty, or property without due process of law, this declaration is not intended as a guaranty against the commission of murder, false imprisonment, robbery, or any other crime committed by individual malefactors."[77] The Fourteenth Amendment was intended to check "the exertion of arbitrary and tyrannical power on the part of the government and legislature of the state."[78] Murder, robbery, and other ordinary crimes "are cognizable only in the state courts, unless, indeed, the state should deny to the class of persons referred to the equal protection of the laws."[79]

Bradley asked about count one of the indictment, which alleged a conspiracy to interfere with the right to peaceable assembly: "Does this disaffirmance of the power of congress to prevent the assembling of the people amount to an affirmative power [of Congress] to punish individuals for disturbing assemblies?"[80] Bradley concluded that Congress did not have such power, but that such punishment "is prerogative of the states."[81]

Bradley proceeded to ask whether anything had occurred since the adoption of the original Bill of Rights to change the situation. To Bradley, the Fourteenth Amendment prohibited the states from violating the rights to assemble and bear arms, but did not apply to a private conspiracy:

The 14th amendment declares that no state shall by law abridge the privileges or immunities of citizens of the United States. *Grant that this prohibition now prevents the states from interfering with the right to assemble*, as being one of such privileges and immunities, still, does it give congress power to legislate over the subject? . . . If the amendment is not violated, it has no power over the subject.

The second count, which is for conspiracy to interfere with certain citizens in *their right to bear arms*, is open to the same criticism as the first. . . . In none of these counts is there any averment that the state had, by its laws interfered with any of the rights referred to.[82] (emphasis added)

Thus, Bradley recognized the incorporation of the First and Second Amendments into the Fourteenth Amendment, but not the latter's application to purely private deprivations of the rights declared therein. The indictment could not stand.

For some, Bradley's opinion spelled the end of civil rights enforcement.[83] Although the opinion precluded further indictments against private individuals, Bradley recognized that the Fourteenth Amendment was intended to incorporate the Bill of Rights against the states. In an earlier opinion, Bradley had written that the Civil Rights Act of 1866 "is in direct conflict with those state laws which forbade a free colored person . . . from having firearms."[84] Unfortunately, *Cruikshank* raised no issues of state action.

THE BRIEFS FILED IN THE SUPREME COURT IN *CRUIKSHANK*

As noted, because Woods disagreed with Bradley's decision, *Cruikshank* was certified to the Supreme Court. The brief for the United States in *Cruikshank* was signed by Attorney General Williams and Solicitor General S. F. Phillips.[85] The brief described the counts of the indictment as alleging the conspiracy's objectives as being the hinderance of citizens of African descent from "(1) peaceably assembling together, (2) bearing arms, (3) enjoying life and liberty."[86] The brief otherwise neglected these subjects altogether, confining itself to discussion of the law of conspiracy. It seems incredible that, given the prosecution's theory of the case in the trial court and the fact that the issues were before the Supreme Court, the government's brief contained no mention of the First or Second Amendments, only one superficial reference to the Fourteenth Amendment,[87] and no discussion of the state action requirement.[88] Williams and Phillips simply abandoned any effort to uphold the counts alleging violation of the rights to assemble and to bear arms, in effect conceding that the indictment was insufficient.[89] As one scholar concluded: "Black Americans did not have their 'day in court' because the Attorney General of the United States did not present the Supreme Court with legal theories of civil rights enforcement most favorable to their cause."[90]

The issue of whether the Fourteenth Amendment incorporated the rights to assemble and to bear arms was not briefed by the defendants either, undoubtedly because only a private conspiracy was shown. Four separate briefs were filed for the defendants. Marr's brief formulated the issue as whether "that power has been conferred upon Congress to protect individual citizens by punitive legislation, against the violation of these right[s] [assembly and bearing arms] by individuals."[91] His answer was, of course, that the Constitution does not "undertake to protect individuals in the several States, against the acts of individuals."[92] The Bill of Rights did not "grant or secure" rights, it "simply recognize[s] them as existing rights, derived from some other source."[93] Moreover, the prohibitions of the Fourteenth and Fifteenth Amendments "are addressed to governments — to organized power alone," and the State of Louisiana had not "violated the provisions of these Amendments."[94]

Marr also argued for restrictive interpretations of the First and Second Amendments. The First Amendment protects the right peaceably to assemble "for the purpose of petitioning the government for a redress of grievances," not, as the indictment alleged, "for a lawful purpose."[95] Similarly, the Second Amendment protected the right to bear arms "for the purpose of maintaining, in the States, a well regulated militia," not, as the indictment alleged, "for a lawful purpose."[96] Marr nonetheless conceded that "the right of self-defence is a natural right; and the right to keep and bear such arms as may be necessary for that purpose cannot be questioned."[97] Even if the Second Amendment guarantees the right to bear arms for a lawful purpose, Marr continued, the indictment "does not charge what the lawful purpose was, for which arms were to be kept and borne, nor does it set forth either the time or place at which they were to be kept and borne, nor the acts by which this alleged right was to be interfered with."[98]

John Campbell, who as counsel for the butchers in *Slaughter-House* argued for a broad interpretation of the Fourteenth Amendment, now represented the defendants and argued for a narrow interpretation. His brief contended that private interference with assemblies and arms-bearing was a matter for state authorities.[99] The First Amendment's prohibition on denial of the right to assemble "contains no implication of control, superintendence, allowance or prevention of such assembles."[100] Campbell added:

The same objections apply to the counts which charge the object of the conspiracy to disturb the exercise of the right to keep and bear arms. This is not a right derived from or secured in the Constitution of the United States. The second amendment to the constitution, denies to the government power to infringe that right. . . . The privilege of citizens to keep and bear arms, for a lawful purpose, is not a right or privilege which the United States granted, nor its government charged to guard and to guarantee; nor is an interference with this right an offense against any law of the United States.[101]

Campbell ended with the obvious point that the indictment alleged private conspiracy, as if "these commands in the first section of the 14th Amendment were addressed to each and every inhabitant in the State," and failed to allege state action.[102] To Campbell, the Fourteenth Amendment was but "an additional guarantee to existing rights and liberties" against "tyrannical legislation" of the states.[103]

The brief of Philip Phillips and David S. Bryon[104] argued that *Slaughter-House* decided that assembly "is one of the rights of citizens of the United States, resulting not from any particular article of the Constitution, but from the general nature of the government."[105] Similarly, the brief continued, quoting a phrase from Woods's jury instruction: "The right to bear arms is not guaranteed by the Constitution of the United States. It has been said that 'a man who carries his arms openly, and for his own protection, or for any other lawful purpose, has as clear a right to do so, as to carry his own watch or wear his own hat.' The right to bear arms . . . is a matter to be regulated and controlled by the State, . . . and the United States have nothing whatever to do with it; either to support the right or abridge it."[106]

A fourth brief was submitted by David Dudley Field,[107] brother of Justice Stephen J. Field, who sat on the U.S. Supreme Court at the time. Consisting of very short arguments, the brief asserted: "That the right to assemble, the right to keep and bear arms, the right to life, liberty and property, the right to vote, and the rights, privileges, and immunities belonging to, or granted and secured to the citizens of the States, are not within the control of Congress, but remain under the exclusive control of the States."[108]

In sum, the brief for the United States made no mention of the First and Second Amendments or the counts alleging violations thereof, nor did it address whether the Fourteenth Amendment protected the rights to assemble or bear arms. The defendants' briefs conceded that assembly and arms-bearing for lawful purposes were natural rights, but argued that these rights preexisted the Constitution and thus were not "granted or secured" by it. All four of the defendants' briefs argued that Congress could pass no law infringing the rights to assemble or bear arms. The common thread in all of the defendants' briefs was the position that the indictment alleged only private action, whereas the Fourteenth Amendment provided protection only from state action.

United States v. *Cruikshank* was argued in the Supreme Court on March 30, 31, and April 1, 1875. Williams and S. Phillips argued for the United States, and Johnson, Field, P. Phillips, and Marr argued for the defendants.[109] Johnson, a Democrat leader in the Congress that passed the Fourteenth Amendment, had prevailed on the same issues in the earlier South Carolina Klan trials. *Cruikshank* was reargued in October 1875.[110]

THE CONGRESSIONAL INVESTIGATION

Before the Supreme Court reached its decision, the House of Representatives convened a Select Committee on the Condition of the South, which held hearings on the Grant Parish massacre and other incidents. Beckwith, who prosecuted the *Cruikshank* case, gave a lengthy statement of the facts.[111] When asked why he had not taken action to prevent the massacre, after Judge W. R. Rutland came to his office and sought criminal complaints against lawless blacks, Beckwith responded that he did not have sufficient evidence and that he thought federal troops had been dispatched to keep the peace, but they had not in fact.[112]

Another witness was Marr, counsel for Cruikshank, who also gave a detailed account.[113] Although his Supreme Court brief gave an equivocal rendition of the Second Amendment, he made no hair-splitting legal arguments in response to questions by the committee about his leadership of what he described as a group of armed citizens in New Orleans who took to the streets in response to mobs.[114]

Louisiana's Governor Kellogg was called to testify.[115] Kellogg traced the troubles back to the Democratic legislature of 1865, which "passed a number of laws reducing the colored people to a condition of virtual peonage," such as the vagrant law and the law "prohibiting carrying fire-arms on plantations without consent of owner."[116] Tracing matters up to the Grant Parish massacre, Kellogg testified that relative quiet prevailed once the prosecutions started. However, Bradley's decision dismissing the indictments "was regarded as establishing the principle that hereafter no white man could be punished for killing a negro, and as virtually wiping the Ku-Klux law off the statute-books."[117] As a consequence, "there were rumors that the negroes were arming."[118]

The Report of the Majority of the Select Committee was unkind to Kellogg, finding that he was elected only through fraud and the use of federal troops.[119] Signaling the end of Reconstruction, the report recommended no civil rights initiatives.

Representative George Hoar, chairman of the committee, and two other members submitted a report with their views.[120] It traced Louisiana's troubles, once again, to the Democratic legislature of 1865, which had enacted a series of laws "designed to restore the negro to a state of practical servitude," including the firearms prohibition that "depriv[ed] the great mass of the colored laborers of the State of the right to keep and bear arms."[121]

Bringing matters up to the Colfax massacre, the Hoar report mentioned what happened when the white forces first confronted the blacks: "a large body of whites rode into town, and demanded of the colored men that they should give up their arms and yield possession of the court-house."[122] This part of the episode, of course, gave rise to the Second Amendment allegation in the indictment.

THE SUPREME COURT'S
DECISION IN *CRUIKSHANK*

In November 1875 the justices decided among themselves that the *Cruikshank* indictments were defective. After initially assigning the writing of the opinion to Justice Nathan Clifford, Chief Justice Morrison Waite later decided to write the opinion himself.[123] The Court handed down its decision on March 27, 1876.[124]

Waite's opinion affirmed the opinion of the circuit court written by Bradley, who joined in the court's opinion.[125] Bradley's lower court opinion unequivocally stated that the Fourteenth Amendment protected the rights to assemble and bear arms from infringement by the states, but concluded that no state action had been alleged.[126]

True to the issues as framed by the United States and the defendants, the Supreme Court did not consider whether the Fourteenth Amendment incorporated the rights to assemble and keep and bear arms against the states. Instead, the *Cruikshank* court resolved that private action cannot constitute a violation of the rights guaranteed by the Constitution.

The court set the tone of the opinion by explaining that the federal government has limited, enumerated powers and that the states are sovereign within their spheres.[127] The court concluded that all rights that are not "granted or secured" by the Constitution or laws — terms of art in the Enforcement Act — "are left under the protection of the States."[128]

As for the indictment for conspiracy to deprive "citizens of the United States, of African descent and persons of color" of "rights and privileges 'granted and secured' to them" by the Constitution and laws,[129] the court stated about the alleged violation of the First Amendment:

The right of the people peaceably to assemble for lawful purposes existed long before the adoption of the Constitution of the United States. In fact, it is and always had been, one of the attributes of citizenship under a free government. It "derives its source . . . from those laws whose authority is acknowledged by civilized man throughout the world." It is found wherever civilization exists. It was not, therefore, a right granted to the people by the Constitution. The government of the United States when established found it in existence, with the obligation on the part of the States to afford it protection. As no direct power over it was granted to Congress, it remains . . . subject to State jurisdiction.[130]

Thus, because the right to assemble predated the Constitution, it was not granted by the Constitution and thus was not protected under the Enforcement Act. The court did not address whether the right was secured by the Constitution, which could have been consistent with the right existing before the adoption of the Constitution.

Noting that the First Amendment prohibits Congress from abridging the right to assemble, the court continued: "This, like the other amendments proposed and adopted at the same time, was not intended to limit the powers of the State governments in respect to their own citizens, but to operate upon the National government alone."[131] For that proposition, the court cited *Barron* v. *Baltimore*, which held that the Bill of Rights did not restrain state action.[132] That case, of course, was decided 35 years before the adoption of the Fourteenth Amendment, which the court did not mention in this part of the *Cruikshank* opinion. However, the court hastened to add: "The particular amendment now under consideration assumes the existence of the right of the people to assemble for lawful purposes, and protects it against encroachment by Congress. The right was not created by the amendment; neither was its continuance guaranteed, except as against congressional interference. For their protection in its enjoyment, therefore, the people must look to the States. The power for that purpose was originally placed there, and it has never been surrendered to the United States."[133]

In other words, Congress could not abridge the right to assemble. For protection of this right from private violence, however, citizens must look to their state government. Because state action was not alleged in the indictment, the court did not consider whether a federal remedy existed if the states should violate the right to assemble.[134]

Regarding the counts of the indictment alleging private infringement of the right to bear arms, the court applied identical reasoning:

The second and tenth counts are equally defective. The right there specified is that of bearing arms for a lawful purpose. This is not a right granted by the Constitution. Neither is it in any manner dependent upon that instrument for its existence. The second amendment declares that it shall not be infringed; but this, as has been seen, means no more than that it shall not be infringed by Congress. This is one of the Amendments that has no other effect than to restrict the powers of the national government, leaving the people to look for their protection against any violation by their fellow-citizens of the rights it recognizes to what is called, in *The City of New York* v. *Miln*, 11 Pet. 139, the "powers which relate to merely municipal legislation, or what was, perhaps, more properly called internal police," "not surrendered or restrained" by the Constitution of the United States.[135]

Once again, like the right to assemble, the right to bear arms was not "granted" by the Constitution and was not "dependent" on the Constitution "for its existence" because the right existed independently of, and long antedated, the Constitution. However, Congress had no authority to protect persons against the private infringement of the right to bear arms, which, like other local crimes, was a liberty or property interest for the states to protect.

Although the Second Amendment declares broadly that the right to have arms "shall not be infringed," the First Amendment states only "Congress shall make no law" abridging the right to assemble. The court nonetheless applied the same analysis to both. The court had no reason to address violation of First or Second Amendment rights by the states or to consider whether the Fourteenth Amendment protected these rights from the states.

The court then applied the same analysis to the counts alleging that defendants intended to deprive the victims of life or liberty without due process of law.[136] The court saw this as an alleged conspiracy to imprison falsely and to murder within a state. "The rights of life and personal liberty are natural rights of man."[137] However, protection of life and liberty from private violence was a matter for state protection. "It is no more the duty or within the power of the United States to punish for a conspiracy to falsely imprison or murder within a State, than it would be to punish for false imprisonment or murder itself."[138]

The Court emphasized that the Fourteenth Amendment's due process clause "adds nothing to the rights of one citizen as against another. It simply furnishes an additional guaranty against any encroachment by the State upon the fundamental rights which belong to every citizen as a member of society."[139] Similarly, the equal protection clause does not "add anything to the rights which one citizen has under the Constitution against another."[140]

The court deemed all of the counts alleging violation of voting rights to be defective as well,[141] and said of counts alleging that the defendants intended to put the victims in fear of bodily harm on account of voting: "Certainly, it will not be claimed that the United States have the power or are required to do mere police duty in the States. If a State cannot protect itself against domestic violence, the United States may, upon the call of the executive, when the legislature cannot be convened, lend their assistance for that purpose. This is a guaranty of the Constitution (art. 4, sect. 4); but it applies to no case like this."[142]

Clifford filed what he called a dissenting opinion in *Cruikshank*, but actually he had only different reasons why he thought the indictment was defective.[143] Noting that in its brief the United States had abandoned the defense of all counts of the indictment except three counts, Clifford stated that only those three counts should have been considered by the court.[144] Under that reasoning, the court should not have considered the counts alleging violation of the First and Second Amendments. Clifford found the three counts not abandoned by the government's argument to be overly general and defective.[145]

Whatever its constitutional grounds, *Cruikshank* did not protect the rights of blacks to assemble and to have arms to protect the assembly — or, indeed, life itself. *Cruikshank* was the death knell of prosecutions of private persons for violation of Bill of Rights guarantees under the Enforcement Act, and heralded the end of Reconstruction.[146] Even so, *Cruikshank* had no occasion to consider whether the Fourteenth Amendment protects the rights to assemble and to bear arms from state infringement.

NOTES

1. United States v. Cruikshank, 92 U.S. 542 (1876).

2. In addition, extensive hearings were held in Congress two years after the event. See House Report 261, 43rd Cong., 2d Sess. (1875). For an early–twentieth century account that included interviews with some of the participants, see Manie W. Johnson, *The Colfax Riot of April, 1873*, 18 LOUISIANA HIST. Q. 391 (1930). For a contemporary analysis of the trials and the Supreme Court decision, see Robert J. Kaczorowski, THE POLITICS OF JUDICIAL INTERPRETATION: THE FEDERAL COURTS, DEPARTMENT OF JUSTICE AND CIVIL RIGHTS, 1866–1876, at 175–228 (1985).

3. "The Riot in Grant Parish," *New Orleans Republican*, Apr. 10, 1873, at 1.

4. "Troubles in Grant Parish," *New Orleans Republican*, Apr. 11, 1873, 1.

5. "The Troubles in Grant Parish," *New Orleans Republican*, Apr. 12, 1873, 1.

6. Id.

7. "The Strife in Grant Parish," *New Orleans Republican*, Apr. 12, 1873, at 4.

8. Id.

9. *The Daily Picayune* (New Orleans, La.), Apr. 15, 1873, at 4.

10. Id., Apr. 16, 1873, at 4.

11. Id., at 1.

12. Id.

13. "From Grant Parish: Horrible Massacre," *New Orleans Republican*, Apr. 16, 1873, at 1.

14. "From Grant Parish: Official Report of Staff Officers," *New Orleans Republican*, Apr. 18, 1873, at 1.

15. Id. John Lewis, a black Louisiana legislator, later recalled: "They attempted [armed self-defense] in Colfax. The result was that on Easter Sunday of 1873, when the sun went down that night, it went down on the corpses of two hundred and eighty negroes." Ted Tunnell, CRUCIBLE OF RECONSTRUCTION: WAR, RADICALISM, AND RACE IN LOUISIANA 1862–1877, at 190–91 (Baton Rouge, La., 1984).

16. Id., Apr. 17, 1873, at 1.

17. Id., Apr. 18, 1873 (afternoon edition), at 1. Further factual accounts are set forth in id., Apr. 18, 1873 (morning edition), at 1.

18. "The Colfax Massacre," *New Orleans Republican*, Apr. 19, 1873, at 1. The *Picayune* complained that the Attorney General was not informed that Beckwith and others had refused to take action, including sending in federal troops, when the Radicals and armed blacks originally took over Colfax. Ten days before the "massacre," why had not Beckwith notified Washington that "a riotous assembly of misguided negroes had driven" both whites and some blacks from Colfax, and "were plundering the neighborhood with impunity?" Governor

Kellogg was also criticized for not taking action before things got out of hand. *Daily Picayune*, Apr. 21, 1873, at 1, 4.

19.   United States v. Cruikshank, 92 U.S. 542, 544–45 (1876).

20.   Id. at 545.

21.   Id. at 548. Although not mentioned in the Supreme Court summary, another 16 counts charged the defendants with murder in executing the conspiracy. United States v. Cruikshank, 25 Fed. Cas. 707, 708 (C.C.D.La. 1874).

22.   *The Daily Picayune* (New Orleans), Feb. 24, 1874, at 1. See also id., Feb. 22, 1874, at 4 (announcing coming trial and naming defendants and attorneys).

23.   United States v. Hall, 26 Fed. Cas. 79 (C.C.S.D.Ala. 1871).

24.   *The Daily Picayune* (New Orleans), Feb. 24, 1874, at 1.

25.   Id.

26.   Id., Feb. 25, 1874, at 1.

27.   "The Grant Parish Prisoners," *New Orleans Republican*, Feb. 18, 1874, at 5. The *Picayune* published a similar summary of Nelson's testimony:

I came from the Mirabean Plantation to Colfax; I was present in the fort and subsequently retired to the court-house with the other negroes; the building was fired and the negroes rushed out — some crawled under the floor and were burned, others were shot, and quite a number were captured. I amongst them; I heard Nash say he had thirty-seven prisoners; the white men then numbered about 300; they quarreled as to killing the prisoners. Nash did not wish to shoot us, but the others compelled him. We were marched out in the middle of the night to the fort in squads and by couples, and shot by the white men. I was marched out with another man, and they fired at us. My companion received five wounds in the head and was killed. I received a wound in the neck, fell down and pretended to be dead. The next morning nobody was there, and I got up and walked home.

The Daily Picayune (New Orleans), Feb. 28, 1874, at 4.

28.   Id.

29.   *The Daily Picayune* (New Orleans), Mar. 6, 1874, at 2.

30.   Id., Mar. 11, 1874, at 8.

31.   Id., Mar. 13, 1874, at 1.

32.   Id., Mar. 14, 1874, at 4.

33.   "The Grant Parish Prisoners," *New Orleans Republican*, Mar. 14, 1874, at 1.

34.   Id.

35.   Id. Instead, he charged the jury that the Fourteenth Amendment protected the right to due process, and thus that it was an indictable federal offense to kill someone because it deprived that person of life and liberty without due process. If Nelson and Tillman were committing a crime, the judge instructed, they were entitled to a jury trial and other elements of due process. Id.

36.   "The Grant Parish Prisoners," *New Orleans Republican*, Mar. 17, 1874, at 1.

37.   Id.

38.   *The Daily Picayune* (New Orleans), Apr. 28, 1874, at 8.

39.   Id., May 19, 1874, at 1. See also id. at 4.

40.   Id., May 20, 1874, at 1.

41.   "The Grant Parish Prisoners," *New Orleans Republican*, May 19, 1874, at 1.

42.   *The Daily Picayune* (New Orleans), May 22, 1874, at 8.

43.   Id.

44.   Id.

45.   Id. See United States v. Avery, 80 U.S. (13 Wall.) 251, 20 L.Ed. 610 (1872).

46.   Id.

47.   Id., June 5, 1874, at 8.

48.   Id., June 6, 1874, at 1.

49.   Id.

50.   Id.

51.   Id., June 7, 1874, at 2.

52.   Id. The reference to "the right of citizens to bear arms peaceably to assemble," while awkward, may have accurately quoted Bryan, because peaceably would modify both bearing arms and assembly, and the assembly was armed.

53.   Id.

54.   Id.

55.   Id.

56.   Id., June 9, 1874, at 2.

57.   Id.

58.   Id.

59.   Id., June 11, 1874, at 1.

60.   Id.

61.   Id.

62.   Id.

63.   Id.

63.   "The Grant Parish Prisoners," *New Orleans Republican*, June 21, 1874, 1.

65.   Id. at 4.

66.   Id.

67.   *The Daily Picayune* (New Orleans), June 28, 1874, at 2.

68.   Id.

69.   "The Grant Parish Case," *New Orleans Republican*, June 28, 1874, at 1.

70.   Id.

71.   Id.

72.   *The Daily Picayune* (New Orleans), June 28, 1874, at 2.

73.   Id., June 28, 1874, at 4.

74.   Id., June 30, 1874, at 4.

75. "The Ku Klux Law in the Circuit Court," *New Orleans Republican*, June 30, 1874, at 2.

76. United States v. Cruikshank, 25 Fed. Cas. 707, 708–10 (C.C.D.La. 1874).

77. Id. at 710.

78. Id.

79. Id. at 712.

80. Id. at 714.

81. Id.

82. Id. at 714–15.

83. Kaczorowski, THE POLITICS OF JUDICIAL INTERPRETATION at 183–88.

84. Blyew v. United States, 80 U.S. 581, 643 (1872) (Bradley, J., dissenting).

85. Brief for the United States, United States v. Cruikshank, No. 609, U.S. Supreme Court, at 27.

86. Id. at 2.

87. Id. at 6.

88. The circumstance of lack of state action perhaps is why "it does not seem to have been argued that the Fourteenth Amendment made the Bill of Rights applicable to the states." S. Morrison, *Does the Fourteenth Amendment Incorporate the Bill of Rights?* 2 STAN. L. REV. 140, 145–46 (1949).

89. Robert J. Kaczorowski, THE POLITICS OF JUDICIAL INTERPRETATION: THE FEDERAL COURTS, DEPARTMENT OF JUSTICE AND CIVIL RIGHTS, 1866–1876, at 206 (1985) concluded about the authors of the brief for the United States: "They capitulated to the opponents of national civil rights enforcement, for they failed to propose a legal theory supporting the broad authority of the national government to enforce civil rights. . . . They abandoned the effort to defend the other counts charging the defendants with infringing specific Bill of Rights guarantees of freedom of assembly and the right to keep and bear arms, and Fourteenth Amendment guarantees to due process and equal protection."

Similarly, Lou Falkner Williams, THE GREAT SOUTH CAROLINA KU KLUX KLAN TRIALS, 1871–1872, at 259 (Ph.D. dissertation, University of Florida, 1991) notes: "The legal representatives of the United States completely abdicated any responsibility to uphold the constitutionally novel aspects of the case. . . . Thus the nation's top legal spokesmen chose never to argue the First and Second Amendment issues before the nation's high tribunal."

90. Kaczorowski, THE POLITICS OF JUDICIAL INTERPRETATION at 207.

91. Brief of R. H. Marr, United States v. Cruikshank, at 7.

92. Id. at 9.

93. Id. at 10.

94. Id. at 21.

95. Id. at 25.

96. Id. at 26.

97. Id.

98. Id.

99. Brief for Defendants, Cruikshank v. United States, No. 609, at 5 (1875).

100. Id. at 5–6.

101. Id.

102. Id. at 25.

103. Id. at 26.

104. Brief for Defendants, United States v. C. C. Nash, No. 609, U.S. Supreme Court. This brief also listed William R. Whitaker and E. John Ellis as of counsel.

105. Id. at 10.

106. Id. at 10–11.

107. Brief for the Defendants, United States v. Cruikshank, No. 609, U.S. Supreme Court.

108. Id. at 6.

109. United States v. Cruikshank, 92 U.S. 542, 547, 23 L.Ed. 588, 589–90 (1876).

110. C. Peter Magrath, MORRISON R. WAITE 125 (1963). The only surviving copy of oral argument is that of Field. It was an eloquent speech on the limited powers of the federal government, but did not mention the rights to assemble or bear arms, or the incorporation of these rights in the Fourteenth Amendment. Argument of David D. Field, United States v. Cruikshank, No. 609, reprinted in 7 LANDMARK BRIEFS AND ARGUMENTS OF THE SUPREME COURT OF THE UNITED STATES: CONSTITUTIONAL LAW at 420.

111. House Report 261, 43rd Cong., 2d Sess., part 3, at 409 (1875) (testimony of Jan. 22, 1875).

112. Id. at 419.

113. Id. at 468.

114. A spontaneous uprising occurred on September 14, 1874, Marr claimed, "because the conviction was upon the minds of the people that they were to be deprived of their right to bear arms, and the negroes were to be armed." Id. at 488. Marr elaborated: "The arms with which the white people were providing themselves in the city of New Orleans were seized, and I am quite sure that a small part of the force that had a conflict with the police down here at the foot of Canal street had gone down to get some arms on the steamship Mississippi, and . . . the outbreak was the result of the seizure of arms, and the apprehension that filled the minds of the people here that the colored people were well provided with arms, and being trained in the use of arms, and the white people were to be disarmed." Id. at 489.

The Daily Picayune (New Orleans), Sept. 10, 1874, at 1, commenting on the above arms seizure, editorialized: "The right of an American citizen to possess and bear arms is guaranteed him by the constitution. The right of a merchant to sell and of an individual to buy arms, is beyond all question." After freedmen had complained for ten years about being disarmed by whites, the whites were complaining about the police disarming them. Perhaps the incorporation of the Bill of Rights into the Fourteenth Amendment was not such a bad idea after all.

115.   House Report 261, 43rd Cong., 2d Sess., part 3, at 242 (1875).

116.   Id. at 243.

117.   Id. at 246.

118.   Id. The Governor also defended police actions directed at Democrats in New Orleans, including seizures of arms shipments, leading the Democrats to charge that their rights to assemble and keep and bear arms were infringed. Id. at 252–54. He claimed that the seizures were made with due process and that the arms were destined to members of White League Clubs. Id. at 253.

119.   Id., Part 1, at 3–4.

120.   Id. at 5.

121.   Id. at 10.

122.   Id. at 13.

123.   C. Peter Magrath, MORRISON R. WAITE 125–26 (1963).

124.   United States v. Cruikshank, 23 L.Ed. 588, 589–90 (1876).

125.   United States v. Cruikshank, 92 U.S. 542 (1876).

126.   Bradley's circuit court opinion would be cited as authority by the court as late as Jones v. Mayer Co., 392 U.S. 409, 441 n. 78 (1968).

127.   92 U.S. at 549–51.

128.   Id. at 551.

129.   Id. at 548.

130.   Id. at 551–52.

131.   Id. at 552.

132.   Id., citing Barron v. Baltimore, 7 Pet. 250.

133.   Id. at 552.

134.   Even though the court stated that the right to assemble "for a lawful purpose" was protected by the First Amendment, but that private interference thereof may not be remedied by Congress, the court stated in dicta that the right to assemble to petition Congress was "an attribute of national citizenship" and that Congress could punish violations of that right. Id. at 552–53.

135.   Id. at 553. New York v. Miln, 36 U.S. (11 Pet.) 102, 139 (1837) upheld a state statute concerning passengers in vessels arriving in New York as a police regulation and not as a regulation of commerce. It did not mention the Bill of Rights.

136.   Id.

137.   Id.

138.   Id. at 553–54.

139.   Id. at 554.

140.   Id. at 554–55.

141.   Id. at 555–56.

142.   Id. at 556.

143.   Id. at 559.

144.   Id. at 561.

145. Id. at 560–69.

146. C. Peter Magrath, MORRISON R. WAITE 130–34 (1963). Justice Thurgood Marshall referred to Cruikshank and similar cases in these terms: "The Court began by interpreting the Civil War Amendments in a manner that sharply curtailed their substantive provisions." University of California Regents v. Bakke, 438 U.S. 265, 391 (1978) (opinion of Marshall, J.).

8

Unfinished Jurisprudence

THE AFTERMATH OF *CRUIKSHANK*

In *Presser* v. *Illinois* (1886),[1] the Supreme Court considered the direct applicability of the First and Second Amendments to state action. Herman Presser was convicted and fined $10 under an Illinois act prohibiting armed parades in cities without a license. On horseback with a sword, Presser led 400 workers with unloaded rifles through Chicago's streets to protest police violence.[2]

The *Presser* opinion was written by Justice William Woods, who as a circuit judge in Reconstruction tried Enforcement Act prosecutions for violation of First and Second Amendment rights. In 1871 Woods wrote that the "rights enumerated in the first eight articles of amendment" are "expressly recognized, and both congress and the states are forbidden to abridge them."[3] In *Cruikshank*, Woods instructed the jury that "every citizen of the United States has the right to bear arms," which is "secured by the Constitution."[4] His opinion that the rights to assemble and to bear arms were federally protected from private conspiracy, contrary to Justice J. S. Bradley's opinion, sent *Cruikshank* to the Supreme Court.[5]

In *Presser*, Woods concluded that the Second Amendment right of individuals to have arms does not protect the unlicensed march in a city of a private military unit: "The sections under consideration, which only forbid bodies of men to associate together as military organizations, or to drill or parade with arms in cities and towns unless authorized by law, *do*

not infringe the right of the people to keep and bear arms. But a conclusive answer to the contention that this amendment prohibits the legislation
in question lies in the fact that the amendment is a limitation upon the
power of Congress and the National government, and not upon that of the
States"[6] (emphasis added).

The court thus held that the armed paraders went beyond the individual
right of keeping and bearing of arms, adding that the Second Amendment
does not apply directly to the states. Similarly, the Court rejected a First
Amendment right of assembly applicable to Presser's band, because "the
right voluntarily to associate together as a military company, or to drill or
parade with arms, . . . is not an attribute of national citizenship."[7]

Presser did, however, recognize that the states may not infringe on the
right to keep and bear arms:

All citizens capable of bearing arms constitute the reserved military force or
reserve militia of the United States as well as of the States, and, in view of this
prerogative of the general government . . . *the States cannot*, even laying the
constitutional provision in question out of view, *prohibit the people from keeping
and bearing arms*, so as to deprive the United States of their rightful resource for
maintaining the public security, and disable the people from performing their
duty to the general government. But . . . *the sections under consideration do not
have this effect*.[8] (emphasis added)

Presser did not consider whether the Fourteenth Amendment protects
the right to keep and bear arms, an issue not raised by the parties.[9] A year
later, Chief Justice Morrison Waite, author of *Cruikshank*, cited *Cruikshank* and *Presser* as authority that the first ten amendments applied to the
federal government but not the states.[10] A separate argument was made
that the Fourteenth Amendment protected Bill of Rights guarantees from
state infringement.[11] The court refused to decide the issue because it was
not raised in the trial court.[12] In a later opinion, Woods interpreted *Cruikshank* to mean that the Fourteenth Amendment prohibits states, not individuals, from violating fundamental rights.[13]

Miller v. *Texas* (1894)[14] confirmed that the court had never addressed
whether the Fourteenth Amendment protects the right to keep and bear
arms. Miller had a shootout with policemen seeking to arrest him for
carrying a pistol contrary to state law. He claimed that the two officers
tried to kill him, but he returned fire and killed one of them. A newspaper
account alleged that Miller had, just before that incident, been arrested for
living "in open and notorious adultery with a young and greasy-looking
negress,"[15] which suggests that racist police may have been out to get

him. After being nearly lynched while in jail, Miller was convicted of murder and sentenced to death.[16]

After his conviction was affirmed on appeal, Miller attacked the Texas law as violative of the Second, Fourth, and Fourteenth Amendments. Citing *Cruikshank*, the Supreme Court found that the Second and Fourth Amendments did not directly limit state action.[17] The court refused to consider whether the statute violated the Second and Fourth Amendments as incorporated into the Fourteenth: "And if the Fourteenth Amendment limited the power of the States as to such rights, as pertaining to citizens of the United States, we think it was fatal to this claim that it was not set up in the trial court. . . . A privilege or immunity under the Constitution of the United States cannot be set up here . . . when suggested for the first time in a petition for rehearing after judgment."[18]

The court did not cite *Cruikshank* or *Presser* on the Fourteenth Amendment issue, because those cases did not address that topic. *Miller* left open the possibility that the Second and Fourth Amendments would apply to the states through the Fourteenth Amendment.[19]

THE INCORPORATION OF BILL OF RIGHTS GUARANTEES INTO THE FOURTEENTH AMENDMENT

Beginning in 1897 and extending through today, the Supreme Court has found substantive Bill of Rights guarantees incorporated into the due process clause of the Fourteenth Amendment. The reasoning in these opinions is a priori, requiring only a sentence or two. No case refers to the intent of the Fourteenth Amendment's framers, even though that intent supported incorporation. Preincorporation cases like *Cruikshank*, if referred to at all, are cited to demonstrate the fundamental character of the right in question.

In 1897, just three years after *Miller* sharply distinguished the direct application of the Bill of Rights to the states from its incorporation into the Fourteenth Amendment, the Supreme Court discussed state laws regulating rights guaranteed in the federal Bill of Rights as follows:

The law is perfectly well settled that the first ten Amendments to the constitution, commonly known as the Bill of Rights, were not intended to lay down any novel principle of government, but simply to embody certain guarantees and immunities which we had inherited from our English ancestors. . . . In incorporating those principles into the fundamental law there was no intention of disregarding the exceptions, which continued to be recognized as if they had been formally expressed. Thus, . . . the right of the people to keep and bear arms (article 2) is not infringed by laws prohibiting the carrying of concealed weapons.[20]

The court would not have asked whether state concealed weapon laws violated the Second Amendment, unless the states were prohibited from infringing on the right to keep and bear arms.[21] The court depicted the right as fundamental, noting that it may be regulated but not prohibited.

A month after the above decision, the court held in *Chicago B. & Q. R. Co.* v. *Chicago* that the just compensation clause of the Fifth Amendment is incorporated into the Fourteenth Amendment.[22] The court referred to "limitations on such power which grow out of the essential nature of all free governments" and "implied reservations of individual rights . . . which are respected by all governments entitled to the name."[23] The court relied on a decision by Justice Howell E. Jackson as a circuit judge explaining why the taking of private property without just compensation violates the Fourteenth Amendment: "Whatever may have been the power of the states on this subject prior to the adoption of the 14th Amendment to the Constitution, . . . since that amendment went into effect, such limitations and restraints have been placed upon their power in dealing with individual rights that the states cannot now lawfully appropriate private property for the public benefit or to public uses without compensation to the owner; and that any attempt so to do . . . would be wanting in that 'due process of law' required by said Amendment."[24]

What were the limitations on state powers in dealing with "individual rights"? In the paragraph before the one quoted by the court, Jackson explained: "The first 10 amendments to the constitution recognized and secured to all citizens certain rights, privileges, and immunities essential to their security. . . . So far as the states were concerned, citizens of the United States were . . . left without adequate protection and security in their persons and property. The fourteenth amendment was adopted to remedy and correct this defect in the supreme organic law of the land."[25]

The First Amendment admonishes only that "*Congress* shall make no law" abridging free speech and press. These rights were incorporated into the Fourteenth Amendment in *Gitlow* v. *New York* (1925) with a single assertion: "freedom of speech and of the press . . . are among the fundamental personal rights and 'liberties' protected by the due process clause of the 14th Amendment from impairment by the states."[26]

Assembly came next. *De Jonge* v. *Oregon* (1937) appealed to *Cruikshank* in support of incorporation of that right into the Fourteenth Amendment as follows:

The right of peaceable assembly is a right cognate to those of free speech and free press and is equally fundamental. As this Court said in United States v. Cruikshank . . . : "The very idea of a government, republican in form, implies a right on the part of its citizens to meet peaceably for consultation in respect to public affairs and to petition for a redress of grievances." . . . The right is one that cannot be denied without violating those fundamental principles of liberty and justice which lie at the base of all civil and political institutions, — principles which the Fourteenth Amendment embodies in the general terms of its due process clause.[27]

Freedom of religion required little discussion to be incorporated. *Cantwell* v. *Connecticut* (1940) held: "The fundamental concept of liberty embodied in that [Fourteenth] Amendment embraces the liberties guaranteed by the First Amendment. The First Amendment declares that Congress shall make no law respecting an establishment of religion or prohibiting the free exercise thereof. The Fourteenth Amendment has rendered the legislatures of the states as incompetent as Congress to enact such laws."[28] A few years later, the establishment clause was welcomed into the incorporation tent with a single nod: "The First Amendment, as made applicable to the states by the Fourteenth, . . . commands that a state 'shall make no law respecting an establishment of religion or prohibiting the free exercise thereof.'"[29]

The Fourth Amendment, which protects both substantive and procedural rights, came next. *Wolf* v. *Colorado* (1949) explained:

The security of one's privacy against arbitrary intrusion by the police — which is at the core of the Fourth Amendment — is basic to a free society. It is therefore implicit in "the concept of ordered liberty" and as such enforceable against the States through the Due Process Clause. The knock at the door, whether by day or by night, as a prelude to a search, without authority of law but solely on the authority of the police, did not need the commentary of recent history to be condemned as inconsistent with the conception of human rights enshrined in the history and the basic constitutional documents of English-speaking peoples.[30]

Finally, *Edwards* v. *South Carolina* (1963) brought the right to petition for a redress of grievances into the fold because "it has long been established that these First Amendment freedoms are protected by the Fourteenth Amendment from invasion by the States."[31]

Meanwhile, the Supreme Court made comments implying that the Second Amendment is incorporated, but never heard a case on the subject. It was recognized that the Fourteenth Amendment was intended to eradicate the black codes, under which "Negroes were not allowed to bear arms."[32] The court held that the Fourteenth Amendment protects from state infringement the "indefeasible right of personal security, personal liberty and private property."[33] The Freedmen's Bureau Act, of course, declared that this right includes "the constitutional right to bear arms."[34]

Although it involved a procedural guarantee — the Sixth Amendment right to jury trial in a criminal case — *Duncan* v. *Louisiana* (1968) is instructive. The court noted: "The Fourteenth Amendment denies the States the power to 'deprive any person of life, liberty, or property, without due process of law.' In resolving conflicting claims concerning the meaning of this spacious language, the Court has looked increasingly to the Bill of Rights for guidance; many of the rights guaranteed by the first eight Amendments to the Constitution have been held to be protected against state action by the Due Process Clause of the Fourteenth Amendment."[35] Justice Hugo Black, concurring, quoted from Senator Jacob Howard's speech introducing the Fourteenth Amendment to the Senate, which stated that the Amendment would protect "personal rights" such as "the right to keep and to bear arms."[36]

With little fanfare and no reference to the intent of the framers, the Supreme Court has recognized that the Fourteenth Amendment incorporates the Bill of Rights generally, particularly the substantive guarantees. It has not explicitly held that the Fourteenth Amendment incorporates the Second Amendment. Probably more evidence exists that the framers of the Fourteenth Amendment intended to protect the right to keep and bear arms from state infringement than exists for any other Bill of Rights guarantee.

THE INTENT OF THE FRAMERS OF
THE CIVIL RIGHTS ACT OF 1871

The Supreme Court has analyzed the intent of the framers of the Civil Rights Act of 1871, today's 42 U.S.C. § 1983, as applied to various issues. The evidence mustered by the court establishes that the right to keep and bear arms was intended to be protected by the Civil Rights Act.

Monell v. *Department of Social Services* (1978) noted that Representative John Bingham drafted the Fourteenth Amendment to nullify *Barron* v. *Baltimore* (1833), which held the Bill of Rights inapplicable to the states.[37] On the same page of Bingham's speech, "the right of the people to keep and bear arms" was characterized as one of the "limitations upon the power of the States . . . made so by the Fourteenth Amendment."[38]

In *Patsy* v. *Board of Regents* (1982), the court noted that Representative Henry L. Dawes opined that "Congress assigned to the federal courts a paramount role in protecting constitutional rights."[39] The Court quoted

Dawes on the judicial protection of "these rights, privileges, and immunities,"[40] which Dawes identified as follows: "He has secured to him the right to keep and bear arms in his defense. . . . It is all these, Mr. Speaker, which are comprehended in the words, 'American citizen,' and it is to protect and to secure him in these rights, privileges and immunities this bill is before the House."[41]

Patsy referenced the remarks of Representatives Benjamin Butler and John Coburn.[42] On the pages of the *Globe* cited by the court, Butler argued for protection of "rights, immunities, and privileges" guaranteed in the Constitution.[43] In a report introducing the civil rights bill, Butler advocated protection for "the well-known constitutional provision guaranteeing the right in the citizen to 'keep and bear arms.'"[44] Also on the page cited by the court, Coburn supported the civil rights bill to prevent the following state infringement: "How much more oppressive is the passage of a law that they shall not bear arms than the practical seizure of all arms from the hands of the colored men?"[45]

Senator Allen Thurman, whom the court cited four times,[46] included among Fourteenth Amendment protections: "Here is another right of a citizen of the United States, expressly declared to be his right — the right to bear arms; and this right, says the Constitution, shall not be infringed."[47]

The authorities quoted by the court to construe the Civil Rights Act of 1871 establish that the act's framers intended to protect the right to keep and bear arms. However, the court has not had occasion to acknowledge this intent.

EXPLICITLY GUARANTEED RIGHTS

In *San Antonio Independent School District* v. *Rodriguez* (1973), the Supreme Court enunciated that "the key to discovering whether [a right] is 'fundamental'" lies in assessing whether it is "explicitly or implicitly guaranteed by the Constitution."[48] The following sets forth the few occasions in the twentieth century when the court has mentioned the explicitly guaranteed substantive right to keep and bear arms.

In *United States* v. *Miller* (1939),[49] the court avoided determining whether a shotgun with a barrel less than 18 inches may be registered and taxed under the National Firearms Act consistent with the Second Amendment. The district court declared the act in violation of the Second Amendment,[50] and thus no evidence was in the record that such a shotgun was an ordinary military arm. The Supreme Court remanded the case for fact-finding based on the following: "In the *absence of any evidence* tending to show that possession or use of a 'shotgun having a barrel of less than eighteen inches in length' at this time has some reasonable relationship to the preservation or efficiency of a well regulated militia, we cannot say that the Second Amendment guarantees the right to keep and bear such an instrument. Certainly it is *not within judicial notice* that this weapon is any part of the ordinary military equipment or that its use could contribute to the common defense"[51] (emphasis added).

In support of this proposition, the court cited a Tennessee decision that stated on the same page about "ordinary military equipment": "If the citizens have these arms in their hands, they are prepared in the best possible manner to repeal any encroachments upon their rights by those in authority."[52] *Miller* did not suggest that the person in possession of the arm must be a member of the militia, asking only whether the arm could have militia use. The individual character of the right protected by the Second Amendment went unquestioned.

Referring to the militia clause of the Constitution, *Miller* stated that "to assure the continuation and render possible the effectiveness of such forces the declaration and guarantee of the Second Amendment were made."[53] The court explained that historically "the Militia comprised all males physically capable of acting in concert for the common defense" and that "these men were expected to appear bearing arms supplied by themselves and of the kind in common use at the time."[54]

Miller cites approvingly the commentaries of Justice Joseph Story and Judge Thomas M. Cooley.[55] Story stated: "The right of the citizens to keep and bear arms has justly been considered, as the palladium of the liberties of the republic; since it offers a strong moral check against usurpation and arbitrary power of the rulers."[56] In the reference cited by the court, Cooley stated: "Among the other safeguards to liberty should be mentioned the right of the people to keep and bear arms. . . . The alternative to a standing army is 'a well-regulated militia'; but this cannot exist unless the people are trained to bearing arms."[57]

The Supreme Court made virtually no further important reference to the Second Amendment until *United States* v. *Verdugo-Urquidez* (1990), a Fourth Amendment case that makes clear that the Bill of Rights protects the rights of the citizenry at large.[58] The court explained:

"The people" seems to have been a term of art employed in select parts of the Constitution. . . . The Second Amendment protects "the right of the people to keep and bear Arms," and the Ninth and Tenth Amendments provide that certain rights and powers are retained by and reserved to "the people." See also U.S. Const., Amdt. 1, ("Congress shall make no law . . . abridging . . . *the right of the people*

peaceably to assemble"); Art. I, § 2, cl. 1 ("The House of Representatives shall be composed of Members chosen every second year *by the People of the several States*") [emphasis added]. While this textual exegesis is by no means conclusive, it suggests that *"the people" protected by the* Fourth Amendment, and by the First and *Second Amendments,* and to whom rights and powers are reserved in the Ninth and Tenth Amendments, *refers to a class of persons who are part of a national community* or who have otherwise developed sufficient connection with this country to be considered part of that community.[59]

The 1992 abortion case of *Planned Parenthood of Southeastern Pennsylvania* v. *Casey*[60] discusses the broad parameters of the Fourteenth Amendment's due process clause, noting that "all fundamental rights comprised within the term liberty are protected by the Federal Constitution from invasion by the States."[61] The court recognized that the Fourteenth Amendment extends its protection to, but is not limited by, the specific guarantees expressed in the Bill of Rights:

The most familiar of the substantive liberties protected by the Fourteenth Amendment are those recognized by the Bill of Rights. We have held that the Due Process Clause of the Fourteenth Amendment incorporates most of the Bill of Rights against the States. . . . It is tempting, as a means of curbing the discretion of federal judges, to suppose that liberty encompasses no more than those rights already guaranteed to the individual against federal interference by the express provisions of the first eight amendments to the Constitution. . . . But of course this Court has never accepted that view.[62]

Fourteenth Amendment protections may be expanded, but certainly not reduced, beyond the practices that existed at the time it was ratified.[63] Bill of Rights guarantees are the floor, but do not constitute the ceiling, of rights guaranteed by the Fourteenth Amendment:

Neither the Bill of Rights nor the specific practices of States at the time of the adoption of the Fourteenth Amendment marks the outer limits of the substantive sphere of liberty which the Fourteenth Amendment protects. See U.S. Const., Amend. 9. As the second Justice [John Marshall] Harlan recognized:

"[T]he full scope of the liberty guaranteed by the Due Process Clause cannot be found in or limited by the precise terms of *the specific guarantees elsewhere provided in the Constitution* . . . [such as] the freedom of speech, press, and religion; *the right to keep and bear arms.* . . . It is a rational continuum which, broadly speaking, includes a freedom from all substantial arbitrary impositions and purposeless restraints."[64] (emphasis added)

As one of the "specific guarantees" of the Constitution, the right to keep and bear arms should be protected from state infringement by the Fourteenth Amendment.

In the Supreme Court's jurisprudence, a substantive right explicitly enumerated in the first eight amendments is a fundamental right and is protected by the Fourteenth Amendment. Incorporation of the Second Amendment into the Fourteenth Amendment logically follows from the Court's pronouncements concerning the individual right to keep and bear arms as a fundamental right coequal with other Bill of Rights guarantees.[65]

THE FREEDMEN'S BUREAU AND CIVIL RIGHTS ACTS AND THE RECONSTRUCTION AMENDMENTS

The declaration of the Freedmen's Bureau Act concerning "the constitutional right to bear arms" has never been mentioned in any reported decision concerning the Fourteenth Amendment or the Civil Rights Act of 1866. The same Congress passed both acts and proposed the amendment by more than two-thirds vote. The 1866 Act is currently codified at 42 U.S.C. §§ 1981 and 1982. The portion codified at §1981 protects the "full and equal benefit of all laws and proceedings for the security of person and property,"[66] which, the Freedmen's Bureau Act declared, includes the right to bear arms.

The Supreme Court has recognized the common origins and purposes of the Freedmen's Bureau and Civil Rights Acts of 1866 and the Fourteenth Amendment. The court has also recognized the fundamental character of the rights to personal security and personal liberty, which the framers of those acts and the Fourteenth Amendment declared as including the constitutional right to bear arms.

Hurd v. *Hodge* (1948) explained that, to understand the Civil Rights Act of 1866, "reference must be made to the scope and purpose of the Fourteenth Amendment; for that statute and the Amendment were closely related both in inception and in the objectives which Congress sought to achieve."[67] A purpose of the Fourteenth Amendment "was to incorporate the guaranties of the Civil Rights Act of 1866 in the organic law of the land."[68]

Section 14 of the Freedmen's Bureau Act, which expressly recognized the right of bearing arms, was noted in *Georgia* v. *Rachel* (1966) in reference to "the enforcement of the numerous statutory rights created under the Civil War Amendments."[69] "§ 14 of the amendatory Freedmen's Bureau Act . . . re-enacted, in virtually identical terms for the

unreconstructed Southern States, the rights granted in § 1 of the Civil
Rights Act of 1866."[70] *City of Greenwood, Mississippi* v. *Peacock*
(1966)[71] repeated: "Section 14 of the amendatory [Freedmen's Bureau]
Act of 1866 established, in essentially the same terms for States where the
ordinary course of judicial proceedings had been interrupted by the rebellion, the rights and obligations that had already been enacted in § 1 of the
Act of April 9, 1866 (the Civil Rights Act) and provided for the extension
of military jurisdiction to those states in order to protect the rights
secured. . . . By the Act of July 6, 1868, . . . the Freedmen's Bureau legislation was continued for an additional year."[72]

In *Jones* v. *Alfred H. Mayer Co.* (1968), the court held that the portion
of Civil Rights Act codified at 42 U.S.C. § 1982 barred both public and
private racial discrimination in the sale or rental of property, and that the
act is a valid exercise of Congress' enforcement power under the Thirteenth Amendment.[73] Outlining some of the same legislative history
presented in Chapter 1 of this book, *Jones* noted the origin of the Civil
Rights Act in S. 60, the first Freedmen's Bureau bill.[74] Even though
Congress could not override the president's veto, S. 60 "was significant
for its recognition"[75] of certain rights. The court noted:

When Congressman Bingham of Ohio spoke of the Civil Rights Act, he charged
that it would duplicate the substantive scope of the bill [S. 60] recently vetoed by
the President, ... Nobody who rose to answer the Congressman disputed his
basic premise that the Civil Rights Act of 1866 would prohibit every form of
racial discrimination encompassed by the earlier bill the President had vetoed.
Even Senator Trumbull of Illinois, author of the vetoed measure as well as of the
Civil Rights Act, had previously remarked that the latter was designed to "extend
to all parts of the country," on a permanent basis, the "equal civil rights" which
were to have been secured in rebel territory by the former [S.60] , . . . to the end
that "all the badges of servitude . . . be abolished."[76]

Similarly, no member of Congress disputed the explanation by both
Bingham and Lyman Trumbull that the Civil Rights Act would protect the
rights explicitly listed in the Freedmen's Bureau bill, which included the
right to bear arms.[77] The court concluded that "conduct reached by the
Freedmen's Bureau bill would be reached as well by the Civil Rights
Act."[78]

Trumbull explained that his bill would, the court observed, destroy the
black codes and would "affirmatively secure for all men, whatever their
race or color, what the Senator called the 'great fundamental rights.'"[79]
The black code provisions that would be eradicated, explained Trumbull

on the same page of the *Globe* cited by the Court, included the "provisions of the [Mississippi] statute [which] prohibit any negro or mulatto from having fire-arms."[80]

The right to keep and bear arms could be found to be protected both by 42 U.S.C. § 1981 and by the Thirteenth and Fourteenth Amendments, according to the standards set forth in *Jones* v. *Mayer*. The court remarked that "history leaves no doubt that, if we are to give [the law] the scope that its origins dictate, we must accord it a sweep as broad as its language."[81] Further, the Thirteenth Amendment clothed "Congress with power to pass all laws necessary and proper for abolishing all badges and incidents of slavery in the United States."[82] The black code prohibitions on possession of firearms were a badge of slavery.[83]

The significance of the rights declared in the Freedmen's Bureau bill and the Civil Rights Act to the Fourteenth Amendment has also been articulated in several other opinions. Justice Harlan noted that the privileges and immunities protected by the Fourteenth Amendment included those set forth in the first section of the Civil Rights Act.[84] Justice William Brennan traced the Civil Rights Act of 1871, 42 U.S.C. § 1983, which protects "any rights" that are "secured" by the Constitution, and which enforces the Fourteenth Amendment, to the Freedmen's Bureau bill.[85] Noting that "the Congress that passed the Fourteenth Amendment is the same Congress that passed the 1866 Freedmen's Bureau Act,"[86] Justice Thurgood Marshall concluded that the rights set forth in the Freedmen's Bureau Act were dispositive of Congress' intent in the Fourteenth Amendment.[87]

In a 1987 opinion, Brennan stated of § 1981: "Clearly, the 'full and equal benefit' and 'punishment' clauses guarantee numerous rights other than equal treatment in the execution, administration, and the enforcement of contracts."[88] Justice Brennan noted:

The main targets of the Civil Rights Act of 1866 were the "Black Codes," enacted in Southern States after the Thirteenth Amendment was passed. Congress correctly perceived that the Black Codes were in fact poorly disguised substitutes for slavery:

"They defined racial status; . . . *forbade owning firearms or other weapons*; controlled the movement of blacks by systems of passes."[89] (emphasis added)

The court does not always seem to be aware that the Freedmen's Bureau Act passed. Four opinions mention only that the bill was vetoed and that the override vote failed;[90] three mention that the bill actually passed in a second override vote.[91] Only a few appellate courts have recognized the passage of the Freedmen's Bureau Act of 1866.[92]

The Freedmen's Bureau Act has never been mentioned by any court in a case concerning whether the Civil Rights Act or the Fourteenth Amendment protects the right to keep and bear arms. The Ninth Circuit, refusing to recognize incorporation of the Second Amendment into the Fourteenth, failed to acknowledge the recognition in the act of "the constitutional right to bear arms."[93] However, noting that today's "section 1981 rests on the thirteenth and fourteenth amendments," the Third Circuit opined *en banc*:[94] "The 1866 Act was a response to burgeoning abuses against former slaves, which threatened to render illusory the freedom granted to them in the thirteenth amendment. . . . This threat came from the growing power of the Ku Klux Klan and the adoption by the Southern States of the 'Black Codes,' which restricted such varied rights as the rights to serve as minister, to receive an education, and to own arms."[95]

CONCLUSION

Jurisprudence concerning the right to keep and bear arms is perhaps on a level with the rudimentary jurisprudence on the rights to free speech and press at the dawn of the twentieth century.[96] Nineteenth century cases held that the Bill of Rights does not directly apply to the states, but in the twentieth century the Supreme Court recognized that Bill of Rights guarantees are generally protected by the Fourteenth Amendment from state infringement. The logic of incorporation of all substantive Bill of Rights freedoms, including the Second Amendment, into the Fourteenth Amendment, as well as explicit statements by the Court, suggest that the right to keep and bear arms is protected against violation by the states. However, the Supreme Court has not definitively resolved this issue of great public interest.

Justice Clarence Thomas discussed the Second Amendment in his concurring opinion in *Printz* v. *United States* (1997), which held that a federal law commanding local law enforcement officers to check the backgrounds of handgun purchasers violated state powers under the Tenth Amendment.[97] Reflecting that the law might also run afoul of the Second Amendment, Thomas continued: "Marshaling an impressive array of historical evidence, a growing body of scholarly commentary indicates that the 'right to keep and bear arms' is, as the Amendment's text suggests, a personal right."[98] Someday, Thomas concluded, the court may "determine whether Justice Story was correct when he wrote that the right to bear arms 'has justly been considered, as the palladium of the liberties of a republic.'"[99]

Although firearms ownership, even by peaceable citizens, is controversial today, it was far more controversial during Reconstruction. Trusting ex-slaves to own firearms was, by any definition, the cutting edge of true belief in civil rights. It remains to be seen whether contemporary society will accommodate the same rights of the freedmen sought to be guaranteed by the framers of the Fourteenth Amendment.

NOTES

1. Presser v. Illinois, 116 U.S. 252 (1886).

2. On Presser's militia, compare GERMAN WORKERS IN CHICAGO 161–67, 235–39 (Keil & Jentz eds., Univ. of Chicago Press, 1988) (group's purpose described as defense against police attacks) with Spies v. Illinois, 122 Ill. 1, 12 N.E. 865, 886, 921–24 (1887) (describing organization as socialist), *writ dismissed* 123 U.S. 131 (1887). On the social context of *Presser*, see L. H. LaRue, "Constitutional Law and Constitutional History," 36 BUFFALO LAW REVIEW 373, 375–78 (1987).

3. United States v. Hall, 26 F.Cas. 79, 81–82 (C.C.S.D. Ala. 1871).

4. "The Grant Parish Prisoners," *New Orleans Republican*, Mar. 14, 1874, at 1.

5. United States v. Cruikshank, 92 U.S. 542 (1876).

6. 116 U.S. at 265.

7. Id. at 267.

8. Id. at 265.

9. S. Morrison, "Does the Fourteenth Amendment Incorporate the Bill of Rights?" 2 STANFORD LAW REVIEW 140, 147 (1949).

10. Spies v. Illinois, 123 U.S. 131, 166 (1887).

11. Id. at 151–52, 166–67.

12. Id. at 181.

13. United States v. Harris, 106 U.S. 629, 27 L.Ed. 290, 293–94 (1893), also relying on Bradley's Circuit Court opinion, United States v. Cruikshank, 25 Fed.Cas. 707, 714–15 (1874). United States v. Sanges, 48 F. 78, 85–86 (N.D.Ga. 1891), noting "the steady adherence" of the Supreme Court to Bradley's Circuit Court opinion in *Cruikshank*, explained:

The chief ground of the [*Cruikshank*] decision is that the clauses in the constitutional amendments relied on to sustain the validity of the enforcement act were guaranties of rights against the action of the government only, federal or state, and not against individuals.

The rights specified in that indictment which the defendants were accused of conspiring to hinder and interfere with were — *First*, the right of peaceably assembling together for a peaceful and lawful purpose; *second*, the right of bearing arms for a lawful purpose. . . . The court held that none of these rights are granted by the constitution, nor dependent upon it for their existence, but are only guarantied against state or federal infringement.

Logan v. United States, 144 U.S. 263, 36 L.Ed. 429, 437, 439 (1892) characterizes *Cruikshank* as having held that "fundamental rights, recognized and declared, but not granted or created, in some of the amendments to the Constitution, are thereby guaranteed only against violation or abridgement by the United States, or by the states."

14.   Miller v. Texas, 153 U.S. 535 (1894).

15.   "Foul Murder," *Dallas Daily Times-Herald*, June 17, 1891, at 1. The author is indebted to an unpublished study by Kenneth J. LaBoone for this reference.

16.   Miller v. State, 20 S.W. 1103 (Tex. App. 1893).

17.   Miller v. Texas, 153 U.S. at 538.

18.   Id. at 538–39.

19.   Brown v. New Jersey, 175 U.S. 172, 174 (1899) cites *Cruikshank*, *Presser*, and *Miller* for the proposition that the first ten amendments do not restrict the States, and does not mention the Fourteenth Amendment in connection with these cases. Arkansas v. Kansas & T. Coal Co., 96 F. 353, 362 (W.D. Ark. 1899), *rev'd on other grounds* 183 U.S. 185 (1901), noted that under the Second Amendment "the federal government is denied the power to deprive the people of the right to keep and bear arms," rhetorically asking: "If this right belongs to the citizens of this state under the fourteenth amendment, can the state pass any law which shall deprive citizens of other states of the same right, under the same circumstances?"

20.   Robertson v. Baldwin, 165 U.S. 275, 281–82 (1897).

21.   The court was referring to state concealed weapon laws, because federal law did not then nor does it today purport to regulate the carrying of concealed weapons, a purely local matter.

22.   Chicago B. & Q. R. Co. v. Chicago, 166 U.S. 226 (1897).

23.   Id. at 237 (citation omitted).

24.   166 U.S. at 238–39, quoting Scott v. Toledo, 36 F. 385, 395–96 (C.C. Ohio 1888).

25.   36 F. at 395.

26.   Gitlow v. New York, 268 U.S. 652, 666 (1925). Fiske v. Kansas, 274 U.S. 380, 387 (1927) added a single explanatory phrase: "the act is an arbitrary and unreasonable exercise of the police power of the state, unwarrantably infringing the liberty of the defendant in violation of the due process clause of the 14th Amendment."

27.   De Jonge v. Oregon, 299 U.S. 353, 364 (1937). *Cruikshank* continues to be cited for the proposition that the Fourteenth Amendment protects persons from state action, not individual wrongs. McDonald v. Smith, 472 U.S. 479, 482 (1985); United Brotherhood of Carpenters and Joiners v. Scott, 463 U.S. 825, 831 (1983); Chapman v. Houston Welfare Rights Organization, 441 U.S. 600, 661 n.

35 (1979) (White, J., concurring).

28. Cantwell v. Connecticut, 310 U.S. 296, 303 (1940).

29. Everson v. Board of Education, 330 U.S. 1, 8 (1947).

30. Wolf v. Colorado, 338 U.S. 25, 27–28 (1949).

31. Edwards v. South Carolina, 372 U.S. 229, 235 (1963).

32. Bell v. Maryland, 378 U.S. 226, 247–48 & n. 3 (1964) (Douglas, J., concurring).

33. Griswold v. Connecticut, 381 U.S. 479, 485 n. (1965).

34. 14 Stat. 173, 176 (1866).

35. Duncan v. Louisiana, 391 U.S. 145, 147–48 (1968).

36. Id. at 166–67.

37. Monell v. Department of Social Services, 436 U.S. 658, 686–87 (1978), citing Barron v. Baltimore, 7 Pet. 243 (1833).

38. CONG. GLOBE, 42nd Cong., 1st Sess., App. 84 (Mar. 31, 1871). As the court pointed out, Bingham "declared the bill's purpose to be 'the enforcement . . . of the Constitution on behalf of every individual citizen of the Republic . . . to the extent of the rights guaranteed to him by the Constitution.'" 436 U.S. at 685 n. 45.

39. Patsy v. Board of Regents, 457 U.S. 496, 503 (1982).

40. Id.

41. CONG. GLOBE, 42nd Cong., 1st Sess., 475–76 (Apr. 5, 1871).

42. 457 U.S. at 504.

43. CONG. GLOBE, supra, at 448–49.

44. H. R. REP. No. 37, 41st Cong., 3rd Sess., 3 (Feb. 20, 1871).

45. CONG. GLOBE, 42nd Cong., 1st Sess., 459 (Apr. 4, 1871). The court continued: "Opponents of the bill also recognized this purpose and complained that the bill would usurp the State's power," citing Rep. Whitthorne. 457 U.S. at 504 n. 6. On the page cited by the Court, Whitthorne asserted that under the civil rights bill, if a police officer seized a pistol from a "drunken negro," then "the officer may be sued, because the right to bear arms is secured by the Constitution." CONG. GLOBE, 42nd Cong., 1st Sess. 337 (1871).

46. 457 U.S. at 504–6.

47. CONG. GLOBE, 42nd Cong., 2d Sess., App. 25–26 (1872).

48. San Antonio Independent School District v. Rodriguez, 411 U.S. 1, 33 (1973).

49. United States v. Miller, 307 U.S. 174 (1939).

50. United States v. Miller, 26 F.Supp. 1002, 1003 (W.D. Ark. 1939).

51. 307 U.S. at 178.

52. Id., citing Aymette v. State, 2 Hump. (21 Tenn.) 154, 158 (1840).

53. 307 U.S. at 178.

54. Id. at 179.

55. Id. at 182 n. 3.

56. 2 J. Story, COMMENTARIES ON THE CONSTITUTION 646 (5th ed. 1891). "One of the ordinary modes, by which tyrants accomplish their purpose without

resistance is, by disarming the people, and making it an offense to keep arms." J. Story, A FAMILIAR EXPOSITION OF THE CONSTITUTION OF THE UNITED STATES 264 (1859).

57.   T. Cooley, CONSTITUTIONAL LIMITATIONS 729. T. Cooley, GENERAL PRINCIPLES OF CONSTITUTIONAL LAW 281–82 (2d ed. 1891) explains further: "The right is General — It may be supposed from the phraseology of this provision that the right to keep and bear arms was only guaranteed to the militia; but this would be an interpretation not warranted by the intent. . . . If the right were limited to those enrolled, the purpose of this guaranty might be defeated altogether by the action or neglect to act of the government it was meant to hold in check. The meaning of the provision undoubtedly is that the people from whom the militia must be taken shall have the right to keep and bear arms, and they need no permission or regulation of law for the purpose."

58.   United States v. Verdugo-Urquidez, 494 U.S. 259 (1990).

59.   Id. at 265.

60.   Planned Parenthood of Southeastern Pennsylvania v. Casey, 505 U.S. 833 (1992).

61.   Id. at 847 (citation omitted).

62.   Id.

63.   Seventeen of the 28 states (61 percent) that ratified the Fourteenth Amendment by July 9, 1868 (the date it was ratified by a sufficient number of states) had constitutions that explicitly guaranteed the right to keep and bear arms. See conclusion to Chapter 3 of this book. To date, 43 state constitutions protect the right to keep and bear arms. A proposed arms guarantee is on the November 1998 ballot in Wisconsin.

64.   505 U.S. 833, 848 (1992) (citation omitted).

65.   Other than the right to keep and bear arms, the only substantive Bill of Rights guarantee not explicitly recognized as incorporated by the Court is the Third Amendment right against the quartering of soldiers in the home. The only appellate decision on point needed only one sentence to find that right to be fundamental and incorporated. Engblom v. Carey, 677 F.2d 957, 961 (2d Cir. 1982).

66.   42 U.S.C. §1981 provides in full: "All persons within the jurisdiction of the United States shall have the same right in every State and Territory to make and enforce contracts, to sue, be parties, give evidence, and to the full and equal benefit of all laws and proceedings for the security of person and property as is enjoyed by white citizens, and shall be subject to like punishment, pains, penalties, taxes, licenses, and exactions of every kind, and to no other."

67.   Hurd v. Hodge, 334 U.S. 24, 32 (1948).

68.   Id.

69.   Georgia v. Rachel, 384 U.S. 780, 796 (1966).

70.   Id. at 797 n. 26.

71.   City of Greenwood, Mississippi v. Peacock, 384 U.S. 808 (1966) (holding that certain criminal defendants were not entitled to removal of their case to

federal court under the 1866 Civil Rights Act).

72. Id. at 817 n. 11.

73. Jones v. Alfred H. Mayer Co., 392 U.S. 409, 413 (1968).

74. 392 U.S. at 423 n. 23.

75. Id.

76. Id. at 424 n. 31.

77. CONG. GLOBE, 39th Cong., 1st Sess., 654 (Feb. 5, 1866) (S. 60 amended to protect right to bear arms); id. at 743 (Feb. 8, 1866) (Trumbull); id. at 1292 (Mar. 9, 1866) (Bingham).

78. 392 U.S. at 428 n. 39. Moreover, "some members of Congress supported the Fourteenth Amendment in order to eliminate doubt as to the constitutional validity of the Civil Rights Act as applied to the States." Id. at 436.

79. Id. at 432.

80. CONG. GLOBE (supra) at 474 (Jan. 29, 1866).

81. 392 U.S. at 437 (brackets in original and citation omitted).

82. Id. at 439.

83. Id. at 436.

84. Oregon v. Mitchell, 400 U.S. 112, 160–63 & n. 13 (1970) (Harlan, J., concurring and dissenting).

85. Adickes v. Kress & Co., 398 U.S. 144, 215 n. 25, 225 n. 30 (1970) (Brennan, J., concurring and dissenting).

86. Regents of the University of California v. Bakke, 438 U.S. 265, 397 (1978).

87. Id. at 398.

88. Goodman v. Lukens Steel Co., 482 U.S. 656, 671 (1987) (concurring in part and dissenting in part).

89. Id. at 672–73, quoting H. Hyman & W. Wiecek, EQUAL JUSTICE UNDER LAW 319 (1982).

90. Oregon v. Mitchell, 400 U.S. 112, 159 (1970) (Harlan, J., concurring and dissenting); Loving v. Virginia, 388 U.S. 1, 9 (1967); Patterson v. McLean Credit Union, 491 U.S. 164, 194 (1989) (Brennan, J., concurring and dissenting); Jones v. Mayer Co., 392 U.S. 409, 423 n. 30 (1968).

91. Georgia v. Rachel, 384 U.S. 780, 797 n. 26 (1966); Regents of the University of California v. Bakke, 438 U.S. 265, 397 (1978) (Marshall, J.); City of Greenwood, Mississippi v. Peacock, 384 U.S. 808, 817 n. 11 (1966).

92. United States v. Timmons, 672 F.2d 1373, 1375 (11th Cir. 1982) (land title claims); Baines v. City of Danville, 357 F.2d 756, 768 (4th Cir. 1966) (postjudgment removal procedures). See Croker v. Boeing Co., 662 F.2d 975, 1004, 1006 (3rd Cir. 1981) (dissenting opinion) (Congress unable to pass bill over veto).

93. Fresno Rifle & Pistol Club v. Van de Kamp, 965 F.2d 723, 730 (9th Cir. 1992) (refusing to consider even "remarks by various legislators during passage of the Freedmen's Bureau Act of 1866, the Civil Rights Act of 1866, and the Civil Rights act of 1871.")

94.   Croker v. Boeing Co., 662 F.2d 975, 987 (3rd Cir. 1981) (*en banc*).

95.   Id. at 988. The Freedmen's Bureau bill, the Civil Rights Act, and the Fourteenth Amendment, the dissent noted, were related "both temporally and politically." Id. at 1004.

96.   William van Alstyne, "The Second Amendment and the Personal Right to Arms," 43 DUKE LAW JOURNAL 1236, 1238 n. 9 (1994).

97.   Printz v. United States, 521 U.S. ___, 117 S.Ct. 2365, 2385 (1997).

98.   Id. at 2386 & n. 2. Among the authorities cited, the following analyze the incorporation of the Second Amendment into the Fourteenth Amendment: S. Halbrook, THAT EVERY MAN BE ARMED: THE EVOLUTION OF A CONSTITUTIONAL RIGHT (1994); Amar, *The Bill of Rights and the Fourteenth Amendment*, 101 YALE LAW JOURNAL 1193 (1992); Cottrol & Diamond, *The Second Amendment: Toward an Afro-Americanist Reconsideration*, 80 GEORGETOWN LAW JOURNAL 309 (1991).

99.   117 S.Ct. at 2386, citing 3 J. Story, *Commentaries* § 1890, p. 746 (1833).

Table of Cases

Bibliography

PRIMARY SOURCES

Federal Records

Condition of the South. House Report No. 261, 43rd Cong., 2d Sess. (1875).
Congressional Globe.
Exec. Doc. No. 6, 39th Cong., 1st Sess. (1867).
Exec. Doc. No. 6, 39th Cong., 2d Sess. (Jan. 3, 1867).
Exec. Doc. No. 27, Senate, 39th Cong., 1st Sess. (1866).
Exec. Doc. No. 29, 39th Cong., 2d Sess. (Feb. 19, 1867).
Exec. Doc. No. 43, Senate, 39th Cong., 1st Sess. (1866).
Exec. Doc. No. 70, House of Representatives, 39th Cong., 1st Sess. (1866).
Exec. Doc. No. 118, House of Representatives, 39th Cong., 1st Sess. (1866).
Exec. Doc. No. 268, 42nd Cong., 2d Sess. (April 19, 1872).
Exec. Doc. No. 329, House of Representatives, 40th Cong., 2d Sess. (1868).
House Miscellaneous Doc. No. 44, 40th Cong., 2d Sess. (Jan. 29. 1868).
House Miscellaneous Doc. No. 64, 39th Cong., 1st Sess. (1866).
House Report No. 22 on Memorial of Victoria C. Woodhull, 41st Cong, 3rd Sess. (Jan. 30, 1871).
House Report No. 30, 40th Cong., 2d Sess. (Mar. 10, 1868).
Kendrick, Benjamin B., ed. *Journal of the Joint Committee of Fifteen on Reconstruction: 39th Congress, 1865–1867.* New York: Columbia University, 1914. Reprint, New York: Negro Universities Press, 1969.
Kurland, Philip B. and Gerhard Casper, eds. *Landmark Briefs and Arguments of*

the Supreme Court of the United States: Constitutional Law. Bethesda,
    Md.: University Publications of America, 1978.
Proceedings in the Ku Klux Trials at Columbia, South Carolina in the United
    States Circuit Court. Republican Printing, 1872. Reprinted, New York:
    Negro Universities Press, 1969.
Report of the Commissioner of Freedmen's Bureau. Exec. Doc. No. 70, House of
    Representatives, 39th Cong., 1st Sess. (1866).
Report of the Joint Committee on Reconstruction at the First Session, Thirty-
    Ninth Congress. Washington, D.C.: Government Printing Office, 1866.
Report of the Joint Select Committee to Inquire Into the Condition of Affairs in
    the Late Insurrectionary States. Washington, D.C.: Government Printing
    Office, 1872.
Senate Exec. Doc. No. 2, 39th Cong., 1st Sess., pt. 1, (Dec. 13, 1865).
Testimony Taken by the Joint Select Committee to Inquire into the Condition of
    Affairs in the Late Insurrectionary States. 13 vols. Washington, D.C.:
    Government Printing Office: 1872.
United States Statutes at Large.
U.S. War Dept., Records of the Army Commands. Record Group 393, National
    Archives.

State Records

Brevier Legislative Reports. Indiana 1867.
Debates and Proceedings of the Convention Which Assembled at Little Rock,
    January 7, 1868, to Form a Constitution for the State of Arkansas. Little
    Rock, Ark., 1868.
Florida Senate Journal. 1866.
Journal of Both Sessions of the Convention of the State of Arkansas. 1861.
Journal of the Constitutional Convention of the State of North Carolina.
    Raleigh, N.C.: J. W. Holden, 1868.
Journal of the Convention of Delegates of the People of Arkansas (1864). Little
    Rock, Ark., 1870.
Journal of the Convention of the State of North Carolina, 1865–1866. 1875.
Journal of Proceedings of Convention (Arkansas). 1836.
Journal of the Proceedings of the Convention of Delegates Elected by the People
    of Tennessee. Nashville, Tenn.: Jones, Purvis & Co., 1870.
Journal of Proceedings of the Constitutional Convention of the State of Florida.
    1868.
Journal of the Proceedings of a Convention of Delegates to Prepare a Constitu-
    tion for the People of Florida, 1838–1839. 1839.
Journal of Proceedings of the Convention of Florida. 1865.
Journal of the Proceedings of the Constitutional Convention of the People of
    Georgia, 1867–1868. Augusta, Ga.: E. H. Pughe, 1868.
Journal of the Proceedings of the Constitutional Convention of the State of

Mississippi (1868). Jackson, Miss.: E. Stafford, 1871.

Journal of the Proceedings of the Convention of the People of Georgia. Milledgeville, Ga.: R. M. Orme, 1865. Reprinted, 1910.

Journal of the Reconstruction Convention, Which Met at Austin, Texas. Austin, Tex. : Tracey, Siemering, 1870.

Journal of the Texas State Convention. 1866.

Laws of Mississippi. 1865.

Legislative Record (Pennsylvania). 1867.

Maryland Code. Baltimore, Md., 1806.

Maryland Code. Baltimore, Md.: John Murray, 1860.

Massachusettes H.R. Document No. 149. Feb. 28, 1867.

Official Journal of the Constitutional Convention of the State of Alabama . . . Commencing November 5, 1867. Montgomery, Ala.: Barrett & Brown, 1868.

Official Journal of Proceedings of the Convention for Framing a Constitution for the State of Louisiana. New Orleans, La.: J. B. Roudanez, 1867–1868.

Perlman, ed. *Debates of the Maryland Convention of 1867.* Baltimore, Md.: Hepborn & Haydon, 1867.

Poore, Benjamin, compl. *The Federal and State Constitutions.* 1877.

Proceedings of the Constitutional Convention of South Carolina. Charleston, S.C.: Denny & Perryu, 1868.

Report of the Debates and Proceedings of the Convention of the Revision of the Constitution of the State of Indiana. 1850.

Supplement to the Code of Maryland. Baltimore, Md.: John Murray, 1865.

Texas House Journal. 1866.

Texas Senate Journal. 1866.

Virginia Convention of 1867–1868, Debates and Proceedings. Richmond, Va., 1868.

Wisconsin Senate Journal. 1867.

Newspapers

American and Commercial Advertiser (Baltimore, Md.)
Baltimore Gazette
Baltimore Journal
Boston Daily Advertiser
Boston Daily Journal
Cadiz Republican
Charleston Daily Courier
Chicago Tribune
Daily Chronicle (Washington, D.C.)
Daily National Intelligencer (Washington, D.C.)
Daily Picayune (New Orleans, La.)
Daily Richmond Examiner

Dallas Daily Times-Herald
Federal Gazette
Harper's Weekly
Loyal Georgian
National Intelligencer
New Orleans Republican
New York Evening Post
New York Herald
New York Times
New York Tribune
Philadelphia Inquirer
The Press (Philadelphia, Pa.)
Springfield Daily Republican
The Sun (Baltimore, Md.)
Weekly Journal (Wilmington, N.C.)

SECONDARY SOURCES

Books

Aristotle. *The Politics*. Transl. T.A. Sinclair. New York: Penguin, 1962.
Aristotle. *Athenian Constitution*. Transl. H. Rackman. Cambridge, Mass.: Harvard University Press, 1935.
Berger, Raoul. *Government By Judiciary: The Transformation of the Fourteenth Amendment*. Indianapolis, Ind.: Liberty Fund, 1997.
Berger, Raoul. *The Fourteenth Amendment and the Bill of Rights*. Norman: University of Oklahoma Press, 1989.
Berlin, Ira, et al., eds. *Free at Last: A Documentary History of Slavery, Freedom, and The Civil War*. New York: New Press, 1992.
Billings, W. and E. Haas, eds. *In Search of Fundamental Law: Louisiana's Constitutions, 1812–1974*. Lafayette: University of Southwestern Louisiana, 1993.
Biographical Directory of the United States Congress 1774–1989. Washington, D.C.: U.S. Government Printing Office, 1989.
Bishop, Joel P. *Commentaries on the Criminal Law*. Boston, Mass.: Little, Brown, 1865.
Blackstone, William. *Commentaries*. St. Geo. Tucker ed. Philadelphia, Pa.: William Young Birch & Abraham Small, 1803. Reprint, South Hackensack, N.J.: Rothman Reprints, 1969.
Bowers, Claude G. *The Tragic Era*. Cambridge, Mass.: Riverside Press, 1929.
Brant, Irving. *The Bill of Rights*. New York: Bobbs Merrill, 1965.
Burgess, John W. *Reconstruction and the Constitution, 1866–1876*. New York: Charles Scribner's Sons, 1902.

Cooley, Thomas M. *A Treatise on Constitutional Limitations.* Boston, Mass.: Little, Brown, 1927.

Cooley, Thomas M. *General Principles of Constitutional Law.* 2d ed. 1891.

Coulter, E. Merton. *The South During Reconstruction, 1865–1877.* Baton Rouge: Louisiana State University Press, 1947.

Curtis, Michael K. *No State Shall Abridge: The Fourteenth Amendment and the Bill of Rights.* Durham, N.C.: Duke University Press, 1986.

Dubois, W.E.B. *Black Reconstruction in America.* New York: Atheneum, 1962.

Evans, W. M. *To Die Game: The Story of the Lowry Band, Indian Guerrillas of Reconstruction.* Baton Rouge: Louisiana State University Press, 1971.

Farrar, T. *Manual of the Constitution of the United States of America.* Boston, Mass.: Little, Brown, 1867.

Flack, Horace Edgar. *The Adoption of the Fourteenth Amendment.* Baltimore, Md.: Johns Hopkins University Press, 1908.

Fleming, Walter L., ed. *Documentary History of Reconstruction.* Cleveland, Ohio: Arthur H. Clark, 1906.

Foner, Philip S. & Walker, George E., eds. *Proceedings of the Black State Conventions, 1840–1865.* Philadelphia, Pa.: Temple University Press, 1980.

Goodell, William. *Views of American Constitutional Law, in its Bearing Upon American Slavery.* 2d ed. Utica, N.Y.: Lawson & Chaplin: 1845.

Halbrook, Stephen P. *That Every Man Be Armed: The Evolution of a Constitutional Right.* Albuquerque: University of New Mexico Press, 1984. Reprinted Oakland, Calif.: The Independent Institute, 1994.

Halbrook, Stephen P. *A Right to Bear Arms: State and Federal Bills of Rights and Consitutional Guarantees.* Westport, CT: Greenwood Press, 1989.

Hyman, Harold & William M. Wiecek. *Equal Justice Under Law.* New York: Harper & Row, 1982.

Kaczorowski, Robert J. *The Politics of Judicial Interpretation: The Federal Courts, Department of Justice and Civil Rights, 1866–1876.* New York: Oceana Publications, 1985.

Keil, Hartmut and John B. Jentz, eds. *German Workers in Chicago.* Chicago, Ill.: University of Chicago Press, 1988.

Madison, James, et al. *The Federalist Papers.* New Rochelle, N.Y.: Arlington House, n.d.

Magrath, C. Peter. *Morrison R. Waite: The Triumph of Character.* New York: MacMillan, 1963.

Malcolm, Joyce. *To Keep and Bear Arms: The Origins of an Anglo-American Right.* Cambridge, Mass.: Harvard University Press, 1994.

Maltz, E. *Civil Rights, The Constitution, and Congress, 1863–1869.* Lawrence: University Press of Kansas, 1990.

McConnell, Roland C. *Negro Troops of Antebellum Louisiana; A History of the Battalion of Free Men of Color.* Baton Rouge: Louisiana State University, 1968.

Owen, Robert D. *The Wrong of Slavery.* Philadelphia, Pa.: J.B. Lippincott, 1864.

Paschal, George W. *The Constitution of the United States: Defined & Carefully Annotated.* Washington, D.C.: W. H. & O. H. Morrison, Law Booksellers, 1868.

Pollard, E. A. *The Lost Cause.* New York: E. B. Treat, 1867.

Pomeroy, John N. *An Introduction to the Constitutional Law of the United States.* New York: Hurd & Houghton, 1868.

Rawle, William. *A View of the Constitution.* 2d ed. Philadelphia, Pa.: Philip H. Nicklin, Law Bookseller: 1829.

Rehnquist, William. *Grand Inquests.* New York: William Morrow, 1992.

Shofner, Jerrell H. *Nor is it Over Yet: Florida in the Era of Reconstruction, 1863–1877.* Gainesville: University Press of Florida, 1974.

Singletary, Otis A. *Negro Militia and Reconstruction.* Austin: University of Texas Press, 1963.

Sterling, Dorothy, ed. *The Trouble They Seen: Black People Tell the Story of Reconstruction.* Garden City, N.Y.: Doubleday, 1976.

Story, Joseph. *Commentaries on the Constitution of the United States.* 5th Ed. 1891.

Story, Joseph. *A Familiar Exposition of the Constitution of the United States.* New York: Harper, 1859.

Tucker, Henry St. George, *Commentaries on the Laws of Virginia.* Winchester: Winchester Virginian, 1831.

Tunnell, Ted. *Crucible of Reconstruction: War, Radicalism, and Race in Louisiana 1862–1877.* Baton Rouge: Louisiana State University, 1984.

Wallace, John. *Carpet Bag Rule in Florida.* Jacksonville, Fla.: Da Costa, 1888.

We The States. Richmond, Va.: William Byrd Press, 1964.

Williams, Lou Falkner. *The Great South Carolina Ku Klux Klan Trials, 1871–1872.* Ph.D. Dissertation, University of Florida, 1991.

Zuczek, Richard. *State of Rebellion: Reconstruction in South Carolina.* Columbia: University of South Carolina Press, 1996.

Law Journals

Amar, Akhil. "The Bill of Rights and the Fourteenth Amendment." 101 *Yale Law Journal* 1193 (Apr. 1992).

Amar, Akhil. "The Bill of Rights as a Constitution." 100 *Yale Law Review* 1131 (1991).

Aynes, Richard L. "On Misreading John Bingham and the Fourteenth Amendment." 103 *Yale Law Journal* 57 (1993).

Blodgett-Ford, Sayoko. "The Changing Meaning of the Right to Bear Arms." 6 *Seton Hall Law School Constitutional Law Journal* 101 (Fall 1995).

Cooley, Thomas M. "The Abnegation of Self-Government." 12 *Princeton Review* 209 (1883).

Cottrol, Robert, and Ray Diamond. "The Second Amendment: Toward an Afro-Americanist Reconsideration." 80 *Georgetown Law Journal* 309 (Dec. 1991).

Crosskey, William W. "Charles Fairman, 'Legislative History,' and the Constitutional Limitations on State Authority." 22 *University of Chicago Law Review* 1 (Autumn 1954).

Fairman, Charles. "Does the Fourteenth Amendment Incorporate the Bill of Rights?" 2 *Stanford Law Review* 5 (Dec. 1949).

Halbrook, Stephen P. "Personal Security, Personal Liberty, and 'the Constitutional Right to Bear Arms': Visions of the Framers of the Fourteenth Amendment." 5 *Seton Hall Constitutional Law Journal* 341–434 (Spring 1995).

Halbrook, Stephen P. "Second-Class Citizenship and the Second Amendment in the District of Columbia." 5 *George Mason University Civil Rights Law Journal*, Nos. 1 & 2, 105–178 (1995).

Halbrook, Stephen P. "Rationing Firearms Purchases and the Right to Keep Arms: Reflections on the Bills of Rights of Virginia, West Virginia, and the United States." 96 *West Virginia Law Review*, No. 1, 1–83 (Fall 1993).

Halbrook, Stephen P. "The Right of the People or the Power of the State: Bearing Arms, Arming Militias, and The Second Amendment." 26 *Valparaiso University Law Review* 131 (Fall 1991).

Halbrook, Stephen P. "Encroachments of the Crown on the Liberty of the Subject: Pre-Revolutionary Origins of the Second Amendment." 15 *University of Dayton Law Review* 91 (Fall 1989).

Halbrook, Stephen P. "The Right to Bear Arms in Texas: The Intent of the Framers of the Bills of Rights." 41 *Baylor Law Review* 629 (1989).

Halbrook, Stephen P. "The Fourteenth Amendment and the Right to Keep and Bear Arms: The Intent of The Framers." *Right to Keep and Bear Arms: Report of the Subcommittee on the Constitution.* Senate Judiciary Committee, 97th Cong., 2d Sess., 68 (1982).

Hall, Kermit L. "Political Power and Constitutional Legitimacy: The South Carolina Ku Klux Klan Trials, 1871–1872." 33 *Emory Law Journal* 921 (1984).

LaRue, L.H. "Constitutional Law and Constitutional History." 36 *Buffalo Law Review* 373 (1987).

Levinson, Sanford. "The Embarrassing Second Amendment." 99 *Yale Law Journal* 637 (1989).

Lund, Nelson. "The Second Amendment, Political Liberty, and the Right to Self-Preservation." 39 *Alabama Law Review* 103 (1987).

Morrison, S. "Does the Fourteenth Amendment Incorporate the Bill of Rights?" 2 *Stanford Law Review* 140 (1949).

Palmer, Robert C. "The Parameters of Constitutional Reconstruction: Slaughter-House, Cruikshank, and the Fourteenth Amendment." *University of Illinois Law Review*, No. 3, 739 (1984).

Scarry, Elaine. "War and the Social Contract: Nuclear Policy, Distribution, and the Right to Bear Arms." 139 *University of Pennsylvania Law Review* 2157 (1991).

Reynolds, G. H. "A Critical Guide to the Second Amendment." 62 *Tennessee Law Review* 461 (1995).

Reynolds, G. H. "The Right to Keep and Bear Arms Under the Tennessee Constitution." 61 *Tennessee Law Review* 647 (1994).

van Alstyne, William. "The Second Amendment and the Personal Right to Arms." 43 *Duke Law Journal* 1236 (1994).

Index

ABOUT THE AUTHOR

Stephen P. Halbrook practices law in Fairfax, Virginia. Cases he argued in the U.S. Supreme Court include *Printz* v. *United States* (1997). His books include *That Every Man Be Armed*, *Firearms Law Deskbook*, and *Target Switzerland*.